PSYCHOANALYSIS AND INFANT RESEARCH

PSYCHOANALYSIS AND INFANT RESEARCH

Joseph D. Lichtenberg, M.D.

 THE ANALYTIC PRESS
1983

Distributed by
LAWRENCE ERLBAUM ASSOCIATES, PUBLISHERS
Hillsdale, New Jersey   London

The Analytic Press

Distributed solely by

Lawrence Erlbaum Associates, Inc., Publishers
365 Broadway
Hillsdale, New Jersey 07642

Library of Congress Cataloging in Publication Data

Lichtenberg, Joseph.
    Psychoanalysis and infant research.

    Bibliography: p.
    Includes Index.
    1. Infant psychology. 2. Self. 3. Psychoanalysis.
I. Title. [DNLM: 1. Psychoanalysis—In infancy and
childhood. 2. Infant, Newborn—Psychology. WS 350.5
L699p]
BF719.L52 1983   155.4'22   83-2842
ISBN 0-88163-002-0

Printed in the United States of America
10 9 8 7 6 5 4 3 2

Contents

v

PART II: THE FIRST YEAR

PART III: THE SECOND YEAR

PART IV: APPLICATIONS

Preface

My approach to the findings of infant research on the first two years of life grows out of my primary professional dedication—I am a clinician concerned with the psychoanalysis of patients. In my 30 years of working and theorizing from within my clinical orientation, I have found it rewarding and fascinating to generate questions based on observations of what is abnormal, and I have attempted to derive hypotheses about how pathological entities develop. In fact, for many years I was so taken by the inherent logic of the answers analytic theory provided, as well as by their clinical utility, that I overlooked how my analytic stance might affect the constructs I was using. As I became increasingly aware of the new wave of infant research, however, I became intrigued not only by the remarkable novelty of the findings, but also by the different stance from which the observations were made. Instead of following the already entrenched, pathology-centered questioning mode, infant researchers were taking a fresh look at early development. Roughly speaking, from the vantage point of an analytic theoretician, who took such concepts as a narcissistic stage as a given, infant researchers appeared as "naive" naturalists. They seemed to start at the very beginning, with the questions: What do I observe? What patterns can I discern from this observation? What hypotheses can I formulate? And how can I test these hypotheses? Their stance seemed much freer of prior constraints than the analytic one, although their research was supported by all the technological sophistication of the space age, with video monitoring, split-screen photography, and computer analysis.

The new information from infant research is exciting, but I believe both fields can benefit from viewing their developmental perspectives side by side. We must ask both questions: What can an infant "do"? And what must infancy be like to explain

neuroses, character disorders, and psychoses? The very contrast
between these two views and the theoretical explanations that have
been evolved from them will sharpen issues for both the psychoanalyst and the infant researcher.

Naturally, any psychoanalyst will approach the infancy findings
guided by his or her own central interests. Since my focus for some
time has been on the development of the sense of self, I am
oriented to findings that bear on this—to me—crucial unfolding in
infancy. The new findings have inevitably led me to reconsider
many of my earlier proposals, and I dare say this would be true of
almost any psychoanalytic theoretician who attempted to come to
terms with the plethora of new experimental evidence. On the
other side, the irrefutable heritage of psychoanalytic discoveries
must be grappled with, in time, by infant researchers. It seems impossible to ignore, for instance, the complexity of awareness and
the "dynamic" unconscious; the lawful organization of dreams,
slips, symptoms, and all mental activity; and the universality of
myth and fantasy cycles.

Whatever their differences, both the infant research and the
psychoanalytic perspectives share a conviction in the significance
of prior developments for an exploration of subsequent ones.
Moreover, both approaches utilize multifaceted, multiply determined, multiorganizational explanatory constructs. These basic
similarities suggest that in time a meeting ground might be
established. For now I believe that pointing up the contrasts il-
luminates the problems in each, indicating the directions of further
inquiries rather than an attempt at a premature integration.

Finally, as a clinician, I believe in the power of an outlook to influence the way both partners in a therapeutic endeavor work.
Thus, if analysts gain a new perspective on infancy, they must perforce see the child-self in their analysands differently. It is in this
way that I hope my study will have value for clinicians. Moreover,
I believe even more direct applications can be made from the
knowledge gained from infant research to the psychoanalytic
situation.

Acknowledgments

This book could not have been written without the vision and creative ingenuity of a remarkable group of scientist-humanists, the researchers who study infants. Largely metaphorically and sometimes actually they have allowed me to look over their shoulders and observe the new vista of infancy they have opened up. With great politeness and forbearance they have welcomed me—a full-time clinician and relative outsider to their immediate daily concerns—I have had discussions about the implications for psychoanalysis of the research data and the theoretical constructs that emerge from it with quite a number of the authors cited in the references. Louis Sander, T. Berry Brazelton, Annamarie Weil, Gerald Stechler, Virginia Demos, Stanley Greenspan, Samuel Kaplan, Robert Emde, Daniel Stern, Mary Ainsworth, Justin Call and others have all discussed directly with me ideas that appear in my manuscript—many offering invaluable criticisms and clarifications. Since I have presented various of the chapters at different meetings—three times as precirculated papers at meetings of the American Psychoanalytic Association—the number of my colleagues who have helped me sharpen my thinking is very large. And it must also include all the members of the Interdisciplinary Colloquium on Infant Research of the American Psychoanalytic Association and the study groups to which I have presented the work in progress in Washington and Puerto Rico. In addition to sharing their thoughts, I received from one group of very dear friends the invaluable nutrient of sustaining encouragement. These include Evelyne Schwaber, Melvin Bornstein, Donald Silver, my deeply missed friend the late Ping-nie Pao, John Gedo, Anna Ornstein, Ernest Wolf, Warren Poland, George Klumpner, George Roark, Morris Oxman, Victor Bernal, and Lawrence Friedman. Special mention must be given to Daniel Shapiro. At a panel on

Object Relations Theory, I had presented a paper on the development of sense of the object in which I advanced a series of speculative proposals based on reconstruction and inference (see Chapter 2). After the discussions, Dr. Shapiro asked me if I was aware that there was an accumulating array of research data bearing directly on the hypotheses I had put forward. It was this question that launched me on a five year Odyssey into the mind of the infant that I now share in this book.

Within my family I have many debts of gratitude: to Charlotte for providing me that proverbial "wife" that every busy professional person (male or female) needs to function, and because she is a professional editor of psychoanalytic writings for offering me continuous counsel and constructive criticism; to my daughter, Ann, for her sensitive "consciousness raising" about the problems of the learning disabled child; and to Amy Lichtenberg, Maryland and William Pao, the other children of my household for their patience as they could see my mind fading off into "book thoughts."

A book requires professional publishing skills and I have received the best from the staff of Analytic Press. Sue Heinemann contributed her uncanny knack for picking up lapses in logic and continuity—and an aesthetic sense of fit. With unvarying good humor, Susan Shrader looked after the production and Judith Abrams, the publicity. Lawrence Erlbaum, in this instance, has been far more than a publisher. Through a period of trial and discouragement, his faith and enthusiasm carried and inspired me and all my colleagues on *Psychoanalytic Inquiry*—our journal and our book series.

PSYCHOANALYTIC INQUIRY
BOOK SERIES

PSYCHOANALYSIS AND INFANT RESEARCH

PART I:

The Neonate

Chapter One

The Challenge for Psychoanalytic Theory from Neonate Research

The data from neonate research pose an exciting challenge to psychoanalytic theory. Before 1960, except to a few pioneers such as Spitz, Benjamin, Fries, Wolff, and others, research on the neonate seemed as esoteric subject and an unpromising source of information for conceptualizing detailed aspects of human development. Since 1960, publications on neonates have grown from a trickle to a flood. Monographs and books now regularly appear, detailing the latest ingenious experiments. Our view of the newborn human has changed accordingly. Instead of a "blooming, buzzing confusion" (James, 1890), a state of undifferentiation, or a tabula rasa, we see an organism whose internal states and capacities for behavioral regulation are already rather complex. From the findings of the new research, neonates emerge as much closer to the tiny replicas of self that delight their parents than to the not-yet-psychologically meaningful, tension-discharging organisms postulated by classical analytic theory.

Nonetheless, it is still possible to question the direct application of this burgeoning mass of data to psychoanalytic theory. After abandoning his *Project for a Scientific Psychology* (1895), Freud opted to make his theory a purely psychological one and the existence of psychic representation became the sine qua non for what psychoanalytic theory could encompass. Some might argue that although the neonate's activity is far more complex than either analytic or nonanalytic theoreticians believed, nothing in these fascinating observations demonstrates an ability to receive or to establish psychic representations: This lack alone might place the

3

neonate research findings outside the realm of psychoanalytic theory proper. In my opinion, however, such an argument for exclusion from psychoanalytic consideration is not convincing. The principal issue, I believe, is whether the data lend themselves to or indeed compel a reexamination of basic psychoanalytic hypotheses.

To begin with, we might look at how the new data from research on the first weeks of life confirm or raise doubts about psychoanalytic drive theory, ego psychology, object relations theory, and affect theory. I should, however, first clarify that some of this research has been conducted by investigators with psychoanalytic training. In distinguishing between "psychoanalysis" and "neonate research," I refer not to differences in training but to differences in the data base and methodology. The distinction is between hypotheses derived from the clinical psychoanalytic setting and those stemming from direct observation in an experimental setting.

SOME QUESTIONS FOR DRIVE THEORY

The bulk of evidence from neonate research lends support to those who criticize two proposals of psychoanalytic drive theory: (1) the economic view that drive discharge or tension reduction (the pleasure-pain principle) is the primary principle orienting infantile life, and (2) the genetic-dynamic proposal that the infant awakens to the world of objects as a consequence of the need to satisfy instinctual drives.

Is Tension Reduction an Adequate Model?

From the perspective of the pleasure-pain principle, the neonate is pictured as resting contentedly asleep until physiological hunger, psychologically represented as the oral drive, rises above a threshold level. The infant is aroused, cries (as a discharge manifestation), and then receives the feeding needed to quell the cause of the tension. After experiencing the pleasure of tension-diminution, the infant returns to the sleep state—tension-free.

The picture from current research data on the neonate is markedly different. During the awake state, neonates do more than feed, they look. They show an ability to fix their gaze and to pursue an object visually at an earlier time than was previously believed. Infants will interrupt their feeding, whether it is by breast or bottle, to look at what interests them. Moreover, they exhibit preferences among the visual stimuli they perceive (Fantz, 1961). When a favored stimulus is offered, rather than withdrawing into quiescence, the newborn will prolong the alert period. In studying the different methods mothers use to soothe their babies, Korner and Thoman (1970) found that putting the infant to the shoulder is the most effective means of diminishing crying. Compared with other methods, this action by the mother involves the most stimulation for the infant. The neonate receives direct vestibular and proprioceptive stimulation; indirectly, being held at the shoulder is a potent elicitor of visual alertness.

Furthermore, sleep does not prove to be a state of absence of tension. On close examination, the newborn reveals an extensive repertoire of well-organized sleep behaviors. The amount of activity present during the neonate's sleep can even exceed that observed during noncrying wakefulness (Emde et al., 1976). There are of course periods of quiescent sleep (non-rapid-eye-movement [NREM] sleep), alternating with REM sleep. Yet the active REM sleep periods are longer in the newborn than in the older infant. One group of researchers speculates that the young organism is programmed not to shut out stimulation, but rather to seek it because it is needed for neural growth (Roffwarg et al., 1966).

Other research suggests that prolonged "quiescence" in the neonate, rather than representing the normal end-point of drive discharge, is an indication of pathological reaction to stress. Prolonged quiet (NREM) sleep has been reported to follow circumcision done with a ligature technique that produced an ischemic necrosis (Emde et al., 1971). This dramatic response has been interpreted to be an adaptive altering of the threshold as a response to continuing pain. A similar explanation of an altered threshold has been offered to explain infantile responses to both over- and understimulation involving tactile-proprioceptive-kinesthetic excitation (Shevrin and Tousseing, 1965). The researchers regard the seeming quiescence in these situations as a pathological loss of the appropriate level of excitation needed for normal development. The import of these findings is that a theory stating that tension reduction is the governing principle of the neonatal period (or later) requires revision. Stimulation and the tension it produces as needed for the newborn's homeostatic balance and ongoing development as any other nutrient. This of course does not eliminate the significance of tension reduction. As I will describe, the infant has a variety of means to turn off in response to stimuli—whether distressing (as the circumcision finding) or simply overly repetitive (habituation experiments). What is suggested by the research is that rather than a stimulus barrier and simple reduction mechanism, the newborn is innately equipped to *regulate* stimuli and tension within optimal threshold limits.

Is Need Satisfaction the Sole Basis of Object Relations?

Traditionally, it has been believed that the infant gradually awakes to the world of objects because of the need to satisfy instinctual urges—built principally around oral needs. The original hunger-centered view of the oral phase was extended to include many aspects of mouth-skin proprioceptive-thermal needs, but the central idea was still that the infant remained in a stage of "primary narcissism," like a chick in its shell, until forced by hunger to attend to the mother as a need-satisfying object. Neonate research raises serious doubts about this simple causal chain. Instead, the neonate emerges as an organism whose responsiveness is centered on and geared to a perceptual-motor-affective dialogue with the mother.

Study after study documents the neonate's preadapted potential for direct interaction—human to human—with the mother. Newborns respond selectively and actively to sound frequencies within the range of the human voice. The focus of their gaze is most accurate for objects about eight inches away—the exact distance from the mother's eyes when an infant is held in the normal breast- or bottle-feeding position (Stern, 1977). Neonates will look for longer periods of time at line drawings of a face than at dots. By two weeks, they will look at the mother's face longer than at a stranger's and will also look at the mother's face longer if she is talking to them (Carpenter, 1974). Films have documented that neonates react in a specifically responsive manner to the mother's chattering at them—in a way that suggests participation in a dialogue (by eight weeks, infants add to their repertoire of responses what appear to be definable pre-speech activities). Presented with a toy suspended in front of them within eight inches gaze focus react actively, but differently—they seem to try to reach and grasp the object (Trevarthen, 1974, 1977). All this suggests that the neonate begins life with different patterns of response to human and inanimate sources of stimulation.

The importance of hunger and its satiation is not contradicted by neonate research, but its significance is diminished. It no longer holds the unique, primary position assigned to it in psychoanalytic theory as the "entrepreneur" for the dialogue between the mother and the growing infant. Some studies in fact confirm the great significance of the feeding experience, but they alter the perspective from which to view it. Sander et al. (1976), for instance, studied two groups of newborns. One group was fed on a four-hour, fixed schedule in a lying-in nursery; a matched group was fed on an around-the-clock, demand schedule in a rooming-in arrangement. This first phase of the study lasted for 10 days. Then, for the 11- to 28-day period, both groups of babies were transferred to a setting with a single caretaker in a rooming-in arrangement. (After this, they were transferred to foster homes). In the initial phase, the newborns fed on the fixed schedule cried and were more active at night than during the day. As soon as they were transferred to the surrogate mother (11th day), however, the day-night activity pattern reversed itself—in the first 24 hours. In contrast, with the demand-fed babies (as is true with demand feeding by the infant's own mother), longer day-activity and longer night-sleep patterns were well established by the 10 days and continued smoothly during the 11- to 28-day period. The abrupt reversal in the patterns of the fixed-schedule babies was followed by "an overcompensation, a precocious advance with greater time awake during the day hours and less sleeping" (p. 185). Surprisingly, this tendency persisted over the whole first month.

In the same study, two surrogate mothers were used. Each of the caretakers was assigned to look after one group of demand-fed babies in the first 10 days and continued with the same babies until the end of the 28th day. These same women were alternatively assigned the care of the fixed-schedule babies after the tenth day. A significant variation was found in the day-night pattern of the infants cared for by each woman, although the experimenters could discern no difference in the women's overt caretaking procedures. According to Sander et al., these findings "suggest the possibility that we are encountering here some mechanism by which temporal adaptation is being effected between infant and caretaker" (p. 198). They postulate that "regulation of feeding behavior may, already in the first 10 days of life, become dependent upon specific adaptation to the one individual caretaker who regularly feeds" (p. 198).

Observations of infants born with esophageal atresia point to the specific importance of the feeding experience in establishing a normal interest in oral intake and competence in using the mouth (Dowling, 1977). In one group of newborns, formula was fed into a stomach bypass, without simultaneous mouth stimulation. These infants did not develop recognizable hunger-satiation patterns or signals (see Lichtenberg, 1978a, for a discussion of the effects on body-self formation). Moreover, these infants' attachment to their mothers was tenuous, and their overall functioning lacked motivation, vitality, intentionality, and mastery of the distorting effect these failures produce on the formation of body-self imagery. Other neonates were given sham mouth feedings along with the actual feeding into the bypass. The mothers were encouraged to put up with the inevitable messiness and to give a full and adequate general response to the baby. If sham feedings were begun early, at a time when the sucking response was strong, a normal level of interest in oral intake developed and the infant became competent in mouth functioning. The infants also showed normal vitality and motivation. If, however, sucking and lip-smacking responsiveness were not activated in the early infancy period, it was very difficult to stimulate interest in oral intake later, once the older infant's esophageal passage had been repaired. Dowling believes these findings confirm the significance psychoanalytic theory has assigned to oral experience as an organizer of motivation.

The research I have cited on different feeding schedules and on neonates with esophageal atresia *does* link the individual feeding experience of infants to patternings that affect the basic attachment and responsiveness to their mother, as well as to oral interests. Certainly, the findings indicate that the feeding experience is an important factor in the neonate's development. Yet to say that the feeding experience is important does not mean it is the centerpiece around which *all* infantile psychological development unfolds. Rather, as Sander et al. explain, it takes its part as one of a number of features of early postnatal development that lead to the establishment and maintenance of "proper phase synchrony within the infant between his various physiological components" (1976, p. 200).

Following this line of thinking, the oral-phase drive, in the psychoanalytic sense, becomes but one aspect of a basic regulatory core (Weil, 1970). In the functioning of this core, neonate research suggests that "*extrinsic* determinants may have a significant role in modifying both rates of change and the temporal organization of intrinsic infant subsystems, that is, the relationship of the phase characteristics of one function in respect to another" (Sander et al., 1976, p. 195). The *intrinsic* factor is the potential for response. The abrupt shift in the sleep-activity pattern of the fixed-schedule babies in Sander et al.'s study, in response to a changed environment, suggests a latent, intrinsic regulatory potential taking hold and making an overcompensating advance. Emde (1981a) refers to a biological predisposition "such that there are built-in self-righting tendencies'' after a defection due to adverse environmental circumstances (p. 213).

There is no simple way of reconciling the findings of neonate research with psychoanalytic drive theory and its related theory of motivation. Many of the infant observations suggest an impelling quality to the neonate's behavior, a general concept that is at least parallel to the psychoanalytic formulation. Sander (1980a) connects the concept of drive with control of the initiation of behavior, a control that must reside with the individual to organize his or her own world. Tomkins (1981) speaks of a drive system, but his definition differs from the psychoanalytic one. In his view, the drive supplies vital information on where and when to do what, but normally affective amplification is needed to make this specific information urgent. As we shall see later, in Chapter 11, this view has special significance for an understanding of how the infant research might be integrated with psychoanalytic thinking on erotogenic zones. Other considerations involving drive theory will be taken up in Chapter 6, in discussing the structural conception of the id and its general property of peremptoriness.

AN AMPLIFICATION OF EGO PSYCHOLOGY

Since the advent of ego psychology, the ''ego'' side of the undifferentiated id-ego matrix has received increasing attention. Neonate research adds substantial evidence of the existence of autonomous organizing, orienting, and controlling functions. Establishing a longer day–shorter night wakefulness distribution, for instance, would appear to be an internal regulation from the ''ego side'' of the basic regulatory core. Another type of control is revealed in newborns' tendency to turn away from unpleasant odors (Bower, 1971), indicating that odors are identified as unpleasant prior to any training. In addition, newborns will turn their eyes correctly toward the source of a sound. They will react with distress if the sound source is experimentally disengaged from their view of the ''speaker's'' mouth. These findings suggest that auditory localization and auditory-visual coordinations are autonomous functions (Basch, 1977).

Another type of control is revealed in newborns' tendency to turn their heads away from the side near which an unpleasant odor has been placed. This indicates that newborns have the capacity to distinguish the direction from which an odor originates prior to any training. Very quickly this preprogrammed capacity to distinguish odors and the direction of their source enters into learned preferential responses. When a breast pad is placed on either side of neonates eight days old, one from the mother and one from another woman, the infants reliably smell the difference and turn toward the mother's pad (MacFarlane, 1975).

I have already mentioned that infants appear to react selectively to human and nonhuman objects placed before them. Their movements indicate they have inborn precoordinations for each of these exchanges. In response to the mother, the neonate will "open his mouth, circle and purse his lips, and sustain this for several seconds. This is often accompanied by tongue thrusts as well as body quivers and small thrusts of the head forward . . . . These responses, especially when accompanied by the widening of the eyes, are as compelling as the social smile at 6 weeks" (Bennett, 1976, p. 87). These "greeting responses" contrast with the neonate's movements in response to a toy, in which visual tracking is combined with precursors of attempts to grasp, kick at, or place the object in the mouth. Stern (1977) suggests that the infant's differentiated responses to humans and to inanimate objects follow separate paths. The interactions with humans eventually lead to internal representations of people in affectively charged units of experience. The reactions to inanimate objects lead to the formation of sensorimotor schemata, as proposed by Piaget (1936).

As early as the second week, infants will reach for an actual three-dimensional object rather than for a photograph of the same object. What this finding suggests is that, from the earliest days, neonates perceive a three-dimensional world and, with minimal learning, can respond differentially to it and a two-dimensional representation of it (Bower, 1971). Another indication of the infant's early capacity for organizing experience is the successful mastery of thumb sucking. Murphy (1973) has observed that on the fifth day, numerous trial attempts were made before the thumb entered the mouth. By the tenth day, bringing the thumb to the mouth was a successfully executed pattern.

Newborns show appreciable ear-hand coordination. They will reach out to grasp objects they can hear but not see. This ability normally disappears at age five or six months, when vision takes over as the primary perceptual mode. Bower (1976) has suggested that this innate skill might be exploited with blind children, to provide them with an active way of scanning their world (similar to the active way sighted children use vision). He devised a sonar mechanism that furnished a congenitally blind child with auditory input reflected from objects. "Not only did auditory-manual behavior not decline, but also the infant actually developed some skills comparable to those acquired by a normal infant at the same age. Furthermore, the experiment clearly showed the flexibility of the newborn infant's perceptual system. No organism in the history of life had ever received the input this infant was given, yet he began making sense of the sounds within seconds after the device had been put on" (p. 44).

Other research has measured the degree of habituation (diminished response) to repetitions of visual, auditory, and painful stimulation (Bridger, 1961). The infant consistently shows diminished responsiveness to repeated stimulation by light, by a rattle, and by a bell. The researchers believe that this "habituation represents inhibition of response to a repetitive stimulus which no longer conveys useful information" (Aleksandrowicz and Aleksandrowicz, 1976, p. 264). Habituation to pinprick, however, did not appear to be consistent, leading the researchers to conclude that persistent or repeated pain is not a "noninformative" message. In fact, infants respond in differing ways to unpleasant stimuli. When their faces were covered with a cloth, some newborns responded by going to sleep; others removed the cloth with both hands. Aleksandrowicz and Aleksandrowicz conclude: "For the infant who is not able to remove himself from excessive sensory stimulation, habituation represents an essential means of controlling environmental input'' (p. 264). They note the similarity of the results of their habituation experiments to Freud's concept of a stimulus barrier, while to me their findings are far more indicative of an innate mode of information regulation than a barrier to stimulation as such. Habituation responses are made to stimuli already perceived, not because of their intensity and therefore overstimulating potential but because of their lack of novelty. A new stimulus of greater intensity will be perceived preferentially.

The existence of a capacity for making time estimates is suggested by neonates' responses in social interactions, especially in the rises and falls in their excitement as the caretaker talks, sings, or clucks to them in varied beats. Stern (1977) comments: "it is difficult to understand how the infant could react as he does, as well as begin to comprehend his social universe, if he . . . were not capable of some fairly impressive time estimating operations" (p. 90). He believes the newborn is equipped with one method for timing intervals of less than half a second and another method for estimating social behaviors longer than half a second.

From birth, motor organization appears as a more or less coordinated unit. Brazelton's (1973) Neonatal Behavioral Assessment Scale measures flexion, extension, and smoothness of movement; ability to hold the head erect; amount of spontaneous and elicited motor activity; and intensity and rapidity of skin color changes both spontaneously and in relation to stimulation. The newborn can even perform a kind of "walking." If properly supported, a newborn will march along a flat surface. This ability normally disappears at about eight weeks, but it does not appear to be a random activity pattern, without significance. "It has been shown . . . that if an infant practices walking at the very early phase, the experience will accelerate the appearance of walking later" (Bower, 1976, p. 39).

All these findings suggest a complex model of basic functioning, which might be seen as amplifying Hartmann's (1964) concept of autonomous ego functions of perception, memory, and control of motility. Observations of the infant's early capacity for differentiating, timing, screening, pattern matching, sorting, and discriminating refine Hartmann's list of autonomous functions. Indeed, neonate research furnishes a broadened empirical basis for Hartmann's astute appraisal: "A state of adaptedness exists before the intentional processes of adaptation begin" (1939, p. 49).

As already noted, in the earliest weeks of life, an infant will pay more attention to the mother's stationary face than to a stranger's face and still more attention if seeing the mother's face is combined with hearing her voice. But what is most indicative of the neonate's discriminatory ability is the infant's response to the unfamiliar. When, for instance, a view of the mother's face is combined with the sound of a strange female's voice, the infant actually turns away (Carpenter et al., 1970). According to the experimenters, this response indicates that the baby has a clear discriminatory sense of the familiar linkage of mother's face with her voice and reacts negatively to the incongruity. The findings also suggest that in the earliest weeks of life the neonate can screen perceptual input with reference to information stored from daily experience and can classify this input in relation to both categories of animate and inanimate and matches of visual and auditory cues. In addition, the neonate rapidly learns to exert an active choice for a preferred stimulus. Already at three days, an infant can be trained to turn the head to one side for a reward, such as a brightly colored object, when a buzzer sounds, and to the other side when a bell sounds (Bower, 1971). Within a month, the baby will engage in more intense nonnutritive sucking of a nipple in order to see a picture or to hear music (Siqueland and de Lucia, 1969).

Neonate research also indicates that the ways in which reactions are organized at the neurophysiological level may have counterparts in current or later psychic organization. To this point, I have reviewed only observations of the newborn and the first weeks of life. At two and a half to three months, dramatic changes occur. There is a shift in perceptual organization. The eight-inch gaze focus expands to a range almost as extensive as that of the adult.

At about nine weeks, the infant's mode of looking at the mother changes from a kind of "searching" eye movement to a more active scanning of her face in the region of the eyes. After three months, the infant can track the mother as she leaves, approaches, and moves about the room (Stern, 1977). Other manifestations of the general organizational change that occurs at two and a half to three months are consolidation of a day-night pattern with a markedly increased wakefulness and a rapid increase in the ability to sustain long periods of sleep. Stimulus conditions required for predicting accelerations of heart rate are different after the first two months. By four to six months, infants show a preference for looking at patterns that convey human activity such as walking and running, a sensitivity regarded by the researchers as resulting from an intrinsic organizational shift rather than being acquired slowly through experience (Fox and McDaniel, 1982).

The advent of social smiling and a dramatically different form of eye-to-eye contact, in which the infant can visually fixate the mother's eyes and hold the fixation, with eye widening and eye brightening, highlight a shift to greater control in a reciprocal exchange guided by the mother's cues (Emde et al., 1976). After this achievement, the infant's interest in and responsiveness to the environment are heightened, and smiling becomes integrated with more complex processes of memory, anticipation, and discrimination.

This dramatic change tends to confirm Spitz's (1959) hypothesis that development occurs in irregular, steplike spurts, with an affective sign such as the social smile serving as an indicator that an organizing change has occurred. In this view of development, a predictable genetic ground plan must coordinate with environmental responses. Some infant observers indicate that this interaction with the environment must occur within limits set by a maturational timetable, or the critical period for the development may be passed (Spitz, 1959; Dowling, 1977). Others cite the power of self-righting tendencies (Sander, 1975; Kagan et al., 1978). I shall discuss the issue of continuities and transformations further in Chapter 11.

A related question concerns the timing and relative influence of conflict during the early stages of life. Clearly, there are polarities—pulls between wakefulness and sleep, between responses to one kind of stimulation and another. There are also pulls between the regulating efforts of the caregiver and accommodating or resistive inclinations of the infant. Infant research has examined how these polarities are dealt with. What interests the psychoanalyst, on the other hand, is how these pulls relate to what analytic theory views as *intrapsychic* conflict. The existing psychoanalytic concept of an undifferentiated id-ego matrix, in which drive patterning has not yet been organized, presents a possible way of integrating the research findings into analytic theory. Basch proposes: "Instincts and drives may be looked upon as blueprints for behavior whose actual implementation depends on the activation of innate perceptual capacities by environmental stimuli" (1977, p. 250). Mahler suggests that when the infant "*is able to wait for and confidently expect satisfaction*—only then is it possible to speak of the *beginning of an ego,* and of a symbiotic object as well" (1967, p. 745). I shall return to the timing and organization of intrapsychic conflict when I discuss the driving force that sexuality exerts, and the struggle every child goes through in attempting to deal with assertiveness and reactive aggression (see Chapter 9).

It seems clear that much bridging must be accomplished before analytic thinking on drives, ego functioning, and early intrapsychic conflict can be integrated with the data of infant researchers. The picture drawn by the neonate researchers is lined in a different frame of reference, using a different vocabulary. They envision the neonate and the caretaker as a developing *interactional system,* in which "each partner is viewed as having separate competencies which affect the other's behavior and as initiating and reinforcing the behavior of the other" (Emde, 1980, p. 89). When they focus on the neonate's contribution to the system, they stress how internal states (active sleep, quiet sleep, active wakefulness, quiet wakefulness, and crying) reveal the importance of biological patterning in defining readiness to act and react

(Emde and Robinson, 1979). In looking at the mother's contribution, they emphasize how the first qualitative steps in development are critically dependent on a background or nonspecific stimulus environment (Wolff, 1969). As Sander et al. (1976) explain: "The mechanisms which make a nonspecific stimulus environment essential may be built around the redundancies which are constituted in the recurring encounters attending periodic fluctuations of behavioral states of the infant, during which patterns of exchange are becoming stabilized . . . . Regulation for the infant as a whole may be inseparable from a stable regularity or redundancy in key exchanges between infant and caretaker" (p. 202). Essentially, what the infant researchers state is that the infant's repetitious patterning of behavioral states and the caretaker's recurring encounter with the infant's fluctuations constitute the key regulatory exchange. The psychoanalytic statement of this would be that the mother provides her mature ego as an auxiliary to the infant's immature one. The psychoanalytic statement is a more general one and has a poetic appeal. The language of the infant researcher is an attempt to arrive at a high level of precision that fits what can be observed, with a minimum of assumptions. Both center their attention on functioning, but the ego concept, with its linkage to the concept of id, has ambiguities for this early period (see Chapter 6).

THE IMPLICATIONS FOR OBJECT
RELATIONS THEORY

From what has been described thus far it is clear that the evidence from neonate research can be used to reinforce psychoanalysts' current emphasis on object relations. But what emerges is a new twist to our view of object relations—the postnatal baby is a participant in and an activator of the dialogue, not simply a recipient. As early as the first postnatal day, microkinesic movie analysis reveals that the neonate moves in precise synchrony with the articulated structure of adult speech (Condon and Sander, 1974). Infants aged 12 to 21 days can consistently copy adults' facial and manual gestures. An outside observer was able to determine from a videotape of the neonate alone which gesture the baby was performing at any one time, without knowing which gesture of the adult had preceded it (Meltzoff and Moore, 1977). For example, newborns can imitate an adult who sticks out his tongue, opens his mouth, or widens his eyes (Bower, 1976). This basic "social" responsiveness requires an innate patterning. In the instance of the tongue gesture, newborns must identify the thing they see protruding from the adult's mouth as the same thing they can feel (but not see) in their own mouths. They must then execute fairly complex muscular movements to complete the imitation.

These findings imply that from the beginning both the newborn and the mother are primed to participate in a social interaction rather than to act as two individuals sending discrete messages. Their attachment is based on this mutual reciprocity. Infants almost immediately demonstrate an expectancy for engagement in their rhythmic cycling of attention and nonattention. If the mother does the unexpected, such as not moving her face, the infant will alter his or her interactive response and will eventually "turn off." The picture that emerges is one of two partners, each prepared to act on and react to the other. The precision of synchronization is so striking in many of these interactions that the researchers emphasize participation within organization forms rather than viewing each partner's contribution as discrete and separate (Condon and Sander, 1974).

Researchers who have observed mothers' reactions believe that their readiness to accept the task of mothering is highest at birth. In one experiment, one group of mothers was allowed extended contact with their newborns while a control group followed the routine hospital procedure of contact only at feeding times. At one month, the extended-contact mothers showed statistically significant evidence of greater concern, physical closeness, and fondling, as well as a greater tendency to hold their infants in an *en face* position during observed feedings (Klaus et al., 1972). In another study, mothers who were allowed 45 minutes of private skin-to-skin contact with their infants immediately after birth showed significantly more affectionate caretaking behavior 36 hours after delivery than those who were given a 45-minute period of contact much later, 12 hours after birth (Hales et al., 1977). In mothers of premature infants, similar differences have also been observed between those who were permitted contact during the first few days and those who handled their babies only at 20 days or later (Kennell et al., 1970). These findings have led researchers to conclude that mothering behavior is primed for the immediate postpartum period and that early separation can adversely affect the developing maternal attachment bond (Barnett et al., 1970; Peterson and Mehl, 1978).

The marked sensitivity of the mother's responsiveness to immediate contact with her newborn may be an unexpected finding, but the significance of the mother's empathic caretaking has long been recognized. What has been less well appreciated in the psychoanalytic literature is the role of the infant as an active force in the dyadic interaction. One study discovered that more than half of the observed interactions were initiated by the infant (Moss and Robson, 1968). Moreover, many researchers believe that the neonate's behaviors are "built in" in order to elicit maternal responsiveness. Sander et al. (1976), for example, note that during the first few days of life the newborn has relatively longer awake arousal states. They suggest that this greater readiness for interaction exists specifically to provide "an opportunity for establishing certain stable patterns in the infant-caretaking interaction" (p. 193).

Crying has long been considered to have a central role in arousing maternal caretaking responses. A similar role has been described for prolonged nonhunger "fussiness": "One could imagine that a tendency toward prolonged fussiness was built into the human infant to ensure survival by promoting closeness with a caretaker at times not necessarily taken up with feeding" (Emde et al., 1976, p. 85). Thus, from birth to two months, "the demanding characteristics of the infant's crying and helpless appearance" serve as a powerful elicitor of maternal response (Emde, 1981a, p. 189).[1]

Recently, some psychoanalytic theorists have emphasized the necessity of the mother's empathic sensing of how and when to soothe and calm the infant (Winnicott, 1953; Kohut, 1971, 1977; Tolpin, 1971). This need has been viewed from the newborn's side through a measure on the Brazelton's (1973) Neonatal Behavioral Assessment Scale. Neonate "consolability" is scored based on how much examiner intervention is required and, if self-quieting occurs, whether it is done by sucking or by "locking" on a visual or auditory stimulus (Aleksandrowicz and Aleksandrowicz, 1976). What the research shows is that differences in infants' requirements for soothing may play a larger role in development than has hitherto been recognized.

By virtue of other individual differences, infants call for differing responsiveness. Some appear to enjoy being cuddled and held close, folding into the holder's arms; others resist physical contact that involves restriction, by kicking and thrashing, and even crying (Schaffer and Emerson, 1964). In addition, sex differences may affect the mother's response. Total sleep for a 24-hour period is significantly greater for female than for male neonates (Sander et al., 1976). Some researchers believe that the female neonate may have greater tactile sensitivity; from this perspective, mothers' greater use of proximal tactile stimulation of their male infants may represent a response to the male's lesser cutaneous sensitivity (Korner, 1973, 1974). Females may also have greater responsiveness to taste, with more mouth activity and tongue involvement during feeding. Korner wonders if the mother may not have an empathic sense of her girl's affinity for oral comforting.

Infant research provides detailed evidence for the importance of

---

[1]This means of eliciting maternal attention, however, can go awry. A study of child abuse indicates that one child in a large family may evoke battering by a shrill cry (Bell, 1975). A follow-up study was made on maternal reactions to eight infants born with a variety of complications. These babies were quite irritable, with rapid and unpredictable state changes. Toward the end of their first year, seven of the eight mothers expressed rejecting and overanxious attitudes toward their infants (Prechtl, 1963).

the mother-infant relationship—a view that has been held by traditional psychoanalytic theory, and ego psychology, and more recently emphasized by object relations theory. But there is a striking difference. While many other relations theorists focus on conflict, on aggressive struggles, and on primitive mechanisms to deal with those struggles, infant researchers focus on the mutuality and "fit" between partners. Thus infant research describes not what the neonate has to overcome in order to enter into emotionally satisfying object relations but the preadaptedness of each partner to actively secure development-enhancing exchanges.

A RECONCEPTUALIZATION OF AFFECTS

Psychoanalytic theory regards affects primarily as discharge manifestations (id phenomena), which in time become tamed as ego components with signal (Freud, 1926), expressive (Schur, 1966), and intersystemic and intrasystemic orienting functions (Sandler and Joffe, 1969; Lichtenberg and Slap, 1971, 1972). Rather than emphasizing the discharge aspect of early affects, neonate researchers see affects as signals that play a significant role in the growth and development of communication within the infant-caretaker interactional system.

In their opinion, immediately after birth, crying serves as a strong social signal, calling the caretaker to come and alter a state of discomfort. Whether different kinds of crying effectively discriminate between different kinds of distress, however, remains a question. Some researchers believe there is a discrete sound variance between a hunger cry and a pain cry (Wolff, 1969). Other researchers contend that mothers do not seem to recognize the nature of the distress on the basis of sound patterns alone; rather, they depend on the context of the current crying, as recognized from past experience.

Ainsworth and Bell (1969) have used longitudinal studies of the effect of maternal responsiveness to crying to show that crying is an inborn signal behavior for eliciting early caretaking. They reason that crying, as a phase-specific early signal, will, if responded to appropriately, in time give way to other developing communicative behaviors. According to classical learning theory, they note, responding to crying should reinforce it and hence lead to its persistence. Their study, however, showed that those infants whose mothers responded to their cries early in infancy cried less in later infancy.

As previously noted, crying is not the only distress signal present in the first month of life. Beginning about the third week, all infants exhibit a degree of "fussiness," which declines at about three months (Emde et al., 1976). The puzzling aspect of this fussiness (which, in its extreme form, is often labeled "colic") is that it seems relatively independent of mothering and does not seem to be a response to either pain or hunger. The decline of nonspecific fussiness coincides with the appearance of the social smile. The researchers thus postulate that nonspecific fussiness carries an adaptive advantage, by promoting concerned closeness with the caretaker during nonfeeding times. Its disappearance is accounted for by its replacement by a better means of activating and ensuring caretaker responsiveness.

Like nonspecific fussiness, smiling and tearing (present only in humans) are believed to have species-specific survival value. Unlike the hairy primates who remain in tactile contact with their clinging infants, human mothers must be enticed and summoned to attend their physically distant babies. Smiling selectively rewards the mother's responses (Kaufman, 1976). Tearing, on the other hand, is regarded as a protection for the infant during prolonged periods of crying. As La Barre (1978) explains: "in crying at length, the passage of large amounts of air over the nasal mucous membranes would tend to dry them out. Lachrymation, then, is . . . a new adaptation of normally present eye lubrication to the additional task of repairing nasal membrane desiccation" (p. 821).

Before the social smiling response appears, infants show two kinds of smiling (Emde et al., 1976). One kind is, from birth on, a consistent correlate of the REM state, either in drowsiness or sleep. Mothers do not respond to this context-less smile as expressive of pleasure or responsiveness to them. A second kind of smiling begins in an irregular fashion during the first month. This smile is elicited by a wide variety of stimuli, in contrast to the specific responsiveness to the human face of the "social smile" (which begins at two and a half to three months). Emde et al. believe that the smiling connected to the REM state is organized and mediated by brainstem control and that it disappears when cortical control introduces a neurological inhibition. In their opinion, the sequence of development from no smiling during the waking state, to smiling while awake, to a surge in nonspecific smiling, followed by the specifically social smile, "seems to argue for a strong maturational thrust in smiling onset. It is as if a shift in the organism's state of readiness, in CNS organization, must take place before smiling appears. Thereafter, learning is increasingly influential, and smiling becomes modified; it becomes adapted to a specific environment. This view supplements cognitive theories which account for infant smiling in terms of a developing ability to recognize familiar objects" (1976, p. 88). In children blind from birth, smiling follows the same maturational timetable, but its persistence as a specific learned response must be shaped to an auditory-tactile stimulus, or the response may be lost (Fraiberg, 1971).

Thus, infant research, particularly Emde's work, argues for a theory of affects in which each affect expression follows a maturational timetable. The affect expression may be inhibited because of further biological maturation (as in the case of the REM smile). Alternatively, it may develop specificity because of learning (as in the case of the nonspecific wakeful smile becoming the social smile). Emde also contends that new levels of biobehavioral organization affect emotional expression. For instance, about two weeks after the social smile's first appearance, the infant adds a cooing verbalization. Cooing is believed to be a definitively new maturational emergent, not a differentiation of crying. Emde augments his argument for a maturational timetable for the development of affects by noting that the stranger distress of the eight-month-old cannot be fully accounted for by a cognitive explanation alone: "We hypothesize that the added factor is a maturational one and that it controls a further differentiation of emotionality, namely the onset of a capacity for 'fearfulness'" (Emde et al., 1976, p. 122).

Emde's research on a maturational timetable for affect expressions and on the impact of biobehavioral organization on affect development is in many ways an outgrowth of Spitz's writings (1957, 1959, 1965). Regarding affects from the standpoint of internal "states," offers a different, less familiar perspective. Viewing affects in relation to the 24-hour organization of states suggests that from the beginning of life there may be emotional linkages to contexts that involve both behavioral modes and communicative exchange. For example, crying, which is both an affect expression and a communication, is also considered a separate state category, with its own particular pattern of activity and reactivity. Contentment or pleasure, on the other hand, has been interpreted as an initial affective concomitant of the state of alert, bright-eyed wakefulness. Could the feeling tone of this state of alertness be the baseline emotion of a lifelong sense of security and safety (Sandler, 1960)? The "contented" affect the infant shows in the state of alert wakefulness and the interest shown in alert activity may be intimately related to the smile. As Basch (1977) remarks: "The finding that a stimulus of a mildly discrepant sort elicits a bigger smile than either a totally unfamiliar or familiar stimulus suggests that a smile is a response to the ordering of sensation. The smile may well be an inherent reaction which communicates that all is well, i.e., orderly" (p. 248). Emde (1980) believes that affect expression in the infant of two and a half months conveys two dimensions of information: hedonic tone (pleasure or unpleasure) and state of activation (high or low). By four and a half months, a third dimension—whether the source is internal or external—is consistently recognizable.

An investigation of affects in infancy raises many questions. Is there, for instance, an affective component to our sleep states from the very beginning of life—with a sense of replenishment that derives from the correct age-appropriate balance of REM and NREM sleep periods? It might also be asked: Is there an inborn affect of anger or, as Kleinian analysts propose, an intense destructive oral rage? Is crying more than a message—is it a statement of anger? I believe it is noteworthy that references by neonate researchers to anger or rage are relatively rare. Eyebrow movements and the set of the jaw and mouth in some infants have been described as suggestive of anger (Trevarthen, 1977, p. 248). For the most part, however, observers of facial expressions and autonomic responses tend to identity rage only in the three-month-old and anger still later. But perhaps there is a suggestion of something related to anger in the choice of the word "fussiness" for the nonspecific activity pattern noted by Emde et al. (1976).

Tomkins (1981) differentiates between biological primary affects and affect complexes. The latter are combinations of affects and elements of drive, perceptual, memory, motor, and cognitive assemblies. Tomkins describes nine innate affects—interest, enjoyment, surprise, fear, anger, distress, shame, contempt, and disgust. Each innate affect is activated by the frequency of neural firing per unit time, varying with stimulation increase, stimulation level, and stimulation decrease. For example, a relatively sudden onset and a steep increase in the rate of neural firing activates an innate startle response; if the rate of neural firing increases less rapidly, fear is activated; and if still less rapidly, interest is activated. A sustained high-level neural firing activates anger; a sudden decrease produces enjoyment. The internal program that controls each affect in turn controls a specific set of facial, autonomic, blood flow, respiratory, and vocal responses. Tomkins regards the *primary* function of affects to be *the amplification of urgency*—to make one care by feeling. In its relation to other assemblies (drive, perception, memory, motor, and cognition), the affect mechanism may shift from being dependent, to being independent or interdependent. Thus, affect can determine cognition at one time, be determined by cognition at another time, and be interdependent under other circumstances. In offering his theory, Tomkins states: "The appropriate minimal paradigm . . . is the miserable, crying neonate who neither knows why he is crying nor what he can do about it, nor *that* there is anything to do about it. It is *not* a 'motive' in the sense in which psychology has used that concept though it provides the core of what may become a motive. Without affect amplification nothing else matters, and with its amplification anything *can* matter'' (p. 323).

Other researchers have postulated innate links between perception and the organized regulation of excitatory-affective states (Stechler and Carpenter, 1967). They group the states according to receptiveness to information—alert wakefulness being the most receptive, crying the least, with alert inactivity, drowsiness, and sleep falling in between.

Implicit in all these studies is the connection of affect expressions in the neonate to the general organization of the infant-mother interaction. In this view, affects are seen as one of the properties of states. As the infant's states are affected by endogenous rhythms of sleep-wakefulness and activity, the affect expressions signal these changes to the mother, pulling her into greater empathic contact. The states are in turn affected by the success or failure of the communicative exchange within the mother-infant dialogue. Besides the information communicated to the mother, affects also play a part in the neonate's own perceptual informational input (e.g., crying limits intake, and alert wakefulness, with its "pleasant affect," potentiates informational pick-up).

All these studies of affect development challenge the view that cognition is the dominant property of human mental activity. Whether regarded primarily as providing communication in human interrelatedness or as a means of amplification, affects are normal developmental building blocks. They are not primitive phylogenetic leftovers that act intrinsically as disorganizers of cognition; rather, they are a means of amplifying all perceptual-action events and thereby enhancing their "meaning."

CONCLUSION

The examples I have chosen from the vast body of research on the neonate indicate new data relevant to each major conceptual area of psychoanalysis. This must, I believe, lead to a reexamination of our theory, for it has been the tradition in psychoanalysis that revisions have followed a confrontation with new findings. Previously the findings derived from an expanding exploration of pathological conditions such as schizophrenia, melancholia, or narcissism and the attempts to adapt to pathological conflict through sublimation (regarded as the source of creativity). The study of each pathological entity opened the ways to new questions. The findings from infant research draw on a different data base—the observation of normal behavioral phenomena, some naturalistic, most explicitly experimental. In these the neonates answer "what they can do" through sucking, looking, and turning their heads—very different means of response from the communications of the playroom or the couch about what is troubling a patient. Despite the unfamiliarity of the means of communication that provide the data, the sheer force of this information must have an impact on our understanding of development. But it is not only the findings that analysts must reckon with; it is also the language the researchers use to give their data organization and meaning. In subsequent chapters I shall continue to compare the epistemological frame used by the researchers with that used by psychoanalysts. The principal effect may be the borrowing of new terms and metaphors for analytic theory and practice—or the recasting of familiar conceptions of drives, ego, object relations, and affect in a new perspective.

Chapter Two

How Can We Examine the Beginning Sense of Self and Object?

My contention is that the data and theories derived from infant research can be used to support or question specific postulates in psychoanalytic theory. In particular, we might ask: How do the neonate findings compare with psychoanalytic thinking about the earliest development of the sense of self and object? I have previously proposed four factors that need to be considered in this process—genetic endowment, the tendency to generalize or particularize experience, the context of the interaction, and the richness of the experience (see Lichtenberg, 1979). Infant research adds a new dimension to our understanding of each of these factors.

GENETIC ENDOWMENT

I suggested that the infant begins with genetically endowed schemata that facilitate the organization of experience into units involving elements of self and object, as well as affect and cognition. These schemata are activated by certain predetermined, time-appropriate responses. For instance, an inborn structure with the potential for organizing the body image may be triggered by particular responses to physiological needs. Another innate schema might promote a general sense of self, beyond the image focused on body parts. In this regard, we might also postulate a specific responsiveness to such human qualities in the object as the face.

That neonate research supports the idea of inborn regulatory potentials activated by predetermined responses should be clear from Chapter 1. Yet beyond this point, the theories seem to diverge. Other than Stern (1977), the neonate studies I have referred to do not speak of a body image, or of a schema of the self and of a human object. This is the language of internal representation. Neonate researchers use a more biological language to address the infant's experience and an interactional model to explain their findings. Sander et al. (1976), for instance, remark: "When infant and caretaking environment can be regarded together as an organic system, research in the area of biological rhythms suggests that the nature of this machinery may include mechanisms of phase control, phase synchrony, entrainment, etc., in the establishing and maintaining of basic regulations" (p. 202).

Sander et al. go on to speak of neonate research language as once removed from the language of relationship:

> In a general way, we have merely been putting our customary language of the infant-mother relationships into a new vocabulary. The formulation of more detailed models of "organization" in the infant environment system provides the means of analyzing events at a more detailed level—within a framework that preserves a meaning, a logic connecting them. It is not intended as a substitute for the traditional concept of "relationship" in early development, but as a bridge to underlying processes [p. 203].

The research language is twice removed from the question of the internal representation of the mother-infant encounters. It does not address the question of an image of the self in an interaction with a to-be-separate object or a to-remain-ambiguously-linked selfobject (Kohut, 1971). I believe my conception of a a schema or template was too static. What are innately preprogrammed are perceptual-affect-action responses to a variety of stimuli. These involve the infant in complex behaviors that employ discriminations based on innate and quickly learned preferences. How useful it is to conceive of these neonatal experiences in terms of a self remains for me an open question. Stern (1983) argues that the neonate's discriminatory powers—including the ability to abstract —warrant using a self concept. I lean to the belief that what is crucial is the sense of self—a later development (see Chapters 8, 9, and 10) and that self and object as psychoanalytic terms are tied up in the whole problem of representation and symbolic process.

GENERALIZING AND PARTICULARIZING TENDENCIES

How, we might ask, does the infant experience the object? Winnicott (1963) proposes that the infant experiences the mother in two ways: as the environmental mother and as the "object" mother. The environmental mother comprises the whole background world in which the infant exists. The air the infant breathes, the warmth of a blanket, the beam of sunlight, the general emotional climate—all these are part of the environmental mother. The "object" mother, on the other hand, is the one who responds to the infant's needs, the mother with whom the infant interacts. She is the mother who feeds, the mother who answers a cry, the mother whose face invites exploration, the mother whose action may jar. This description of the infant's experience of the mother—as environment and as "object"—serves as a paradigm for the tendency to generalize and the tendency to particularize. As I have stated elsewhere: "Particularizing establishes the sense of borders and boundaries; generalizing crosses boundaries within the sense of self and between self and object" (Lichtenberg, 1979, p. 379).

The concept of an environmental mother receives support from neonate researchers' references to a background or nonspecific stimulus environment (Wolff, 1969; Sander et al., 1976). The idea that an "object" mother becomes particularized out of the background finds a parallel in accounts of the social smile. Yet the frames of reference are strikingly different. My hypothesis is meant to address the question of regulating inner and outer perceptions of "people" images and representations. It explicitly makes reference to "experiencing" as a psychological happening. With the exception of Stern (1977), neonate researchers for the most part avoid this speculative area. Condon (1977) recognizes this difference:

> The infant probably does not put his world together in the way the investigator goes about dividing it in order to study the infant's reaction to it. Many things happen at once in the infant's world, yet it is completely organized and he may be aware of ordered coherences or unities in that complexity. A gentle gaze is not the warmth of the caressing hands, the quiet voice is not touch or the smell of perfume or being held; but all of these in their coherence are the mother's presence for the child. The other sensory modalities may each track their relevant stimulus modes in a fashion similar to auditory perception and all may then be integrated together, reflecting coherent perceptual unities of the surround [p. 175].

I believe that more consideration must be given to which "ordered coherences or unities" the infant is aware of if neonate research is to make its fullest contribution to our understanding of human psychology. It may well be that the neonate researchers are particularly well-situated to ask the crucial question: When does awareness in a true psychological sense begin? Stechler (1982) offers promising clarifications. He notes that awareness, in the sense of perception of stimuli and their monitoring, is assumed to be present from birth on. If, however, awareness is conceptualized as implying a sense of the self as actor, doer, or initiator, this awareness comes later in development. Specifically, Stechler proposes that the level of awareness of self as doer comes into being when monitoring functions are transformed to a higher level of organization (see also the discussion in Chapters 7 and 8).

Traditionally, then, awareness is equated with psychology, and earlier functioning (such as perceptual monitoring in the neonate) with neurophysiology. Rubinstein (1976) contends that such a mind-body dichotomy is a false premise. For the language of structural theory, he advocates substituting terms such as information processing, perceiving, classifying, selecting, anticipating, storing, relaying, matching, and comparing. In a somewhat similar vein, Basch states: "The recognition that brain function is what we should mean by 'mind' relieves us of the burden of hypothesizing a mythical mental apparatus whose nature, essence, and function must then be established" (1977, p. 249). A different alternative is proposed by Weil (1978), who employs a system of complementary concepts from psychology and neurophysiology, with translation of terms back and forth.

My own opinion is that unless issues such as the relationship between consciousness and the dynamic unconscious and the timing of the origin of fantasy are addressed, the gap between the bedrock of psychoanalysis and neonate research will remain relatively wide. Spitz (1959) has offered a possible bridging suggestion, in claiming: "the smiling response is an indicator *only* of a far-reaching process of organization which has taken place in the infant's psyche. It indicates that conscious and unconscious have been separated from each other. The recognition, the act of smiling, is manifestly a conscious, directed, volitional act" (p. 20). Following Stechler's (1982) definition of awareness, we might see the social smile as an indicator of a rising level of perceptual sensitivity and of the monitoring function, although it is not, I believe, an indicator of awareness of the self as doer.

The point is that both psychoanalysis and neonate research would be enriched by the formulation of a testable hypothesis that introduces levels of "experiencing" into infant studies. At the moment, the psychoanalyst reaches backward from empathic intuitive reconstruction, based largely on the transference, and the neonate researcher constructs models of regulation and functional organization from experimental observation. It is difficult for the two to meet and move forward on the common ground of human experience.

THE CONTEXT

Let me turn now to the context of our experience of self. This context includes an object and an affect, as well as perceptual and cognitive aspects. From our psychoanalytic understanding of the transference, it would seem that memory traces of significant experiences contain a basic unit consisting of elements of self, object, feeling, and cognition. Thus, it seems inappropriate to discuss the development of the sense of self and the development of the sense of the object as separate entities. Instead, we must look at how the sense of self and the sense of object develop in an interrelated context (see Lichtenberg, 1979).

Neonate research clearly views early development as occurring in a "context"—the mother-infant interaction. Stern (1977) is most explicit in this regard:

> I am suggesting that, at least in the realm of human interactive behaviors, there is a basic process unit of interactive experience. This process unit is not necessarily the smallest unit of perception in any modality, but rather is the smallest unit in which a temporally dynamic interactive event with a beginning, middle, and end can occur. Such a process unit is like the briefest incident or vignette that can contain a sensory, motor, and affective element of experience and, accordingly, have signal value as an interpersonal event . . . . From the infant's viewpoint . . . powerful internal changes and sensations are probably not experienced as belonging exclusively to the caretaker's stimulation (the sensory experience) nor are they experienced as belonging exclusively to his own actions (the motor experience). It is more likely that they are experienced as part of an undifferentiated compound experience including what the caretaker does, what the infant does, and what that feels like internally [pp. 99, 104].

The more detailed accounts of the infant's "states" (e.g., Stechler and Carpenter, 1967) also suggest a group of contexts, involving affects and some specificity of perception and informational exchange. As Condon (1977) states: "The central hypothesis emerging is that interactional synchrony may be an indication of a primary phase of the responding process and that this phase is simultaneously the beginning of a discrimination function, laying an essential organized groundwork for later operations. This would also apply to the adult responding process as well. A different way of stating it may be that interactional synchrony is an early stage in the discrimination/cognition process" (pp. 168–169).

Yet a distinction needs to be made. The context referred to in psychoanalytic theory is intrapsychic and the one described by neonate researchers is interactional. Moreover, the concept of states, although close to certain psychoanalytic ideas (ego states, mood states), is primarily physiological and behavioral rather than psychological. The limitation of this focus becomes clear when Emde et al. (1976) ask: "What about the state concept at later ages?" They themselves admit: "The amount of scientific literature dealing with state-related variables drops off precipitously after the newborn period . . . [and] one gets the impression that the concept of state is in fact much less useful in studying the older child." They explain that "most psychological studies are carried out when the subjects are alert and attentive, when psychological differences in readiness to respond are complex, subtle, and less likely to show obvious physiological correlates. Hence, readiness to respond is more likely to be defined in terms of attitudes, set, cognitive style, and psychological structures" (p. 30).

We can equally well ask: What about the interactional concept at later ages? Interactional models, such as Sullivan's interpersonal theory, have long been used in psychiatry. Stern (1977) believes that the analysis of virtually all complex human social activities, including most interpersonal exchanges, requires the simultaneous consideration of two paradigms. The first is the traditional view of two separate individuals engaging in a sequential stimulus-response exchange, one with the other. The second aspect involves the programmed behavior sequence in which organized motor, sensory, and affective responses are carried out and sustained, more or less in synchrony. "In every situation we encounter," Stern explains, "both are operating. At moments the interaction is best conceptualized [and experienced?] as a stimulus-response dyadic process and at other moments as a programmed dyadic behavioral sequence. It switches back and forth" (p. 89). Sander (1980) proposes a third paradigm for the infant's interaction. He hypothesizes an "open space" in the infant's changing states, a transition point where the infant is neither in a state of need, nor asleep, nor involved in a direct interaction with the caretaker, but remains alert. The infant is, in Winnicott's (1963) language, alone in the presence of another. It is this "open space" that the infant responds to stimuli—a mobile, thumb, rattle—with the mother supplying a nonimpinging, supportive background presence (environment).

The question remains, however: How well does this emphasis on the interactional "context" explain the growing child's behavior? Psychoanalysts, in contrast to infant researchers, employ an intrapsychic model, focusing on a representational world internalized from, and more or less reflective of, interactional happenings. The problem is that the intrapsychic model has been applied to infancy without careful regard for developmental landmarks to establish the existence of symbolic structures. On the other hand, this model makes a specific contribution to our understanding of behavior, once development has reached a level where an intrapsychic representational world can be demonstrated. The psychoanalytic model recognizes and gives importance to the distorting effect on perception and interactive relations of fantasy, unconscious memory, unresolved intrapsychic conflicts, and the tendency to repeat past solutions, both adaptive and maladaptive. In my opinion, this model of intrapsychic regulation or conflict becomes more useful than the interactional one in studying the growing child during the second half of the second year (see Chapters 9 and 10). At the same time, it may be that psychoanalysis overstates our separateness, our degree of independence from our animate and inanimate surround. Rather than simply eliminating the interactional concept with an intrapsychic model, we need to retain a view of the interactional context as an explanatory concept with considerable validity throughout the life cycle. The model proposed by the infant researchers of experiences with another dominated by synchrony, experiences with another dominated by sequential contingencies, and experiences as though separate and alone but with a sense of a background of support (or malevolence) may be applied to the entire life cycle. Only after symbolic process has developed can internal representation be given to each of these experiences encoded along with aspects of cognition and affect.

SCHEMATIC FORMALISMS VERSUS
RICHNESS OF EXPERIENCE

As I have already indicated, development follows an inborn plan, a pathway that is probably common to all humans. Yet "the full potential experience involves far more richness, complexity, and subtlety then a mere ritual of passage" (Lichtenberg, 1979, pp. 382–383). To understand the full development of the sense of self and object, beyond the archaic prototype, we must examine how the bare schema is transformed into a rich experience.

Neonate research details the possibilities for richness in the newborn's experience of the interactional matrix. It points clearly to the readiness of both mother and newborn for immediate postnatal interaction. It underlines the significance of rooming-in with ample opportunity for skin-to-skin contact, and the importance of attunement to feeding needs for establishing day-night and other rhythms. Yet not all babies receive an optimal opportunity for attachment and optimal stimulation. What does neonate research tell us about the differential effect?

Call and Marschak (1976) state: "Infants who experience physical care without reciprocity with the human being offering such care, or infants who have inconsistent mothering, or those with multiple mothering experience are likely to show developmental deviations such as marasmus, rumination, autism, and repression because of the lack of opportunity to identify with a steady, reciprocating, caring person whose style becomes consistently manifest in the life of the infant" (p. 111). Sander et al. (1976), however, make a far more guarded statement: "Obviously, in the human we have no idea as yet what the early or later effects of neonatal stress are, or of early stability or instability, or of shifting the developmental rate of change in one function relative to another, or the kind of basic regulatory organization the individual will have, or on the intrinsic coordination between his various physiological subsystems. What may be gained adaptively by the adult for one kind of a later environment may be lost by the same adult for another kind of later environment" (p. 197).

Kagan et al. (1978) have reported on infants raised in the Guatemalan highlands, who were restricted for over a year inside a windowless hut, often in a sling on their mothers' back. They had no toys and little interaction with other adults. At one year they were quiet, nonsmiling, minimally alert, and physically passive. Compared with children raised in the U.S., they were three months to a year behind in cognitive development. Kagan et al. then discovered that in the middle of the second year, when the infants became mobile and were allowed to leave the hut, their development leaped forward dramatically. On retesting at 10 to 11 years, their cognitive and perceptual abilities were at the same level as those of urban Guatemalan and American middle-class children.

Some infant researchers stress the "considerable resilience and recovery potential in the face of non-optimal conditions" of the "mechanisms underwriting mental development" (Wilson, 1978, p. 346). Using IQ scores on general psychometric tests, Wilson found that with the passage of time monozygotic twins, even quite premature ones, became increasingly concordant in intellectual development. Indeed, they even paralleled each other's spurts and lags. In contrast, dizygotic twins became less concordant with age and eventually matched their siblings as closely as they did each other. Wilson argues that mental development, sensorimotor and cognitive, is backed up by the genetic blueprint; it results from "canalization" of behavioral attributes that have fostered adaptation and survival.

Both Wilson and Kagan, then, focus on cognition as the most important aspect of development. By emphasizing its relatively autonomous continuity, they conclude that early experience has been overrated as a factor determining later outcome. Certainly, these researchers findings on the resiliency of perceptual-cognitive development must be recognized in psychoanalytic theory (see Emde, 1981a). Yet their view is limited to the single pathway of cognition. If we conceptualize an interactional matrix, followed by an experiential unit of self, object, emotion, and cognition, we can broaden the field of inquiry and study each component in its interrelationship with the others. In this way, I believe we can come closer to an understanding of the complexity of human experience. Both psychometric-observational techniques and empathic-introspective approaches can be exploited, to the mutual advantage of both.

Some infant researchers (Greenspan, 1981) are already examining the functional relationship of behaviors to each other and to environmental demands—an approach that comes closer to the psychoanalytic view. Predictions are made from one transaction with the environment to the next, with long-term outcomes predicted only on the basis of repeated, cumulative assessments. Yet, as Emde et al. (1976) point out, it is much easier to "trace the red thread backwards" than to predict its forward course (p. 164). Moreover, they underline the problems in looking at development as a mechanistic linear sequence. With their model of biobehavioral field shifts, they propose instead a stepped progression, which may move in a variety of new directions at any one point. This model suggests the potential contribution of richness.

But how do we define "richness" psychoanalytically? One way is to look at the experiencing of age-appropriate conflict (Lichtenberg, 1979). Conflict, however, is a difficult concept to apply to the neonate, considering that, in psychoanalysis, conflict implies intrapsychic structure. Still, in a broader sense, we might view conflict in relation to Sander's description of polarities. In his words: "polarities in the arrangement of the forces with which the adapting organism must cope are so ubiquitous in the natural world (e.g., night and day, heat and cold, activity and rest, input and output) that it would not be surprising if a key to the comprehension of adaptive mechanics in development could be found in the organism's confrontation with and resolution of oscillating and opposing tendencies" (1975, p. 131). Sander adds: "Psychopathology can be viewed as a failure of integrative mechanisms just as easily as it can be viewed as a consequence of conflict" (p. 131). The concept of an integrative function might also be seen as a bridge to the psychoanalytic view. Weil (1978) believes that the most important factor in tracing maturational variations and their effects is the organizing, integrative function.

This principle, present in the neonate's physiological functioning, "nurtured by maternal care, also continues to mature in accordance with a constitutional timetable. It coordinates the child's functioning at a given time within and between spheres, as well as within the context of ongoing development" (pp. 483–484).

Through interpretation and reconstruction, psychoanalysis has studied unresolved intrapsychic conflicts in order to identify what has gone wrong with development. Neonate research suggests an alternative. The sequence of syntheses, integrations, organizations, and reorganizations can be studied to identify whether development is going right. Has the newborn synthesized the multiple physiological subsystems into the coherence of a well patterned "state"? Has phase synchrony between mother and infant been established, and, between three and six months, do mother and infant enter into a reciprocal social interchange characterized by joy and delight? Between six and nine months, is the infant organized enough in basic 24-hour state regulation to begin to disengage from the dominant social interaction and show an active exploratory initiative (see Sander, 1975, pp. 137–139)?

"Richness" of experience, then, can be defined both by the experiencing of age-appropriate conflict and by the sequences of syntheses, integrations, organizations, and reorganizations. The concept of organizing, integrative mechanisms is, I believe, a promising perspective from which to identify how a given infant is able to overcome less-than-optimal caretaking or less-than-optimal physiological resources. The identification of the process of integration at work (Weil, 1978)—including the later one of the development of a cohesive sense of self (Kohut, 1971, 1977; Lichtenberg, 1975)—is both a sound scientific pursuit and a means to establish an empathic understanding of great therapeutic value.

PART II:

The First Year

Chapter Three

Toward an Adaptational
Perspective on the First Year

Hartmann viewed psychological events with a remarkable broadness of perspective. He stated that in the infant a state of preadaptedness exists prior to the point in development where the organism can function on its own to secure its adaptation (1939, p. 49; 1956, pp. 245-247). In delineating what he meant by "preadapted," Hartmann pointed to the infant's capacity to perceive, remember, and control movements—functions that he conceived to be primary (inborn) and autonomous (developing as a separate organization in response to stimuli, rather than developing as a result of conflict). Hartmann reasoned that certain functions must be present to give psychological registry and meaning to the impulses that make for the confict. Hartmann's premise is based on the view that conflict is created only when a desire to *re*experience satisfaction has to be subjected to delay.

Hartmann's conception of preadaptedness was largely inferential and deductive. Yet it is clear from the description of the neonate presented so far that Hartmann's assumption of a state of preadaptedness is confirmed by a vast amount of research data. It is true that the infant researchers make assumptions that are at variance with Hartmann's view of a hypothetical average expectable environment for the infant. For Hartmann, the average expectable environment was a useful assumption, a way of holding constant the variable of external reality, while studying in detail the other variable, that of intrapsychic maturation and development. Infant researchers, on the other hand, believe that the infant's biological-neurophysiological-behavioral maturation and development are embedded in a dyadic system of reciprocal interactions between infant and caretaker. Preadaptedness reflects a state that can be discovered in the feedback loops characterizing interactions between infant and caregiver. Many infant researchers, including some who are psychoanalysts, do not follow Hartmann in his core assumption of the preeminence of the structural hypothesis as a conceptual tool for understanding this period of life. Thus, such terms as "id" and "ego," are frequently absent from their discussions, and the psychoanalytic concepts of libidinal and aggressive drives are not generally used to explain what is observed.

In reflecting further on the first year of life, then, I intend to depict the characteristics of an early state of biological-neurophysiological-behavioral preadaptedness, and to sketch in the beginning steps by which this early preadaptedness gradually becomes transposed into a form of adaptedness that is psychoanalytically meaningful. This I define to be a minimal unit of experience, comprising an image of the self and of others (animate and inanimate), an affect, and some perceptual-cognitive processing such as thoughts, fantasies, and orientation in time and space. It is this minimal experiential assembly that can be communicated or reconstructed in the clinical setting.

STATE ORGANIZATION AND THE STRUCTURING OF RESPONSE

We have already seen that human infants begin extrauterine life with demonstrable functional capacities. Rather than being amorphous organisms, beset by hunger and molded by the mother, infants show a lawful ordering of their functioning, with five organized behavioral states: alert wakefulness, quiescent wakefulness, REM sleep, NREM sleep, and crying (Wolff, 1966; Emde and Robinson, 1979). The degree of differentiation of these states is contingent on intrauterine maturation. From birth on, in the full-term baby, these states organize the neonate's life in temporal sequences, in conjunction with the stimuli of the extrauterine environment. Each state has different formal characteristics, suggesting differentiated brain patterning. As maturation and development proceed, changes occur in each of the states, but the states retain their initial formal characteristics, at least through most of the first year. As Sander (1975) describes it: "The state of the infant represents a first level of synthesis or coherence within the multiple physiological subsystems of the infant and is characterized by periodicity or rhythmicity" (p. 137).

This state organization represents what I call the biological-neurophysiological-behavioral level of organization. It is biological in that it represents the total bodily state. It is neurophysiological in that synthesis or coherence of the changing biological conditions (maturational and periodic) is mediated through the brain. It is behavioral in that the outcome of neurophysiological mediation (such as changes in state, affect expression, and motoric action viewed holistically) interdigitates with the "behavior" of the caretaker. Feedback loops develop between the biological-neurophysiological-behavioral state of the infant and the caretaker's activities, resulting in mutual regulation.

The infant's impelling tendency to seek the bodily satisfaction of hunger, elimination, sensual pleasure, and sleep has been singled out by psychoanalysis as the paradigm of the infantile state. In contrast, infant research underlines how these satisfactions fit within the states of alert or quiescent wakefulness or the transitions between. In looking, for example, at the time-circumscribed but intense domination of behavior by hunger and the lustiness of the sucking response, infant researchers note that these events occur during the state of active alertness. It is also at this point in alert wakefulness that the mutual interaction between infant and caretaker is heightened. Nonnutritional mouth activity, on the other hand, may be present during alert wakefulness or at the transition to quiescent wakefulness. It is this activity, with its mixture of pleasure to the mucous membrane, reduction of tension through sucking, and working out of mouth-hand-eye coordinations, that leads to what is possibly the first "problem-solving" action response—the ability to bring the hand to the mouth—a skill often achieved by the tenth day (Murphy, 1973). Yet interestingly, in terms of the mutual interaction, this activity occupies a place in the "open space" (Sander, 1980), when the neonate is not being stimulated by the mother (her "presence" is more that of a supportive background). Turning to elimination, especially of the bowel, we find an equally intense grouping of pleasure to a sensitized body part, reduction of tension, and working out of physical coordination. This occurs in the state of active alertness but here the focus of the active alertness shifts from external to internal stimulation. Interest in an outside stimulus is abandoned, the face reddens, the eyes may turn inward, and the whole body tenses during expulsion, relaxing at completion. In the interplay between mother and infant, through touching, soothing, holding and moving about, skin eroticism and whole body tactile-equilibrium sensations are a major means by which caretaking through shared pleasure adjusts the level of infant alertness in the state of wakefulness. Sleep, too, needs to be looked at within the total organized pattern. It reveals not only the powerful pull of need satisfaction, but also the intertwining of the infant's neurophysiological maturation and the caretaker's regulatory activities. In this regard, one might recall how the caretaker's feeding procedures affect the neonate's awake-sleep distribution (Sander et al., 1976).

The transition between states—between sleep and wakefulness, between hunger or high-level motor activity and quiet alertness—may represent moments of stress for the growing infant. The regulatory activities of the mother are important in smoothing over these transitions (Brazelton and Als, 1979). Gradually infants become able to delay a transition. They can stay awake longer if necessary, or wait for food, or restrict their motor activity—all by means of their own control. This control is a consequence of the infant's growing range of capabilities, including by the end of the first year self-soothing techniques, such as play with "transitional" objects (Gay and Hyson, 1976).

This view of the organization of the infant's states and the advancing coordinations within states carries implications for our thinking about development. We might picture the infant beginning with biologically primed activity, moving on to early instances of learned actions, then passing rapidly from simple responsiveness to more complex discriminations and finally to behaviors conveying a sense of choice and intentionality. The infant's smiling can serve as an example. As I mentioned in Chapter 1, before two months of age, smiling occurs both as a situationally unrelated phenomenon during sleep (this later disappears) and as a nonspecific, probably pleasure-related response during wakefulness. With the biological maturation at two and a half to three months, smiling becomes a specific response to limited aspects of the human face (Emde et al., 1976). This stimulus-response reaction is rather rapidly transformed into a recognition reaction when the infant's mother approaches. At this point we can say that the behavioral act of smiling expresses the impelling push to seek or evoke a social response.

The act of smiling then enters into the mutual interactional regulation of mother and infant. The infant's smile "turns on" the mother, and the mother's enthusiasm for entering into the "play" encourages (or limits) repetition. Smiling subsequently occupies a place in the whole evolving repertoire of communicative modes and affect expressions within the active alert state. At six months, a marked brightening of the smile occurs as the result of a further neurophysiological progression. Later the smile reflects the increasingly complex situations that determine pleasure, joy, and interest versus distress, fear and aversion. Thus for the nine-month-old the smile is no longer a greeting response to any friendly approach. The familiarity or unfamiliarity of the approaching person is registered and the state of security of the infant—usually a measure of the proximity of the mother—will often determine whether the baby smiles and makes eye contact or looks away in distress. By one year the full-faced smile of the younger infant is replaced by smiles that are more graduated in their expression of levels of joy. The smiles of this period convey more of a sense of intention and inner-directed control. This affective tone becomes more and more dominant, so that pleasure is communicated by the smile, conveying intentionality.

STIMULUS-SEEKING ACTIVITY AND
BEGINNING COMMUNICATION

Infant research has directed attention not only to the impact of state organization, but also to the neonate's active engagement with the world. From birth on, the neonate is biologically primed to seek stimulation. Very young infants will interrupt their feeding to roll their eyes up and gaze at the mother's face about eight inches away (Stern, 1977). The mother automatically responds to this heightened alertness and speaks to her baby in a rhythmical tone. The infant's arms begin to move in a rhythm synchronous to her speech. As she turns away and prepares to resume feeding, the baby signals with his or her eyes for a repeat contact "run." The mother responds and then resumes feeding.

Another example of stimulus seeking is seen when a toy on a string is dangled before a neonate, in an area 10 to 12 inches in the midline (Trevarthen, 1977). Everything about the baby changes. The eyes fixate on the toy, the pupils dilating. The whole body goes into immediate motion. Fingers, toes, and mouth point toward the object; shoulders hunch forward. At a slightly older age, the infant will instantly swing an arm toward the object, with the fingers contracting to a grasping position. Trevarthen describes one infant who initially missed contact with the toy, his arm overshooting it by a wide margin. He then made three more attempts, coming closer each time, until on the fourth he hit the toy and reacted with excitement.

Using stop-frame photography, Brazelton (1980b) has observed a total body response pattern occurring at a regular rhythm of four times a minute. Each incident of concentrated attention is followed by a collapse and then a further buildup. When the infant is presented with an object, the whole sequence is characterized by the jerky movements of all the body parts. If a familiar person enters the infant's perceptual field, everything about the baby will soften. Although the same sequence of buildup and collapse of body movements occurs in response to the mother, the movements are smoother, with the mother entering into a "courting dance" of rhythmic coos, eye contact, and mouth movements.

As we saw in Chapter 1, the infant begins with certain perceptual preferences, e.g., preferences for specific visual configurations (Bower, 1971; Carpenter, 1974) and auditory ranges (Condon and Sander, 1974; Terhune, 1979). From the start, perception consists of an active organizing of stimuli, guided by the inborn preferences and primed by the impelling urge to seek both animate and inanimate objects. The action responses are in turn differentially patterned depending on whether the activities are *with* humans or *on* nonhuman objects. Brazelton and Als (1979), for instance, remark: "The contrast of the infant's behavior and attention span when he was interacting with his mother, rather than an inanimate object, was striking as early as 4 weeks of age . . . . You could indeed tell from looking at a toe or a finger whether the infant was in an interaction with an object or a parent—and by 4 weeks of age, even which parent it was" (pp. 357–359).

As Brazelton and Als observe, mothers will approach their babies to help collect or contain them. They will smoothly reach around the baby's body to provide support, or they will make eye or voice contact to engage the baby's attention and regulate the stimulation level. Fathers commonly approach their babies in ways that heighten stimulation. They may engage in games of poking or playful grabbing. Their talk to the baby may be rhythmic, but the pace is usually faster and more staccato, with the voice louder. In diapering, mothers will gently lift the baby by the buttocks, slide the diaper in, and smooth the baby over as the process is completed. Fathers commonly pick the baby up by the legs, shove the diaper under, and let the baby plop down onto the table. By three weeks, a baby talked to from behind by the mother will show the smooth, controlled response. When the father's voice is heard the baby will respond with jerky excitement. Each parent thus becomes a partner in a feedback loop patterned according to expected mutual responses.

Infants, however, do more than receive, delight in, or react against the communications of their caretakers. They actively signal their preferences in order to stimulate responses (Moss and Robson, 1968). A *reciprocal* exchange takes place from birth on, with the infant being regulated by verbal and nonverbal communications from the caretaker but also furnishing cues to the caretaker.

In the earliest neonate period the baby "communicates" readiness for interaction as a property of the active wakeful state. The mother must furnish the correct reciprocal feedback to capture the baby in eye-to-eye contact. Even though adultomorphized, the mother's often-stated conviction that her baby is looking at *her* connotes the remarkably rapid appearance of a recognition response. By seven to 10 days, the mother can count on consistent eye-to-eye contact as the baby builts up a response pattern of shared regularity. By four weeks, the baby will usually give the mother recognizable cues of readiness to prolong the state of playful interactive attentiveness. Utilizing this readiness, the mother and baby gradually expand the contact runs, until by three months these have become conversational "games" (Stern, 1977). Communications with more formal characteristics normally develop at about four to five months. At this time the infant undergoes a general expansion of the whole state of alertness, probably associated with a neurophysiological maturation and reorganization. The infant gives much clearer signals of when to initiate and terminate the play activity. It is now that the mother's sensitivity to the infant's indication of preferences reflects on the process of making choices on the part of the child.

Looked at this way, body language signaling, nonverbal vocalizing, verbal signal comprehension, and verbalizing form an additive developmental chain, extending from birth through the second year and beyond (Bruner and Sherwood, 1980; Call, 1980). On the one hand, this sequence leads to increasing discreteness and precision in the exchange between caregiver and child; on the other hand, it leads away from the unique bond of intimacy between infant and mother. It is, however, the dancelike synchrony of the initial behavioral communications that provides the substructure for the deepest level of empathic contact underlying later verbal communication (Stern, 1977).

THE PATTERNING OF PERSONALITY ELEMENTS

The organized patterns observed in the infant also contribute to relatively permanent elements of personality. *Gender patterning* demonstrates the interplay of biological and experiential factors. Defining the specific force in infancy that impels gender differentiation, its timing and its relative specificity, is difficult. Hormonal variations exist and their effect on behavioral functioning must be presumed. Sensory responses, for instance, seem to be less organized in boy newborns than girl neonates, who show greater responsiveness to taste, greater mouth activity, and more tongue involvement during feeding, as well as greater overall tactile sensitivity. As I have already noted, mothers may respond to these differences, empathically sensing the girl baby's affinity for oral comforting, or the boy baby's greater need for proximal-tactile stimulation (see Korner 1973, 1974). Yet, at this point in our understanding, it is the differentiating effect of role assignment that has received the most attention (Stoller, 1968). Mothers are described as having a greater tendency to maintain physical closeness with six-month-old girls than boys (Goldberg and Lewis, 1969). By the end of the first year, "girlness" and "boyness" seem well established in the reciprocal social interplay of infant and family (Fast, 1979). In free-play situations at one year, girls will remain close to their mothers whereas boys move farther apart, spending less time in actual physical contact with their mothers (Messer and Lewis, 1970). It is well to remember that gender identity and sexual object preference, though obviously interrelated, are not identical. It is possible that more thorough observation of the differential responses to mother and father may reveal positive preferences, but what are possibly more important are the aversion responses that may adversely affect the openness of later choices made in the oedipal period.

Imitative responses, which can be seen within the first month of life, also have implications for personality development. Newborns can imitate facial expressions clearly enough for an observer to identify the expression without seeing the mother's face (Meltzoff and Moore, 1977). This kind of imitation begins a complex process, in which the infant becomes the particular baby of the particular mother (and father). The "shaping" is a reciprocal one, in that the baby also activates and alters the mother's reactions. Let us take a neonate who is an active, rapid eater. One mother may be delighted and pick up easily on the baby's rhythm. Another mother may react with mild anxiety. She is afraid her baby is too greedy and gradually introduces social interactions into the feeding situation to prolong it. By slow increments, the baby's eating rate is altered, although the mother sensitively does not hold back on alimentary gratification beyond the baby's tolerance at any one point. In all these intimate reciprocal interactions, multiple small "imitations" occur. Facial expressions and action rhythms are picked up and build into the infant's "personality." These early responses might be considered behavioral preidentifications. They later easily merge into the psychic representations of the "true" identifications traditionally regarded as central to mature personality development (Jacobson, 1964).

Automatisms also increase during the first year, as the infant moves toward more functioning in terms of behavioral action patterns. From the time infants can reliably support themselves in a sitting position, they develop ways of responding to stimuli, with postural-auditory-visual coordinations that persist throughout life. Crawling and walking, once achieved, function as automatisms, although grace or awkwardness may correlate with emotional security or insecurity. In addition, the greeting reaction becomes an automatic affectomotor response, relatively static and universal in all humans.

The contributions by infant research to gender patterning, imitative and shaping responses, and automations blend easily into psychoanalytic concepts of personality and character formation.

Again, it is noteworthy that they do so without employing hypotheses of internal representation. Personality elements are construed as built up by the interaction of the specific qualities of infants' and caretakers' responses to each other. This replaces the concept of an "average expectable environment" but remains solidly within the emphasis placed by ego psychology on an adaptative perspective.

THE REGULATION OF
DYSTONIC STIMULATION

A final consideration in surveying the infant's adaptive patterns is the response to dystonic stimulation. From birth on, the neonate is biologically primed to signal and to react to unpleasure. Infants will cry in response to hunger, abdominal cramping, or physical insult. They show special sensitivities to tactile over- or understimulation (Shevrin and Tousseing, 1965), vestibular disequilibrium, and food allergies (Lichtenberg, 1978a). Nor is crying the only impelling reaction to unpleasure. There are also variations of the fight-flight response, such as whole body reactions (Moro reflex) and total switching off into NREM sleep (Emde et al., 1971). An intermediate form of aversion can be seen in infants' responses when a person looms over them and makes a quick hand gesture forward and down toward them. Just as infants respond in a compelling fashion, with eye fixation, to a face, they will, from the second week, react defensively to a looming head. They will move their heads back and away, widen their eyes, and show a "negative" facial expression (Beebe and Stern, 1977).

   In addition to these extreme responses, infants also display subtle responses to unpleasure. Just as they exhibit a range of positive responses to stimuli that interest them, they show a range of negative responses to repetitions that no longer interest or novelties that disturb them. They may simply withdraw attention (Bridger, 1961; Aleksandrowicz and Aleksandrowicz, 1976); they may shut their eyes or turn away, averting their gaze (Beebe and Stern, 1977). More intense unpleasure leads to fretfulness and crying. Other unpleasure reactions include postural tensing, hitting and kicking, and postural flacidity, with the body becoming a limp dead weight. Prolonged absence of the caretaker may lead to a reduction in functional capacities and states of low-keyed "conservation-withdrawal" (Engel, 1962; Kaufman, 1976).

Experiments in which the mother purposely does not follow anticipated reaction patterns reveal the infant's repertoire of defensive responses. Call (1980) reports that when the mother, after initiating nursing with a hungry infant, removed the breast or bottle, the infant responded at first with increasingly agitated behavior, intensifying approach and sucking patterns. This response was followed by a withdrawal into quiescence. Beebe and Stern (1977) discuss a "visual violation" experiment, in which the mother fixes her gaze above the infant's eyes, keeping her face expressionless and immobile. Infants will first attempt to recapture the mother's expected response by trying to meet her eyes, moving their hands and eyes, reaching with their arms, legs, indeed, their entire bodies. When this is unsuccessful, the infants collapse into an attitude of withdrawal. The cycle of attempt at contact followed by collapse is then repeated, with increasing evidence of distress.

These experimentally induced distress-protective responses are suggestive of the pathological interactional sequences that may occur with mothers who are depressed, withdrawn, or hyperanxious. Violation situations can promote powerful repetitious patterning, affecting both partners in the interaction. Massie (1978) has studied home movies of children who were later diagnosed as autistic. The interaction between mother and infant in these movie sequences followed one form or another of the protest-aversion behaviors described by Beebe and Stern (1977), including dodging, inhibition of responsivity, and escape to the environment. In one case, when the mother tried to engage her baby, at times looming over the infant and tugging at him with increasing frustration, the four-month-old infant averted his eyes, ducked his head, moved his body back, turned or pulled away. Increasingly, this "chase and dodge" interaction resembled a fight, with the infant lapsing more and more into nonresponsiveness. "No matter how vigorously the mother pulled, poked or bounced, the infant would remain motionless, head hanging limp on the chest, head and eyes rigidly averted'' (p. 49). Eventually, he "swung his whole body weight around in the direction opposite his mother, and turned his eyes searchingly on the environment, losing any possibility of peripheral monitoring of the mother, and essentially 'escaping' her presence, at least visually'' (p. 50). Later, in response to the slower, calmer engagement efforts of the experimenter, the infant was able to regain and maintain a normal visual gaze experience with positive affect, an indication that he did not have a perceptual-processing disorder. Such wariness and deliberate eye aversion may be behavioral precursors of paranoid reactions that occur at later stages of development (see Beebe and Stern, 1977, p. 53).

In this chapter, I have described the infant researchers' portrayal of the first year of life as lawfully organized in complex ways. The ordering of biological-behavioral states and the structuring of responses, the seeking of stimuli, the laying down of personality patterns, and the reaction to dystonic stimuli indicate the preparedness of the infant for active involvement with the world. The more we tease out these remarkable functional capacities, the more we can appreciate Hartmann's adaptational perspective. But when we describe behavior only in terms of functional capacities, we may end up indicating the facts of engagement without fully grasping its experiential import. We must consider what mode of explanation consistent with the research data will best allow us to achieve a greater sense of experiential attunement with the infant in this period.

Chapter Four

Do We Need to Postulate Self-Object Differentiation in the First Year?

The infant clearly shows a variety of behavioral responses and functional capacities in the first year. What is not so clear, however, is how the developmental findings relate to the psychoanalytic perspective on intrapsychic functioning. In Chapter 2, I raised several questions that need to be asked about the beginnings of a sense of self and of object. I should now like to reexamine this issue from a slightly different perspective, taking into account the data from the first year of life. Much in the psychoanalytic perspective depends on an understanding of intrapsychic representation. It is therefore important to clarify how and when this developmental advance is made.

INTRAPSYCHIC REPRESENTATION

Clear, differentiated, cognitively organized representations in contexts that parallel experience probably do not exist during the first year. Psychoanalytic theory has tended to take it as a given that the infant lacks boundaries between self and object. Accordingly, self-object differentiation has been regarded as a crucial factor in development, with various times assigned to its occurrence (most commonly about nine months). Support for the assumption that the infant cannot differentiate self from object comes from the ubiquitous existence of merger and oceanic fantasies in adults and from the boundary disturbances found in borderline and schizophrenic patients. At the same time what is usually meant by a self and an object (as a psychological entity) is an intrapsychic representation. In contesting the Kleinian timetable, for instance, it has generally been argued that representations of self and object could not occur as early as the first few months. The traditional view is that such representations only develop more gradually, with the passing of the "symbiotic phase." Yet neither of these views pays much attention to whether representations develop *at all* during the first year, or what the criteria are for making or rejecting such an assumption.

In my opinion, the findings of infant research point in two different directions: (1) The neonate is more highly differentiated than has been thought, and (2) the perceptual-cognitive steps necessary to form an intrapsychic representational world have been underestimated. My suggestion, then, is that intrapsychic self and object representations are developments of the second, rather than the first, year. A correlated idea is that the infant or early toddler can show a remarkable degree of complex *behavioral* activity without our having to assume constant, reliable representations.

The existence of some degree of differentiation from birth is indicated by the differentiated responses neonates make to different stimuli. As I have indicated, young neonates react to the mother's voice; they make eye contact with her and search her face. To the father, they react differently and, to a toy, still differently. These responses appear to be biologically programmed, with the patterns described appearing in the first weeks. The responses then increase in clarity of differentiation with each maturational spurt—at two to three months, there is increased alertness; at six months, brightening; and at nine months, more complex affective changes and discriminations. Thus, a four-month-old can be seen to react in a changing series of differentiated modes. With one set of behaviors, the infant responds to the mother in a complementary mode: The infant supplies initiating cues concerning his or her needs, and the mother responds with the feeding or changing or other caretaking that fills the need. If the time interval for the mother's response falls within an optimal range, the frustration permits the infant and mother to work out coping routines that preserve attachment while increasing discrimination. Another set of behaviors constitutes a social engagement, approaching or achieving synchrony of reactions. With split-screen photography, mother and infant can be observed to perform a repertoire of eye widening, mouth opening, and vocalizings, with temporal gradients of speeding up and slowing down. These synchronous actions build up and collapse, to build again, in patterns suggesting a neurophysiologically based behavioral mode of "being with" mother—a type of "we" rather than a "you and I." When a stranger attempts to introduce a similar response sequence, the fit is not likely to be as great. Synchronous runs may alternate with runs in which one or the other partners overlaps the ending of the other. These overlaps may turn toward play patterns in which the exchanging position of initiator is ordered more as turn taking. Still another set of behaviors can be observed in play intervals. Here the pattern is one of establishing a causal sequence. An entire series of experiments in which infants activate lights or recordings of voices or mobiles by turning their heads, kicking, or sucking at certain rates illustrates instances of learning by consequence. In these examples infants intiate a movement sequence of their own to "cause" a result perceptually outside themselves. Grasping, mouthing, sensory exploration, hitting, kicking—all are play activities that operate in a sequential mode, but at a different rhythm and with different coordinations than in the social exchange.

It is tempting to place pronouns on these differentiations, as long as it is understood that we are *not* using these pronouns to suggest a symbolic process—a level of organization definitively different from that of the biological-neurophysiological-behavioral level found in the first year. With this caveat in mind, we might conceptualize the complementary mode as a big "you" and a little "me," the synchronous social mode as a "we," the alternating social mode as a "you" and a "me" making an "us," and the sequencing play mode as a "me" and an "it" with a "you" in the supportive background (Stern, 1983). Although this use of pronouns gives a false impression of the level of organization in the four-month-old, it does suggest a considerable amount of *differentiation* of the infant (self) in *behavioral* responses to an "object."

Each of these differentiated behavioral modes undergoes further development. Stechler (1982) describes Donna at six months. When her mother attempted to feed her food from a spoon, Donna backed off, turned her head away, and assertively pushed the spoon away. Her mother acquiesced and interrupted the feeding. After an interval, the mother instituted nursing, to which Donna assented. Donna reached up, touched the area around her mother's mouth and while still sucking herself put her fingers into her mother's mouth. Her mother joined happily into the interchange and for a few moments they sucked on each other. With her toys, Donna scanned the area, decisively selected one, reached toward it deftly, slapped it, picked it up, and vigorously banged it on the floor. Her gaze was firm and directed.

In the complementary mode, six-month-old Donna can exert an affirmative and a negative, and her mother can set up an accepting follower's position, an oppositional one, or a leadership alternative—with the initiative shifting back and forth. In the mode of synchrony, new variations can be instituted, the timing varied. In the sequencing mode with play objects, the properties of the object and the potentials of selection become more defined and under the command of the child's preferences.

If differentiations exist from birth and continue to become more developed and refined, what is it that psychoanalysts assume occurs at around nine months? I suggest the principal developmental events of the second half of the first year are (1) the buildup of behavior patterns that evidence increased action planning, and (2) a shift within the interactional matrix, from a predominance of experiences of synchrony and complementarity to increasing experiences of causal sequences of planned actions. An infant at eight or nine months can see a favorite toy in the hands of another, go toward it, overcome obstacles to get to it, refuse a substitute that has been offered, wait until another child puts it down, and finally carry out the anticipated play routine with the toy. This sustained, flexible sequence of anticipation, expectation, overcoming obstacles, planning, and carrying out a plan is, I believe, the overriding organizational change of the second half of the first year (see Stechler, 1982). Whereas the younger infant's activity involves more of the need-satisfying complementary and synchronous social exchanges, here the balance tilts to a greater degree of causal, sequential activity. This shift implies a greater freedom for planned behavior and a greater degree of monitoring of the infant's own activity and that of others through increasingly refined expectancies.

At about nine months, the affect system matures to the point where a particular form of dystonic reaction—fear—occurs. This affect is then available to amplify the infant's averse response to a disturbance in expectancy. At nine and a half months, Becca is taken to visit her grandmother. Her mother carefully introduces Becca to her new surroundings and, by the second day of the visit, Becca is comfortable with her grandmother. At one point, when the mother is out of the room, the grandmother enters with a stranger. Becca, who has just begun to stand, is noisily pulling herself up and down, using the sides of her crib. She interrupts her activity to glance first at her grandmother and then at the stranger. In a fast-paced sequence, her face goes from a flicker of a smile of greeting at her grandmother, to a look of apprehension as she glances past her grandmother to the stranger, to a look of fear and a decomposing of her fearful look into crying at a full glance at the stranger.[1] Becca's mother, hearing her cry, calls to her from the hall. Becca stops crying and, by the time her mother approaches her, she is pulling up in a standing position with a beaming smile.

---

[1] In Becca's case and in most reports of infants in this period, the distress appeared to be apprehension mounting to fear. Broucek (1982) suggests that in some instances the distress may be shame. Broucek draws an analogy to the experience of an adult approaching a person assumed to be a friend only to discover he has made a mistake and the person is a stranger. The embarrassment-shame response is presumably the same as that in infants. The schema for the shame response (based on Tomkins, 1963) would be that the baby anticipates first with rising pleasure an expected face or play pattern, only to suddenly discover that there has been a mismatch.

Placed on her mother's lap, Becca ignores the stranger, playing a familiar game with her mother's earrings. She gives the stranger a few fleeting glances. Finally, her curiosity seems to win out over her apprehension; she reaches out to the stranger to inspect her necklace and then her face. Yet she positions her body so that she remains in or very near physical contact with her mother. As she moves toward the stranger, she glances back three different times, seemingly to inspect her mother's face. Her mother senses this as a request for reassurance and responds with encouragement.

This arresting behavioral sequence might be explained two different ways. We might, for instance, claim that Becca has developed a part or whole psychic representation of her need-satisfying object (her mother). She is thus able to differentiate this internal mother representation, with its good affective memories, from that of the unknown person—the not-mother. Building on this line of reasoning, we might hypothesize that separation concerns or anger at the mother fuel a displaced anxious reaction to the stranger. Becca's libidinal ties to her mother then allow her to overcome the negative reaction. She restores contact with her mother (so the self representation becomes linked or fused with the good-mother representation intrapsychically), and this permits the pleasurable outcome. By remaining in physical contact with her mother while touching the stranger, Becca might draw the representation of the stranger into a loving self-mother representation, much as Leonardo da Vinci does with Christ, the Madonna, and St. Anne.

From a different perspective, we might say that Becca has developed an increasingly rich set of behavioral expectancies. The activity patterns surrounding the interchange with her sensitive and affectionate mother yield the highest pleasure for her. We can see this in Becca's greeting response and in the rapidity with which her fear is allayed in her mother's presence. What elicits the greeting is the sound of her mother's voice and her mother's approach, as well as the reinforcement of auditory with visual stimulation. But what of the fear response to the stranger? Is it that the stranger does not correspond to an inner representation of the mother? Not necessarily.

Nine-month-olds have already gone through a series of transformations in their responses to objects, both animate and inanimate. Beginning at four to five months, infants are more attentive to the activity of their hands as they pick up and drop an object. At about six or seven months, they are more observant of the activity of the object itself as it rises, falls, bounces, or rolls. By nine months, infants tend to observe the object for its properties, moving it around to see its other sides or moving themselves around it. None of this requires an internal representation of the object. All these activity sequences require is perceptual awareness and some form of encoding of prior behavioral experiences so that the activity and properties of the object can be coordinated with perceptual cues. With the human "object," the same developmental sequence occurs, but with one important modification. The activity patterns involve affectively charged exchanges, in which synchronous activities move to turn taking and then to much more active initiation by the infant. When the "properties" of people are discerned with increasing focus, a major property looked for is familiarity within a preexisting activity pattern or its absence: fit or mismatch. In these instances, a balance is struck. Enough familiarity offers supportive assurance, and initially interest will be the predominant affect. If there is too great a weight of strangeness, fear will predominate. With the familiar person, the principal property is the affective tone, and this the nine-month-old is already capable of reading and responding to as an action guide.

Thus, with her mother out of the room, confronted by a stranger who is outside her perceptual-action expectancies, Becca responds with fear. In the presence of her mother, the balance tips to interest, but Becca is responding to two properties—a potential for exploratory action with the stranger and her mother's facial expression, giving affective orientation. Emde (1981a) has demonstrated experimentally that at one year infants exposed to a potentially fear-arousing situation (an illusory step or "visual cliff") will overcome their fear with a silent smile of encouragement from the mother or will stop dead in their tracks if the mother gives a silent look of fear. Certainly, for this to happen there must be an encoding of behavioral patterns and expectancies involving facial cues as signal communications, as well as a means to read or decode the facial cues. These are, as I shall indicate, important steps toward internal representations, but in themselves they are perceptual-action responses, not necessarily a symbolic process.

In summary, although the neonate begins extrauterine life primed to perceive and react differentially to a number of different objects, the evidence indicates that it is not until much later, probably during the second year, that the growing child gradually develops the capacity to represent self and others at a conceptual level (Basch, 1975, 1976; Beebe and Stern, 1977; Greenspan, 1979, 1981, 1982; Friedman, 1980). Stated another way, to an outside observer, the infant perceives and reacts behaviorally in increasingly complex ways within an affectively toned interactional matrix of self and caretaker. However, only with the maturation of many capacities, beginning after the end of the first year, does the ability develop to create an image of the self, and to place that image in space and time, with boundaries that delimit the self as a body unit. It is also at this time that one finds the ability to create an image of the other, placed in the space and time of the interactional matrix in which the infant exists. As a result of a gradual development during the second year (and continuing into the third), the toddler is enabled to form psychic representations that coincide with the context of moment-to-moment experiences—to give representation to what I consider the "basic unit of experience," encompassing self and object, affect and cognition.

CONCEPTUAL REPRESENTATION OF INTENTIONALITY

A critical distinction is that between an intentional action response and a conceptual representation of intentionality, in which there is a representation of the self as intender (agent) coordinated with a representation of the action. I believe Hartmann failed to make this distinction in stating that intentionality begins at three months of age (1939, p. 51). For example, when Becca reached for the stranger's necklace she clearly intended to explore it. But was there a "she" who intended this? Or was there an eye-hand-action response pattern triggered by a specific percept amplified by an affect response of interest? To illustrate this, let us say I ask someone: "What would you do if I throw you a ball?" They might answer: "I will look at the ball, judge its height and speed of trajectory, and reach my hand up to grasp it as it comes to me." If I then throw it suddenly, no such "planned" response occurs. A hand goes up and grabs the ball out of the air. If this is called a reflex, that does a disservice to the learned perceptual-action-affective response involved. But catching the ball in this way requires neither a self-aware intender nor the capacity to form and retain an internal representation of a ball or of the self catching a ball. Of course both a self-aware intender and an internal representation are functions an adult has. The full weight of evidence from sensorimotor and other cognitive studies of infants (Greenspan, 1979, 1981) indicates the infant does not. Becca reaches only for the necklace she sees. In her second year she will be able to make up a game in her mind that involves a necklace without one being present and even seek one out in her mother's drawer. Then there will be a she who knows what she wants and intends to get it—now there is only a perceptual-action-affective response to a stimulus that is present.

Ambitendency in behavioral action responses is observable in the infant. An infant crawling toward a toy may stop—look at mother—and then look back and forth, with a puzzled or troubled expression. This ambitendency may be the precursor of the conceptual representation of opposing urges and functions. Infants at this point can recognize contrasting possibilities for responses and can anticipate positive and negative outcomes in familiar situations, but they require sensory perceptual cueing to trigger the responses. However, until the self can be conceptualized (represented) as the originator of the urge, with an idea of the means of functional completion, opposing pulls on the self cannot be embodied in fitting conceptual representations. And until opposing conceptual representations can be clearly organized, the polarities of the infant's life may lend to turbulence within the infant-caretaker interactional matrix but not to intrapsychic conflict in the infant (see the discussion in Chapter 3).

AFFECTIVE ATTITUDES TOWARD OTHERS

Cruelty, concern, gratitude, hatred, and envy are affective responses that can be said to characterize a child's behavior only when the self as agent reacts to an object conceptualized as present and subjectively meaningful in the child's psychic world. Cruelty will serve as an example. A nine-month-old boy crawls across the room, grabs a toy out of the grasp of another infant, and pushes the other child down in the process. This action may appear cruel, but it is not psychically so in its meaning. The infant's goal is the toy, his assertiveness probably lacks both a representation of the self as director of the effort and a representation of the other infant as a person to whom something "cruel" has occurred. The symbolically organized cruelty of the older toddler involves the self, psychically represented as agent, acting to relieve situationally triggered, pent-up frustration and anger by the perpetration of a cruel act (Parens, 1979a). When the older child takes a toy and deliberately shoves down a victim, there is a pleasure component, derived from the achievement of a specific conceptual goal: to inflict pain.

Similar to this distinction between what is and is not cruel is the differentiation of many early action patterns of the growing infant from the later, psychically represented complex actions of the self on an object that they simulate. Patting the mother who looks sad or "making nice" after hitting or pulling mother's hair is probably an affectively significant antecedent of the later, conceptually complex, actual or potential (trial-action) expression of concern. These behavioral antecedents unfold as imitative transactions within the interactional matrix. They are not yet psychically represented as intentions directed from the self toward an object.

We can hardly speak of such a complex action pattern as the sequence: I hurt mother, I love mother, I make up to mother, I feel good. Indeed, it is only some time after the formation of a conceptual representation of self as intender that the child develops the capacity for reflective self-awareness. "I hurt mother" as an actual action precedes a psychically represented "I" who wishes or intends to hurt mother, which in turn precedes the reflection: "I am aware of myself as one who wishes to or acts to hurt mother."

As a *behavioral* manifestation, envy can be observed toward the beginning of the second year. The one-year-old evidences an awareness of ownership. In an experiment reported by Emde (1981), a one-year-old is in a room with an observer and his mother when a robot toy enters. The toddler looks to the observer—a finding Emde takes to mean the toddler regards both room and toy as possessions of the observer. In their study of the development of normal envy, Frankel and Sherick (1977) begin with observations of two 15-month-old girls: A. and B. "were playing with basins of water. A. repeatedly attempted to pull B.'s basin of water away from her. She seemed more interested in B.'s basin than in her own. Later on, A. walked up to B. and began to play with her shoe. Repeatedly, A. came up to B. and played with an article of her clothing or took a toy with which she had just begun to play away from her" (p. 262). In contrast to the observable manifestations of children after 18 months, these behaviors were directed at the possession, not at the possessor per se. "While the taking of the thing involves interaction with a second person . . . it is not yet an object-related phenomenon" (p. 263). The onset of the emotional side of envy—the hurt, the anger, the sadness, and the yearning—seems to coincide with the development of full symbolic representation toward the end of the second year.

The findings I have reported in this chapter call for a reexamination of three questions asked by psychoanalysts: How do self and object representations become differentiated within the first year; how does the infant move from a narcissistic or autistic stage (without awareness of the object) through symbiosis (with its merger of representations) to separation from the object and individuation of the self; and how does the infant cope with innate aggression, envy, and cruelty and achieve concern? Each of these questions contains an inference that seems unwarranted by the information at hand. From one standpoint, differentiation between self and object exists, from the earliest postpartum days—but the readily observable discriminations are made at the level of perceptual-action responses. Nor does the infant need to emerge from a psychological shell or stimulus barrier to discover there is a world of objects—all the infant needs is for a face to appear or a voice to be heard. The relationship is tilted—infants are cared for by a mother they depend on, but the merging or fusing of the helpless infant portrayed in the presumed symbiotic phase is belied by the active input, the *behavioral* intentionality of the infant. It is the infant's behavioral assertiveness that emerges from the observations —not a world of primitive destructiveness. But the crucial problem lies in the assumption that representations of self and object exist. It is this hypothesis that essentially supports the notion of the need to differentiate fused or merged representations into separate ones. Mahler's postulated developmental stages rest on this assumption. Similarly, the concept of cruelty depends on a self inflicting pain on another, while envy depends on the self coveting another's property or trait. From infant research, the infant emerges as a sensory perceiving, acting, feeling person by virtue of preprogrammed and learned perceptual-action-affective response patterns. If what the infant can "do" in the first year can be explained in these terms, should we not recast our questions to ask about different "levels of learning and awareness," to borrow Greenspan's (1982) term?

Chapter Five

Additional Timetable Considerations

I have just argued that intrapsychic representations do *not* come into being until after the first year. Yet there are other capacities for which the timing seems less certain—they may or may not be a part of the infant's repertoire within the first year. In this group I would place fantasy, emotion (in contrast to affective response patterns), anticipation as a conceptual capacity (as opposed to a behavioral action capacity), the organization of memory, and the use of specific mechanisms of defense. Each of these capacities brings up developmental issues that I believe are unresolved; they thus provide a fertile area for future research (although they may tax the remarkable ingenuity displayed by infant researchers). In general, these capacities touch on the question of how early in life the infant can move from a behavioral approach, organized around bodily action-response patterns and their neural control, to the uniquely human symbolic capacity to conceptualize an actual, planned, or fantasied behavior and response.

FANTASY

Fantasy is a most enigmatic aspect of infantile life. Whereas each infant's life is highly individual and the patterns of the caretaker-infant interactional matrix vary across cultures, the fantasy contents that surface in anthropological studies of superstitions, dreams, and myths are amazingly similar. The universality of blissful responses, for instance, appears in the myths of the Garden of Eden and the land of the lotus eater. Freud's appealing speculation was that these similarities coincide with our phylogenetic heritage as creatures with a long period of dependency in infancy, during which gratification and attachment (first intrauterine and then within an interactional matrix) are biologically and experientially necessary for survival and growth. From a different perspective, our phylogenetic heritage as carnivores has been regarded as providing a genetic commonality that also can be observed behaviorally (biting reflexes, grasping, tearing, scratching, etc.). The question that is bypassed in these assumptions is whether in infancy the action pattern of, for example, blissful sucking or aggressive chewing or painful teething is accompanied at the conceptual level by images of a bountiful breast or a cannibalistic attack or a dangerous predator-enemy. The alternative possibility is that it is not at the time of the action experience but later, in the course of the full development of a representational world, that these oral images arise. This symbolism may be activated by the earlier oral-phase experience, and gives the related impelling pressures their special quality (see Blum, 1978; Call, 1980). If this is so, then, as I shall propose, primary-process imagery develops concurrently with secondary-process ordering of percepts (see Chapter 11).

Traditionally, psychoanalytic theory has suggested that the presence of fantasy activity is indicated by hallucinatory wish fulfillment, which is seen as occurring as early as the third month. The observational evidence cited is an awake baby who begins to cry in an early hunger stage, but who then sucks a finger or a pacifier. The cry is replaced temporarily by a relieved, even smiling, look. Another example is the sleeping baby who, as hunger mounts, passes from the NREM stage to the REM stage, with sucking movements and a brief smile.

Yet there are two explanations that might be offered for these findings. According to one explanation, the infant has a memory of past satisfactions with feeding. This memory includes an image of the breast or bottle and/or of the sensation of being fed. As hunger arousal occurs, this image is activated by the primitive psychic apparatus and brings about, or is accompanied by, the pleasurable affect associated with the tension diminution that is a result of feeding. The second explanation also assumes that there are memories of past experiences with feeding. These past experiences involve a sequence beginning with a hunger signal (a sensory sensation) and an intimately related motor activity—sucking. The motor activity itself stimulates, or is associated with, a pleasurable affect. The pleasurable affect may be accentuated as the sucking activity temporarily relieves the mounting tension from the hunger stimulation. This sudden drop in tension triggers the smile. Yet this effect is short-lived; the smile disappears, and restlessness and crying resume or begin.

Both these explanations involve memory, affect, and tension-state changes. The first involves an image or internal representation; the second does not. The one testable aspect is the existence of memory. Three-month-old infants exposed to play material in a particular context respond with a learned reaction to the play situation if reexposed to it in the same context up to eight days later. After eight days, the learned (remembered) response is lost (forgotten), although if the situation is reinstated briefly 24 hours before testing, the infants show no forgetting after intervals of two to four weeks (Rovee-Collier et al., 1980). Of all the activities of a normal infant, none is more consistently reinforced than the feeding experience. It will not only be remembered, but also all aspects will be developed into expanding patterns of expectancy. Parenthetically, if reinforcement of experience does not occur (as in the babies who received stomach tube feedings rather than mouth feedings because of esophageal atresia), the whole pattern of sucking, anticipation, mouth expectancy, and mouth pleasure is permanently interfered with (Dowling, 1977).

What presuppositions might explain a fantasy world of images associated with the memory function? One is that of a phylogenetic heritage in which images are laid down as deep structures that are then activated by the reinforcing experience of feeding. This hypothesis cannot be proved or disproved; still, at this time I don't know of any confirmatory evidence for it. Another hypothesis is that the memory of repeated perceptual experiences build up an inner world of images. All the experimental evidence of image buildup (especially the work of Piaget and his followers) argues against this until the second year. An argument that might be raised to meet this objection is that the infant reacts differentially to the mother and to a toy. The proposal is that the caretaking, feeding mother is so significant that the infant will retain images (part-object images) of her—the breast or bottle—and build hallucinatory fantasies around this image. There is no question of the differential response or of the motivational incentive for the infant to build memories of the mother. On the other hand, there is no experimental evidence that the infant retains an image of the mother when she is no longer perceived. The infant's joy on the return of the absent mother signifies her importance to the infant—not necessarily her internally represented image.

Another question about fantasy arises with respect to the infant's play. Children 10 to 12 months old may pick up a comb, touch their hair with it, and then drop it. Sitting next to mother in the kitchen, they may imitate her actions with pots and pans. They can pick up a play telephone receiver and put it to the ear, or turn the dial. Is this behavior an indication of fantasy? Stechler (1982) states: "The distinction between dramatization and fantasy is drawn around the question of whether the play is in the main a reenactment or an imitation of something the child has witnessed, versus something which is in the main a creation *de novo* out of the child's imagination. Fantasy may include snatches of actual encounters, but is restructured into a new format" (p. 81). An analysis of the play noted above with the comb, the kitchen utensils, and the toy phone indicates that the child has learned the use of the object at the action level. But it is the present object's properties that serve as the stimulus to the play. These children give no indication of pretending and their demeanor is serious rather than playful. A contrast is provided by the pretend games of older children, who may simulate drinking from a toy bottle or close their eyes, as if asleep. At a still older age, children extend the form of their play beyond their own actions to include others in the actions, or they may pretend to be a dog or a fire engine. Finally, with or without props (or by changing props to suit the plan), toddlers in the second year will build up combinations of play activities in which the image must precede the action. At this point there is a clear indication of a symbolic process and of fantasy activity (see Nicholich, 1977).

If it is assumed that the infant does not form internalized images or representations but instead has memories only of action patterns, what in infantile life corresponds with fantasies? My suggestion is that affect dispositions supply the link between the infant's behavioral activity and the older individual's fantasies. For example, when we, as adults, see a baby contentedly sucking on his mother's breast, with his eyes looking up and his fingers touching the breast, we may, if we are at all in a receptive state, smile and share the sense of contentedness. Or if we see a baby gurgling with excitement as she is held high by her father, we may experience a sense of thrill and heightened body tension. I suggest that in perceiving these exchanges between infant and parent, we recognize the bodily feeling and emotion accompanying the physical action. Certainly fantasy images may simultaneously congeal into our adult experiences, but I submit they are not necessary for the recognition to occur.

My conception is based on several propositions, which will become clearer in the next section. First of all, an affect system develops at birth; affects are differentiated processes from the beginning of life, each component of which has a maturational timetable. Bodily feelings and emotional responses to external stimuli amplify the experience to meaningful levels and are, along with the action pattern of the experience, the unity that persist in memory. Extensive learning, based on the memory of such experiences stimulated by recognition of similar or analogous situations, builds expectancies and makes possible increasing complexity of behavioral intentionality. All of this complexity proceeds, and does not require, cognition at a representational level.

EMOTION

Emotion, in contrast to affective response patterns, may or may not be conceptualized as a feature of the experiential life of the infant in the first year. We have seen that a series of affective response patterns (observable as body reactions with characteristic facial expressions) already exist in the neonate. The birth cry, hunger distress, startle reaction, smiling, and capacity to mimic facial expressions—all are affective manifestations present within the first week or 10 days of extrauterine life.

I have already mentioned Tomkins's (1962, 1963, 1981) view that these manifestations indicate a separate affect system, in which specific affect responses can be activated both innately and as a result of learning. Tomkins identifies a series of affective-behavioral groupings recognizable by muscular responses: surprise–startle, interest–excitement, enjoyment–joy, distress–anguish, anger–rage, fear–terror, contempt–disgust, and shame–humiliation. Each affect is conceived of as controlled by an inherited program of neuronal firing, which in turn controls not only the facial muscles, but also autonomic, blood-flow, respiratory, and vocal responses. Each affect is capable of being activated either innately or via learning by a stimulus from a drive, a perception, a movement, a thought, a memory, or another affect. In the neonate each affect must be capable of being activated by a variety of unlearned stimuli; a cry, for instance, may be elicited by hunger, loud sounds, pain, or a breathing restriction. The same innate activity pathway for the cry (and any other affect) must be accessible to learning. The mother's leaving the room or the expectation of scolding can activate the same pathway for crying as is activated by the unlearned stimuli. Tomkins believes that each pathway is characterized at the neurophysiological level by the "density" of neural firing—the frequency per unit time. As noted in Chapter 1, stimulation increase at a moderate rate triggers interest; at a greater rate, fear; and at a still steeper rate, startle. A steady (unrelieved) stimulation at a high level of firing triggers distress; at a still higher level, anger. A rapid decrease in stimulation triggers joy; a still more rapid drop, laughter. An abrupt interruption of a pleasurable experience triggers shame.

Tomkins believes his conception explains the observation that many different sources can lead to the same affect. For example, a hungry 15-month-old, his face contorted in distress, observes his mother put his food down to answer the phone. His fist contracts. Tomkins notes that each of these elements—drive (hunger), affect (distress), thought (the inference that mother is not going to give him the bottle), and motor reaction (the clenched fist)—conjointly add up to the density level of neural firing required to innately trigger anger. In addition, the same affect may arise because a number of sources have the same abstract property (such as deceleration). For example, if enjoyment is triggered by any sudden deceleration in neural firing, the innate phenomenon of smiling would result from such diverse sources (present later in life) as the sudden reduction of pain, or the sudden reduction of tension at the moment of orgasm, or even the sudden reduction of another affect, as when fear need no longer be maintained or when a high level of interest (puzzlement) is relieved by the sudden awareness of the solution to a problem.

To reiterate: Tomkins regards *the primary function of affect to be the amplification of urgency—making one care by feeling.* For Tomkins, drives supply vital information of where and when to do what, but it is the additional affective amplification that gives this information its impelling quality. In this way affects are not motives themselves, but they can be the core of any and all motives. That affects can be attached to a wide range of motives is a result of the freedom of the affect system to combine with a variety of other components into a central assembly, an executive mechanism upon which messages converge from all sources. Thus, in feelings of inferiority, shame (Wurmser, 1981; Broucek, 1982), or certain kinds of guilt, the affect itself may be identical, but the central assembly may be the result of a host of different disturbing elements—such as doing something that brings oneself down in personal or public estimate, or brings others one loves down.

To return to the first year of life, we can ask: What are the possible implications of Tomkins's formulations for the occurrence of emotions in the developing infant? First, they cast doubt on conceptions that treat affect manifestations such as the "endogenous" smile or the startle "reflex" as precursors of affects, rather than as innate patterns present from birth that later become integrated via learning into increasingly complex assemblies. But are these physical affect manifestations, including those that are later stimulated by learning, "emotions"? Basch (1975) argues that they are not. He accepts Tomkins's concept of the independence of the affect system:

> . . . regardless of its origin, a sudden stimulus leads to an attitude of alertness and readiness to evaluate the situation; a more gradual rise in stimulation promotes interest in its source as evidenced by exploratory behavior; a massive rise in stimulus intensity, regardless of cause, promotes a pain reaction, and prolonged stimulation at such a high level creates active attempts to eliminate the stimulus through fight or flight behavior; on the contrary, a sudden decrease from high stimulus intensity brings relief and behavior appropriate to a state of contentment. These basic adaptive patterns become associated with the sensorimotor record of the organism's perception and of its reaction to experience. When such a sensorimotor pattern is recognized at a later time, the particular associated adaptive behavior, be it fight, flight, attraction, etc. is activated [p. 503].

Basch contends that although this series of increasingly complex responses exemplifies sensorimotor learning, it is not based on reflection. He therefore concludes that it is only when the affective behaviors of joy, anger, etc., "are conceptualized symbolically much later in life" that these behaviors can be "experienced as an emotion or a feeling" (p. 505). In another paper, he adds: "Once conceptualization becomes possible for human beings, after age two, and with the development of the capacity to describe concepts discursively through speech, there is a beginning translation of various behavioral patterns into emotional experiences" (1976, p. 769).

Yet a different conclusion from Tomkins's proposals is possible. Affects can be regarded as present in some significant experiential form, albeit different from the forms of the later, reflective-symbolic state. For the infant and the older child, the experience of joy or distress may be more similar than dissimilar. The infant, however, does not experience joy or distress as part of a complex central assembly, only the older child does. Nor are the complex central assemblies of the toddler the same as those of the five-year-old. These assemblies themselves grow and change with each maturational and developmenal step.

We might, in this regard, reconsider Spitz's concept of "organizers" (1959, 1965). Spitz views a specific affective behavior as the indicator of a far-reaching process of organization. In each case, an affect indicates a link with a cognitive process, i.e., the smile is linked with recognition of the human face; eight-month anxiety, with discrimination of mother from others; and the toddler's negativism, with the availability of volitional choice. In each instance, infant research brings us evidence that the cognitive processing at a behavioral level precedes the "organizer." Recognition, discrimination, and volition have long, detailed histories of gradual and graduated development. Thus, it would seem that we should shift our conceptualization of the first year of life away from the idea of dramatic stage-specific indicators toward a view of gradual development of systems and their mutual accommodation and assimilation.

Should we regard affects as appearing behaviorally as a result of neurophysiological maturation and then undergoing refinement as they become parts of complex central assemblies with other developing systems? If so, then joy can be joy, and anger anger, from their first appearances. And each can be interrelated with whatever mode of response or learning (perceptual-action, sign-determined, or symbolic) is present at any time. If we accept the suggestion that the primary function of affect is the amplification of urgency, then affects—whether or not we follow Basch in thinking of them as emotions only if reflection exists—have a continuity from birth throughout life. Making one care by feeling, to use Tomkins's phrase, exists as a continuous general property whether one knows one cares or not. To my mind, this suggests that there is more conceptual benefit to be gained by regarding emotions as present in the first year than by holding to a definitional distinction based on the mode of response or learning that is being amplified into urgency.

ANTICIPATION

With anticipation, a similar question arises about its timing as an intrapsychic conceptual operation. Behaviorally, children in the second half of the first year may look toward the door through which they expect mother to return. If, at a particular time, they want to crawl freely, they may start to raise a fuss when placed in a playpen. But they will then stop and after a minute take up a toy. It can be said that they anticipate the displeasure they would arouse in mother if they were to fuss. It might be conjectured that this evidence of "delay" indicates a conceptual organization of a memory of a past unpleasure signaled by an affect (anxiety) associated with an action (fussing in the playpen). Careful observation of many such behavioral samples, however, tends to indicate that the baby, when starting to fuss, casts a quick glance to the mother's face and receives a look of "don't." This suggests that anticipation during the second half of the first year is based on action recognition guided by an increasingly sensitive affect signal exchange. In contrast, the view of anticipation as an intrapsychic conceptual operation implies that an affect that the infant clearly has, has assumed a signal function in an internally coded action sequence (Basch, 1975).

In the first year, affects both amplify the nature of the infant's experience and provide a major feature of the infant-mother communication. The special discovery of psychoanalysis has been their signal function as an internalized guidance system for anticipation. Infant research would seem to suggest that, in the *neonate,* affect and action responses to stimuli do not include a capacity for anticipation. Beginning probably in the third month, affect and action are integrated with recognition, making possible a limited form of behavioral anticipation. Between the sixth and the twelfth month, sign-signal functions of intercommunication (affect reading) between caretaker and infant add an informational base to the capacity for anticipation. But only during the second year do affects seem to become integrated into a system of symbolic representation in which they can function as signals in an intrapsychic anticipatory capacity, without external guidance.

When psychoanalysts propose that anxiety, depression, and guilt are complex affects, I believe what is meant is that the affects have become incorporated into complex assemblies with cognitive units. In these situations, the affects carry their own internally reinforcing informational properties. A threat, for instance, stimulates fear, with inclinations toward flight; absence of a loved and needed person stimulates sadness, with inclinations toward crying; a foul "taste" stimulates disgust, with inclinations toward vomiting; frustration of assertiveness stimulates anger, with inclinations toward hitting, biting, or pushing away; novelty stimulates interest, with inclinations toward alertness and exploration; and so on (see Jones, 1981). As these affects become a part of a full experiential unit during the second half of the second year, they can be "read" for their information in monitoring behavior. It is only then that anticipation becomes possible in the absence of perceptual cues.

MEMORY

Infant research has indeed confirmed the supposition of ego psychology that memory exists as an autonomous function. Neonates' action responses to the mother's voice, face, and odor confirms the presence of short-term memory. The trigger for this memory is a perceptual cue—not the evocation of an inner representation without external cueing. It is therefore spoken of as recognition memory rather than evocative memory (Fraiberg, 1969).

A recent experiment has helped us to discover how long recognition memory lasts and how it can be prolonged. Rovee-Collier et al. (1980) placed three-month-old infants in a crib with a mobile that moved by a string attached to their feet. The infants rapidly mastered the kicking technique needed to make the mobile move and evidenced pleasure in their accomplishment. Until eight days later, if the infants were brought back to the same crib with the same mobile, they would begin to kick at a high rate even though there was no string and no movement of the mobile. The memory that triggered this action response could be extended well beyond the eight-day extinction period if the infants were shown the moving mobile before the experiment was repeated. Memory thus reinforced by the cue of the moving mobile could be prolonged for several weeks. If the crib and the remainder of the setting were constant but a different-looking mobile substituted, the kicking was less or absent.

Stern (1982) has reported an experiment that indicates the effect of emotion on memory. Six-month-old infants were shown two hand puppets: a frog and a rabbit. No infants smiled until a game of peek-a-boo was played, using either the frog or the rabbit. This elicited a smiling response from many of the infants. A week later the infants were again shown the puppets. Those that had smiled the week before smiled at the now-still frog or rabbit and looked longer at the puppet that had been used in the game. The infants who had not smiled during the peek-a-boo game did not smile a week later and looked longer at the puppet not used in the game. The experimenters believed that the affective response was remembered by both smilers and nonsmilers so that their preferences were affected, but in opposite directions.

This experiment raises a question: Did the infants who smiled during the game smile a week later at the nonmoving puppet because they remembered smiling or because they saw a funny puppet? I believe neither is the best explanation. I suggest that the infants smiled at the nonmoving puppet previously used in the game for the same reason the infants kicked in the crib with the mobile—they anticipated that the perceptual-action-affective sequence they remembered would be repeated.

The question that remains unanswered at this time is: How do the memory systems of the infant—those cued by perceptual stimuli—relate to the memory activities of the older child and adult? Are memories coded in action-affect pattern responses replaced by later conceptual remembering? Do all or some recognition and enactive memories become transformed into evocative memories? Or do some memories remain in the form of perceptual-action-affect responses, without symbolic representation? These questions are of clinical and theoretical relevance. Psychoanalysts generally believe that the experiences in the early weeks and months of life are a significant determinant of later development, yet the means by which they are recorded and the ways in which the recordings are organized remain elusive. The suggestion I should like to offer is that affects serve as the principal encoding vehicle—although never in isolation from the perceptual-action mode in which they are experienced (see Chapters 11, 12, and 13).

DEFENSIVE ORGANIZATION

Psychoanalysis has evolved a rich, complex understanding of the means by which an individual deals with the full range of stimuli, from positive and orienting to negative and dystonic. The concepts of a defensive organization and especially of the mechanisms of defense have increased our knowledge of mental functioning immeasurably (see Lichtenberg and Slap, 1971, 1972). It seems natural to assume from the workings of the defenses in adults that the child in some archaic fashion functions similarly. Indeed, many efforts have been made to conceptualize a developmental timetable and sequence for the individual defense mechanisms (A. Freud, 1936; Lichtenberg and Slap, 1972). Moreover, Lustman (1957) has tried to interrelate some defense mechanisms with behavioral precursors. He postulates an inborn, primary defense mechanism of imperceptivity to external stimuli.

In Chapter 4, I described the means available to the infant in the first year to deal with dystonic stimuli. These included the Moro reflex, crying, withdrawal into sleep, active pushing away, habituation, gaze aversion, and signal indicators of "no." Are these operations, which occur at the biological-neurophysiological-behavioral level of organization, the only means available in the first year? Or, as has generally been assumed, are defense mechanisms also a part of the infant's functional capacities? This question pertains especially to such early-developing mechanisms of defense as denial, projection, introjection, incorporation, and splitting.

I believe that each specific defense mechanism develops, not as a separate entity, but as a component of the general regulation provided by perceptual-cognitive-emotional control structures (Lichtenberg and Slap, 1971, 1972). Even the earliest mechanisms of defense, however, appear to be associated with some kind of representational capacity, so that the timing of this development seems intimately related to the unsettled question of when perception and action in conjunction with self and object gain internal representation. For example, Beebe and Stern (1977) describe a very troubled infant, in a constant state of gaze aversion with respect to his mother, who looks "paranoid"—that is, his facial expression appears angry and fearful. I believe it is a plausible assumption that the infant experiences affects—anger and fearfulness—that characterize the adult's or older child's paranoid rage and suspiciousness. But can we assume the defense mechanism of projection? Since projection involves the attribution of an aspect of self (psychically symbolized in some representational form) to another person (psychically symbolized in a representational form), the infant's angry and fearful affective state does not involve projection unless these exchanges of "ownership" of the repudiated (projected) aspect of self can occur conceptually. For an explanation of the infant's angry and fearful state, nothing more is required than recognition of steady mismatch of need and anticipation in the caretaker-infant pairing. Similar reasoning would explain the sad-faced, hypoactive, uninterested infant of a depressed, withdrawn mother. The assumption of incorporation or introjection, beyond behavioral imitation (mirroring) (Greenacre, 1941), is neither a required explanation nor consistent with the level of organizational functioning of the infant during the first year.

A last example may seem somewhat more equivocal. In this case, the mother-infant pair has formed a more than adequate attachment. The mother returns after a two-week absence and discovers, to her surprise, that her eight-month-old daughter ignores her for some time—looking instead to the replacement caretaker. Is this an indication of the defense mechanism of denial? Is the infant saying: "I've been so hurt by your abandonment, I won't look at you. I won't give recognition to your presence lest it remind me of my hurt"? Or is it protective denial: "I am so angry at your abandonment, I would kill you if I noticed you"? Each of these formulations assumes intrapsychic symbolic representations of self and object. Is there an alternative explanation? It might be said that in the two-week interval the infant has built a new pattern of interaction in which her activities with the substitute caretaker have become familiar—a security giving match between need and expectation. Her mother on her return is thus a threat to the infant's immediate behavioral pattern and is treated as outside and unfamiliar. This example, however, is a more equivocal one because if the mother were simply outside the familiar she would be a novelty and could arouse interest, and with memory cueing, recognition of her former place of central attachment.

It is not, I believe, easy to unravel this knot at this time, but a great deal can be learned from attachment-departure-reunion studies (Ainsworth, 1979; Sroufe, 1979). In experiments involving three brief separation scenes in an unfamiliar play environment, the responses on reunion of 12-month-olds regarded as attached fell into three groupings. On the second or third reunion after the brief separation, 65% of the children actively sought closeness with the mother and resisted being put down too soon. Another 20–25% showed no distress at the time of separation and tended to avoid the mother on her return. It is of special interest that these same infants, when observed in the home setting, were demonstrably anxious at signs of the mother's departure. In the experimental situation, where the anxious, fussy response did not occur, these infants diverted their attention from the perception of the mother's leaving or returning by hyperattentiveness to some element in the playroom. The last 10% were acutely distressed on departure and during the separation. Then, on reunion, they reacted to mother with strong ambitendent behavior—they demanded to be picked up but at the same time would push off angrily.

I believe these experiments indicate that departure-reunion experiences in infants who have formed attachments are complex aspects of behavioral-affective interaction patterns. The infant has a repertoire of possible behaviors with which to respond. A securely attached infant, after a brief (familiar) departure, may respond to the reunion by giving cues of a desire to be close and remain held until fully comforted and reassured. But after prolonged (unfamiliar) departure—of two weeks, as in our example—even a securely attached child may utilize the means employed in the experiment by anxious, avoidant infants who diverted their attention from the returning mother to some element in the playroom. Turning to the more certain expectancy of the replacement caretaker is the means that I suggest the securely attached eight-month-old girl used to deal with her mother's return after the, for her, extraordinary break in expectancy of the two-week absence.

My explanation does not eliminate the possibility of defense mechanisms such as denial in the infant. However, it seems that until the infant can be thought of as functioning definitively on a symbolic level, it is more appropriate to speak of biological-neurophysiological-behavioral defensive measures and to regard defense *mechanisms* as components of the general advance to a symbolic-representational psychic world. In other words, the conception of defense mechanisms and of a defensive organization cannot be studied in isolation from the unsettled problems of psychic representation of self and objects and of the broad development of organizations of perceptual-cognitive-affective regulation at a symbolic level.

Chapter Six

Reflections on Id and Ego
in the First Year

I have indicated that infants are already accomplished action in-
itiators and responders before they achieve psychic representation
of the purpose of the action or of themselves as the originators of
the action. They are skillful seekers of stimulation and solvers of
problems through refinements in action-response patterns. They
respond to inner impelling forces and to opportunities to exercise
all manner of functional capacities. In all these actions, they seem
pressed to move toward competence (Brazelton and Als, 1979;
Broucek, 1979). Most significantly, they organize their reaction
patterns within the interactional matrix with the caregiver. Yet it is
probably only gradually, beginning possibly after the end of the
first year, that the actor achieves an image of the self doing the acting. I believe this extremely significant event comes about as the
result of an affective-cognitive achievement in imaging, and I shall
describe this process in discussing the second year. The imaging
capacity leads to an advance in objectivization of the external environment. Through a greater appreciation of contingency sequences, aided by pre-speech language acquisition, the imaging
capacity results in an increasing sense of self. But, again, all this
takes place during the second year.

This epigenetic timing bears directly on what we can mean by
the terms "id" and "ego" as they apply to the first year of life. Of
the various traditional and contemporary attempts to define id and
ego (Gill, 1963; Moore and Fine, 1967; Laplanche and Pontalis,
1967), the one that appears to be most applicable to research findings from the first year of life is that which hypothesizes two
psychic organizations according to the characteristic mode of tension regulation employed. Rapaport (1959) assigns immediacy of

discharge (peremptoriness) to the id and delay of discharge to the ego. Processes attributed to the id have the quality of being impelling, that is, of providing a compelling autoplastic pressure. The ego is characterized as an organization of many complex capabilities, which serve and restrain the id's impelling activation, as well as respond to pressures from the environment of greater or lesser intensity. The ego's response to both the id and the environment takes the form of motivated behavior rather than peremptory discharge. A series of questions logically arise from these definitions. What can neonates and older infants during the first year of life be regarded as impelled to do? What functional capacities do children in the first year possess that enable them to respond to this autoplastic pressure as well as to pressures from the environment? Can the pressure that impels action be differentiated sufficiently from the functional capabilities inherent in these infants' actions to justify our speaking of id and ego as two separate organizations?

As we have seen, the traditional psychoanalytic view of the impelling quality of the urge for satisfaction is supported by observations of the infant's tendency to seek and react to the bodily experiences of hunger, elimination, sensual pleasure, and sleep. But when observed, the infant seems to be impelled equally powerfully to seek and react differentially to human and inanimate stimuli. The power of the neonate's response to a toy entering the visual field and the strikingly different response when mother comes into view point to a compelling biological priming. This is id-like in its peremptoriness. But if we were to take all the infant's impelled behaviors as indicators of an id, we would find ourselves at considerable variance from a traditional definition of the id and thereby add confusion, rather than achieving a useful extension of the concept.

The infant's mouth activities can serve as an example. Sucking and salivating indicate the compelling urge to satisfy hunger. Nonnutrient sucking and sensations obtainable from the mucous membrane of the lips are powerful sources of pleasure. These oral cravings are rapidly established as behavioral motivations for solving the problem of coordinating hand-to-mouth movements. But the mouth is equally impressively activated as a sense organ in the whole pattern of attention-fixing behavior in relation to toys or mother. One extremely interesting experiment was performed on three-week-old infants. The infants were blindfolded, and a nipple was placed in the mouth. For half of the infants, a normal rounded nipple was inserted; for half, the nipple had multiple nubs sticking out from the surface. After an infant had time to feel the round or nubbed nipple with mouth and tongue, it was removed and the blindfold taken off. Each infant was shown the two nipples, the one mouthed and the one not. The infants looked more at the nipple explored with tongue and mouth (Meltzoff and Borton, 1976). This finding indicates that the compelling sensory perceptions from the mouth are coordinated with the brain's processing of patterns, connecting them across modes (oral tactile and visual).

It appears that the compelling nature of stimulus seeking extends along far broader lines than are traditionally drawn for the sensual satisfaction of the oral libidinal drive. Nor is there much conclusive support for the concept of an aggressive drive as such, unless we conceptualize this drive as simply a strong general trend toward assertiveness. Anger as an observable affect has not been consistently reported until three months of age or later. Some reflection of aggression may be embedded in the infant's crying and fussiness. Yet crying is often nonspecific and fussiness usually disappears when the smiling response is consolidated at three months, so that these behaviors do not conclusively support the thesis that crying or fussiness derives from a compelling push for aggressive action, differentiated from action or affective neural firing in general.

Support can be found, however, for the traditional view that the id's goal is discharge. The collapse phase of the four times a minute pattern of buildup of eye, mouth, finger, toe, and shoulder reactions to human and inanimate objects can be considered an obligatory discharge phenomenon. Crying may also be a part of a regular compelling pattern of discharge for stimulation. This view seems to be supported by the observation that after periods of crying, the level of integration of behavior in other areas may be higher. In addition, the neonate's extended REM sleep activity and non-stimulus-related smiling can be pointed to as discharge activities—closer probably to the neurophysiological conception of neuronal firing than to what is usually meant by "id." The massive reactions to unpleasure, violent crying, whole-body reactions (Moro reflex), and severe withdrawal reactions likewise appear to be impelling means of discharge. However, a unitary view of accounting for these behaviors as simply discharge phenomena cannot be supported. In each observable pattern of infant behavior, stimulus *seeking* is so compelling a force that stimulus seeking and discharge must be seen as complementary regulatory governors. All these attempts to relate the infant's behavior to one or another traditional view of the id, therefore, seem to me to stretch the conception to or beyond the edge of its usefulness.

Functions suggestive of ego activities are rather easily deduced from the infancy findings. An organizing tendency (albeit one closely relatable to biological patterning) can be inferred from the infant's capacity to regulate a 24-hour period through organized behavioral states, with increasingly complex behavioral modalities within the states, and increasing control of the transitions between states. The infant's capacity to organize and react to perceptual input by action responses and to participate in behavioral communications can be further broken down into functions of pattern matching, discrimination along the lines of preferences, and elemental learning and problem solving (as in bringing the thumb to the mouth). Gender patterning, imitative responses, and the formation of increasingly complex behavioral automatisms all fit in with the idea of a primitive ego organization at work. Similarly, many behaviors, such as gaze aversion and the turning off of attention to repetitious or dystonic stimuli, suggest regulatory and defensive functions associated with the concept of an ego. It is my impression that these and other easily inferred functional capacities fit rather well into the traditional definition of the ego—more so than those I was able to deduce for the id.

Yet there are difficulties, and they have to do with the interface between innate biological-neurophysiological-behavioral organizations and a psychological organization. For example, does the clearly demonstrable learning that allows three- to four-month-olds to take part in the game of looking and smiling, to swing their arms and legs in response to the particular timing, sequencing, and vocalizing of mother, have a form of registry that could be described as psychological "thinking"? If we were to apply the term "ego" to an unbroken sequence between, for example, the genetically patterned, perceptual-behavioral functions present in the neonate, the sign-organized consequence learning of the infant, and the symbolically organized cognitive functions of the older toddler (Basch, 1975; Blum, 1978), then it would not matter at which point in development we inferred psychological, as compared with biological-neurophysiological-action, functioning. However, to do so would again take a familiar term, "ego," and alter, at least for the early infancy period, its traditional reference to psychological functioning. Core issues that bear on the timing of a psychological ego, in contrast to a behavioral "pre-ego," are related to questions about the timing of self and object representations, anticipation, fantasy formation, intentionality, and intrapsychic conflict (see Chapters 4 and 5). The general conclusion that seems to me to fit the data best is that there is as yet no definitive criterion for identifying the timing of the first appearance and subsequent maturation and development of a psychological ego organization as such.

Even if we take those impelling pressures which might be considered an infantile id, and those functional capacities which might be regarded as an infantile ego, is there sufficient distinction between them to warrant the concept of two organizations? The overwhelming evidence, I believe supports the idea of an "undifferentiated phase" (Hartmann et al., 1946). In each instance of behavior, the component that is impelling exists as a gradient along with the component that can be regarded as more characteristic of ego functioning.[1] At one moment, for example,

---

[1]Loewald (1978) challenges the conception of ego apparatuses having primary autonomy: "Perception and memory in their primitive conformations, which remain basic ingredients of their later transformations, . . . are . . . unconscious instinctual activities, aspects of libidinal processes that only later gain a comparatively autonomous status" (p. 467).

the baby's hunger sucking may be impelling and at another the search for eye contact with mother may also seem intensely compelling. Thus the intensity of both hunger and of social seeking may rise and fall or alternate in compelling the infant to act. As observers, we might compare what is impelling or drive-like with what belongs more in the area of "delay," yet it is difficult to define a consistent organizational or structural unit underlying this distinction.

Another example reveals the paradoxical nature of these qualities of impelled (id) and functional (ego) behavior. Older infants not only become captivated by mother's face and vocalizing, but pursue facial and vocal configurations as a perceptual puzzle and a source of novel stimulation. The intensity with which they do this, the rapt expression on their faces, indicates the impelling quality of this learning activity. Its ego side is implied in Call's suggestion that "the infant's engagement in the task of deciphering the human face is a protype of what is involved in the decipherment of vocal and written symbols" (1980, p. 220). Hartmann et al. (1946) recognized this dual aspect: "The child does not only experience deprivation when one of his demands is denied—the demand for food, care or attention—but also when the adult interferes with one of his spontaneous activities, whether they serve the gratification of a drive or the solution of a problem. In the child's life, various types of activities tend to be not as sharply delimited from each other as they normally are with the adult. All action is closer to instinctual drives" (p. 41). I believe Hartmann's (1933) studies of the Zeigarnik effect were early efforts to bring an aspect of these questions into focus. The relatively impelling nature of task completion for the older child may have its roots in a genetically blueprinted, caretaker-supported push for competence or effectance, demonstrable in the infant. Broucek (1982) has suggested that the pull executed by the desire for competence pleasure is augmented by shame that is triggered when a sudden decrement occurs in a pleasure-giving action. Successful completion of a problem-solving action would be the prototype for competence pleasure. An interruption in the completion of the problem-solving action would be the prototype for shame. (This view may help to resolve the controversy that surrounded Hendrick's [1942] proposal of an instinct for mastery, a controversy that could receive no satisfactory solution in the metapsychology of the period.)

Let us consider an experiment by Papousek and Papousek (1975) in this light (see also Broucek, 1979). Four-month-old infants were exposed to five seconds of multicolored bursts of light. They oriented themselves toward the stimulation with interest, and then, typical of responses to unvaried stimuli, their orientation diminished after repetition. The experiment was arranged so that when the infants in the course of their movements rotated their head 30 degrees to a predetermined side three times successively within a time interval, the light display was switched on. As soon as the infants turned on the light presentation by their own head movements, their behavior changed dramatically. Their orientation reactions increased in intensity and they continuously made all kinds of movement to try to switch on the visual stimulation again. If successful, they repeated their head turnings over and over with gestures and vocalizations of joy. But what is most striking is that while the infants eagerly repeated their movements, they watched the visual display less and less. The pleasure and the impetus to repeat the head movements appeared to originate more from the effectiveness of this action (efficacy or competence pleasure) than from the visual stimulus itself.

My conclusion is that we need to lay less stress on distinct structural organizations, and place a relatively greater emphasis on understanding how each developmental finding fits into a pattern of adaptation. The issue then shifts away from a question of whether a form of problem solving is drive-inspired or ego-inspired, and, if ego-inspired, whether the ego has its own independent source of energy. Instead, the questions to be answered become: How does the particular form of problem solving fit into the infant's interactional matrix? How does the infant move toward disengagement from the interactional matrix? And what relatively independent collateral functioning of child and parents facilitates the development of the toddler's intrapsychic life on a symbolic level?

A core issue that refers to differentiation is that of internal arousal. Clearly, in many of the examples I have given, arousal has an internal source, such as the need for food, sucking, or sleep. In other instances, however, it has an external source, such as the mother's face or a toy in the infant's perceptual field. Traditionally, psychoanalytic theory has recognized this problem in accounts of development and has conceptualized a symbiotic closeness that is followed by self-object differentiation. Internal arousal experiences are regarded as helping to stimulate cognitive awareness of the self as separate, and this sense of the self as separate helps to further differentiate internal arousal. At the behavioral level, as we have seen, a degree of differentiation exists from birth, with complex discrimations in the infant's responses to a variety of experiences. Some of these experiences of course involve high internal arousal, but many—even most—do not. Thus, it may be that the significance of internal arousal for differentiation may have been overstated. In any case, I believe that existing psychoanalytic accounts of the first year of life may understate the significance of the fitting together of the mother-infant pair across a range of experiences, from low to high states of internal arousal, and the power of synchronous, biologically primed behavioral systems. Once the power of the interactional matrix that dominates the first year is appreciated, then the need to study the step-by-step movement by which the child emerges from this basic dyadic mode of regulation becomes a central focus for later development. What we commonly mean by an id or drive urge (i.e., the experience of internal arousal arising from a coherent drive organization) can be hypothesized to occur only when disengagement from domination by interactional responsiveness has become a reasonably consistent experience.

In appreciating the power of mother-infant synchrony (positive or negative), then, we need to look for the signposts of emergence from it that occur during the first year. Synchronies and attachment behaviors dominate the young infant's waking life. Feeding

(Call, 1980), visual-vocal interplay (Stern, 1977), and games such as the cough-smile-raspberry (Call, 1980), are examples in which mother-infant reciprocity is maintained by split-second responsiveness. "Some of the mother-infant or infant-mother sequences occur almost synchronously, others overlap (in that one starts before the preceding behavior of the partner is completed), and in other cases, there is a short lapse between the end of one partner's behavior and the onset of the other's 'response'" (Beebe and Stern, 1977, p. 41). This mutual entrainment, the fitting together of mother and infant, develops so rapidly that by three weeks regularity of expectation occurs in the 24-hour organization of states and in the active alert interchange. At this time mothers often state they "know" their babies and that they feel their babies know or recognize them. The bond of this attachment, based on the relative certainty of mutual reactions, provides a basis for the spirit of confidence and trust on which successful adaptation depends. What we find is a powerful and economic system that allows the mother and infant to lock into and pay attention to each other for relatively long periods (Brazelton, 1980a, b).

At the same time, within a period of weeks, the infant can detect some contingencies (finding his or her thumb), which constitute the origins of learning at an action level. Much of this learning takes place when the infant is not impinged on, either by need urgency or by the mother's active intrusion (Sander, 1983). An important milestone in the movement toward emerging is reached when the infant is able to inhibit what had been obligatory responses within the interactional synchrony. For example, with the neurophysiological change that occurs at six months, the infant no longer smiles with a completely lit-up face but begins to smile in a more graded manner (Fraiberg, 1974). The infant can then more definitively initiate and terminate reciprocal exchanges. Other behaviors that have been coupled with the smile, such as vocalizing, may become separated, or, like concentration or surprise, loosely related, giving the infant a greater range of initiative. This advance is followed in the second half of the first year by a series of developments that increase the infant's scope of affective contingent play both alone and with the caretakers. With their caretakers, infants can express anger as well as joy, coyness, or fear, as a clear communication. Alone, at about 10 months, they will babble a form of echolalic speech, a spontaneous dialogue with themselves, imitatively starting them on the road to an active use of verbal signs and symbols. Thus, during the first year, infants institute various trends toward emerging (Call, 1980). But I would emphasize that they do not accomplish disengagement behaviorally or conceptually until considerably later. In fact, at the end of the first year, the infant's movement is toward focusing demands on the mother in preference to others, including the father, as the specific person to meet the infant's specific needs (Sander, 1980). In the independent play activity that begins at this time, the infant's functioning is in the orbit of the nearby mother. The epoch-making events of self-assertion and cognitively self-represented intentionality that affect this relative harmony of the one-year-old are yet to come.

The uncertainties I have noted and the tentative conclusions I have reached in these reflections on the first year of life place me at some distance from the mainstream of psychoanalytic theory on this period (see Weil, 1976). Nevertheless, in adhering to an overview of adaptation as a general concept with which to integrate the new observations about the first year with the psychoanalytic, clinically based observations of later life, I believe I remain close to the tradition of Hartmann, Erikson, Spitz, and Winnicott. As Sander (1980c) has noted, even before 1960, these observers and theoreticians had presented a "view of interactive process in personality organization."

[This view] could be based on the model of adaptation as an actual behavioral fitting together between individual and environment, with the shaping of character organization on the basis of individual strategies arrived at in negotiating a ground plan of a sequence of adaptive tasks, common to all infant-environment systems, but negotiated differently for each. The active negotiation of the adaptive tasks in turn each constructs a part of the individual's perceptual world of interpersonal relationships, each being in turn epigenetically synthesized and integrated in the act of initiating new behavioral adaptations, later to emerge as the broadly generalized behavioral strategies, such as we know in "transference predispositions."

To serve as such a unifying construct, adaptation must be regarded as referring to the biological, neurophysiological, behavioral, and interactional fitting together of the first year as well as to the fitting together that relates to both the symbolically organized intrapsychic functioning and the social mores of the older child and adult.

PART III:

The Second Year

Chapter Seven

The Beginnings of an Imaging Capacity and Sign-Signal Informational Exchange

The second year of life begins poised between the relative interdependence of the infant-caretaker unit and the relative independence of the toddler's initiating behavior. The focus is still on the mother, but the child's activities while "alone" (in the presence of mother) set the stage for a variety of developmental achievements. Of particular importance is the emergence of a sense of self during the second year. As I have already suggested, this sense of self is contingent on certain cognitive developments. With this in mind, I would like to reflect on the import of the toddler's imaging capacity.

My premise is that the way the child perceives an image undergoes a series of changes. Before acquiring what I refer to as an imaging capacity, the infant perceives an image of an object as a component of an action sequence in which the object plays a part. The toddler's imaging capacity raises perception to a new level. Now the object is perceived as having an image (and other properties) even when it is not the source of immediate perceptual input. Through the imaging capacity, an object (including the self) comes to be construed as a discrete, persisting entity, whose appearance functions as a sign conveying information. For example, when toddlers look at the mother's face, her expression acts as a sign signaling affective consonance or dissonance, and the information has regulatory importance. The sign image, with the information derived from it, is at first an object of contemplation;

later, it is employed by the toddler for the deductive, inferential reasoning of this period. The imaging capacity of the first half of the second year is therefore transitional between learning-by-action in the first year and learning through increasingly verbally centered, symbolic representation in the second half of the second year.

THE SHIFT TOWARD AN IMAGING CAPACITY

The developments I am considering transpire during the period from eight to 21 months, and are suggested by a number of easily observable behaviors. The observations are of course verifiable, whereas the speculations I shall put forth concerning the experiential and psychic structural meanings of these behaviors are either not verified or, in some instances, not verifiable (although inferential support for them might be sought).

To begin with, we might look at several developments during the period of the ninth to the twelfth month. Infants will use a finger to point (Call, 1980). They increasingly focus their attention on their mothers for ministration of their needs (Sander, 1980), are often fearful of others and anticipate the mother's departures. Moreover, they employ an increasingly differentiated set of signals to indicate their wishes, whether to be picked up, fed, put down, played with, or given this or that toy (Greenspan, 1979). All of these behaviors, I suggest, indicate a changing relationship between the infant and the "out there." Using the finger to point comes about subsequent to a physical maturation (the ability to move the thumb in a prehensile manner) and is probably only a refinement of the neonate's global pointing of fingers, toes, head, shoulders, and mouth in response to a captivating stimulus. Nevertheless, it adds two properties: the behaviorally efficient demarcation of an object in space and the establishment of the outer limit of the body's reach and the space between the body and the object.

Focusing on the mother adds another dimension to the biological-neurophysiological-behavioral interactions with her. From the earliest period in neonatal life, infants evidence preferences for the mother (caregiver). Within a week, they respond preferentially to her face and voice in contrast to those of the father or another female (Brazelton, 1980a). An alteration in her usual behaviors (seeing her face while hearing another voice, seeing her face held immobile, etc.) is a "violation" of the interactional order that exists between them and the source of distress responses. I suggest the focusing on the mother in the last trimester of the first year adds a new dimension to these long-developing preferences and discriminations. The new dimension takes two forms. First, the emotional exchange is more discrete. The infant is able to respond to the mother's actions (including especially her emotional state) via the rather full repertoire of the infant's affective range—a development that culminates in the last trimester (Sroufe, 1982). Second, the mother's actions are the source of intense scrutiny, because, as a result of the infant's developments in the behavioral (sensorimotor) sphere, they convey more valuable information as indicators of what is to come. In short, mother is a person who means more emotionally than any other person and her actions mean (signify) more. Her reaching for her coat indicates *she* is to leave; her reaching for the infant's coat and her coat means *they* are to leave. The growing capacity for anticipation, for prediction, makes her moves, her expressions, her state of being, a source of focus adding "meaning" in rapidly increasing increments to the well-established system of preferences. Elementary linguistic sign comprehension on the infant's part adds to the richness of the informational exchange.

Another link in the changed relationship is the infant's increasingly complex repertoire of signals—ones that the mother is likely to be most adept at "reading." These include gestures, facial expressions, vocalizings, and general body attitude (a less discrete indicator, but possibly a more significant one). The infant's own body-level awareness of these signals may be far more holistic than what is visible to an observer. What an observer sees as pointing, for instance, may be a whole-body restlessness to the infant. The infant's perfecting of his or her own signals, believing in their fit

into the world of predictions and anticipations, is the counterpart
to the infant's focused responsiveness to the mother's signals. This
is the climax of the development of the signal or gesture as a
behavioral transaction.

This development of the signal as a *behavioral* transaction is
followed in the second year by a system of signs, which call for
(signal) responses at a cognitive level of deduction and inference.
In my opinion, it is the imaging capacity that plays a significant
role in this transition. What the imaging capacity does is to create
what Werner and Kaplan (1963) call "things-of-contemplation,
that is, objects that one regards out there, rather than things upon
which one merely acts" (p. 67). The properties of the image (its appearance, attributes, and the information it conveys) are conceived
as having an existence independent of the perceiver's presence:
"My mother is there whether I see her or not." "My room is there
whether I am in it or not." (Of course, the symbolic representation
involved in the language I am using for illustrative purposes does
not apply to the initial experience of the imaging capacity.)

Before the development of the imaging capacity, the same data
of immediate sensory perception that will later be treated as objects of contemplation are responded to a stimuli for action. If,
for instance, something is construed as a novelty, it arouses interest, approach, and motor response, and perhaps later habituation and discard. Or, if something is construed as threatening, it
arouses wariness, aversion, and flight. In other words, before
the imaging capacity, infants do not distinguish between an object (a toy, the mother, a toe) and their activities with that object—the object is nothing but a prolongation of the infants' activities (Piaget, 1937). It is with the development of the imaging
capacity that the object is construed as having a particular appearance (image), along with other sensory properties (sound, tex-
ture, smell, activity pattern), whether or not it is the source of immediate perceptual input.

The earliest evidence of the imaging capacity coincides with
Piaget's Stage IV (eight to 13 months), when infants begin to attribute some degree of objectivity to an object screened from their

perception. Infants at this stage become fascinated with the problem of size and shape consistency of objects. During stage IV infants begin to conceive space differently. Previously they were aware of displacements of objects when they occurred close to their bodies. Now the range of spatial comprehension is extended and the space away from the body, which had been responded to as a relatively single plane, is now reacted to as having depth (Flavell, 1963; Greenspan, 1979). Clearer evidence of the existence of the imaging capacity comes in Piaget's Stage V (13 to 18 months), when toddlers will search for an object under two or more screens, provided they have seen the object disappear each time. It is at this age that children will pick up a comb and touch their hair or place a telephone to the ear. These activities indicate a response to objects in terms of their functions—although at an imitative, gestural level, rather than a symbolic, pretend one (Piaget, 1945; Nicolich, 1977).

The full development of the imaging capacity is complete with the achievement of what Piaget calls object permanence (see Décarie, 1962). After 18 months, the toddler will continue to search for an object that has disappeared behind a screen, even if the disappearance occurs without the toddler's seeing the object moved. It is also at this stage that the child introduces pretending into the handling of functional objects. In simulating drinking from a toy baby bottle, the child will appear playful, as if aware of pretending. Play activities extend from direct involvement with the child's own body to include other actors and receivers of action: A child will put an empty cup to mother's mouth, to a doll's, and then his or her own (Piaget, 1945; Nicolich, 1977).

THE IMPACT OF THE IMAGING CAPACITY

The imaging capacity provides data first for recognition memory, unrelated to action, and later for evocative memory. Before the imaging capacity, recognition is highly developed but is action-bound; that is, what is recognized is not the object per se, but the whole action sequence connected with the object—a bottle is to put in the mouth, a ring is to grab, a smiling mother is to smile back at. As the action dissolves, so presumably does the "image." The properties of the object and its independent existence have not become abstracted out of an action sequence. The object (bottle, mother, self) has not become an "object-of-contemplation" in its own right (Werner and Kaplan, 1963). Once the imaging capacity develops, the toddler can sustain the mental image of a vanished object through successive disappearances. During the 13- to 18-month period, the object must be discovered and verified between each hiding, or the memory image may not persist. After 18 months, recognition does not require the immediate perceptual cue; the toddler is able to evoke the image of the absent object and pursue it (Fraiberg, 1969).

The imaging capacity is directly related to learning (mentation) through sign recognition. The object perceived conveys not only an appearance conducive to recognition but information to be used in the deductive process appropriate to the early toddler period. The child is able to use the image of the screen and of the examiner's action in placing the object behind the screen as a sign that the screen is a thing for hiding behind, the game is hide-and-seek, and the signal to the child is "seek." In other words, the image formed is related to the specific problem-solving orientation of this period—problems previously dealt with by actions patterned to immediate response are now dealt with through deductive inference.

This change from direct response to a stimulus via an action sequence to a contemplative response is marked by an affective change. In general, the change is from a joyous response to novelty to a more pensive, even wary, response to the problem posed by an identical percept. The response of the nine- or 10-month infant to the "stranger" may be examined in this light. I would like to suggest that the most developmentally normal response to the not-mother person (often no "stranger") is one of wary exploratory interest; that is the approaching person becomes in Werner and Kaplan's (1963) phrase an object of contemplation—a problem to be puzzled through. My thesis is that the approaching not-mother person may be the first of a group of objects that is responded to as an image that has become objectified. Put another way, the response to the stranger may be the first example of the functioning of the imaging capacity.

It is significant, I believe, that the contemplative response to the slowly approaching, friendly stranger that eight- to 10-month-olds who are securely placed in the mother's lap demonstrate coincides in time with Piaget's Stage IV, when appreciation of space in depth occurs and the consistency of the size and shape of objects becomes a source of fascination. The response to the stranger is, however, so complex that it is difficult to tease out the facet of it I wish to comment on now. Previously it was regarded as the result of two developments: a cognitive advance by which the discrimination of mother from others was accomplished and the maturation of the affect of fear. Let us reexamine the cognitive side of the explanation. As we have noted, a neonate is capable of discriminating the mother's face, voice, and odor. It therefore seems unlikely that the response to a stranger is a matter of discriminatory capacity; it is more a matter of meaning. Previously the stranger meant another novelty to smile and giggle at and with. In fact being not-mother actually enhanced the novelty value of the visiting aunt. Instead of representing the advent of the capacity for discrimination, the change results from the infant's increasing selective attachment to the mother that occurs during the second half of the first year. In other words, it is not that the eight- to 10-month-old *becomes* able to discriminate; rather it is that the infant now has a *need to exercise* the preexisting capacity to discriminate through what I call the imaging capacity. That is, the infant treats the not-mother person with somewhat sober-faced curiosity through the visual and tactile exploration described by Mahler et al. (1975).

What is the basis of the need to exercise this capacity? As the infant's attachment to mother intensifies, each approaching person is scanned to see if that person raises or lowers the infant's sense of security, the central pivot of which lies in the mother's presence. It is not the presence of the relatively familiar grandmother or the totally unknown visiting aunt that determines the response, but the status of the mother's security providing support, measured against other factors such as the startle pressure exerted by the stranger. Thus infants in their own homes, with their mothers available for physical contact, will react to the not-mother person in a way that indicates that it is important that he or she is not mother. This person is lifted out of the surround and regarded as an object in his or her own right. An experiential parallel for this is when we suddenly really look at a familiar object—like a painting we have owned for years—and say: "Oh, I never noticed the symmetry of that tree and the house beyond." For the infant, removing an object from its familiar surround and particularizing discrete aspects of the object (mother = security and not-mother = someone outside of security to be explored differently) is, as I hope to illustrate, an important means by which the infant comes to a sense of self. The imaging capacity is the means by which the self becomes objectified.

The Mirror and the Self

In contrast to the stranger, whose appearance stimulates the response of sober puzzlement, a mirror elicits a response of delight in infants between nine and 12 months of age. They will laugh, coo, and jiggle their bodies with excitement, indicating an action-patterned response. At this age, if the mirror is distorted, they show no change in reaction, and if a label is placed on their foreheads, they display no notice of it. The reaction to the mirror builds on the infant's response pattern to any novel experience; only a new element is added. The mirror elicits an action response —but one of the infant's own making. Each movement the infant makes instantly influences the percept. The mirror has the same property to entertain as a mobile or an animated cartoon, but with the infant as creative director.[1]

Infants between 13 and 15 months, however, react quite dif-

---

[1]In one experiment, infants viewed themselves through a videotape monitor. As soon as the picture frame of the monitor was frozen, the infants stopped being delighted and highly active (T. Modarressi, personal communication).

ferently to the mirror. When confronted with their mirror images, these toddlers grow sober, pensive, and less active. If the mirror is distorted, they focus on it intently, without pleasure. They will notice a label surreptitiously placed on their foreheads, and may even reach for it *in the mirror,* but they do not touch it on their own faces. They will purposefully create a "show" in the mirror by their own movements, without apparent recognition that the mirror contains information relative to themselves (the label on the forehead). These findings suggest that the mirror and the image in it have become, through the imaging capacity, a discrete entity "out there," an object of contemplation, but not a reflection of the self as such (Modarressi, 1980).

Between 15 and 21 months a dramatic change occurs. Toddlers who have surreptitiously had a smudge placed on the nose (Brooks and Lewis, 1976; Lewis and Brooks-Gunn, 1979) or a label on the forehead (Modarressi, 1980; Modarressi and Kenny, 1977) will, when exposed to a mirror, reach up and touch *their* noses or foreheads. (Amsterdam and Levitt [1980] find this reaction more reliably between 18 and 22 months.) What this interesting bit of behavior suggests is that at this age children have discovered that the mirror will not only "capture" and reflect visual information about an image, but convey information "out there" about *themselves.*

What are the earlier developments that make this discovery that the mirror conveys information about the self possible? The fact that objects convey information is given with the very first object that enters the newborn's visual focus area. Moreover, the fact that objects convey differing information is given in the infant's differentiated reaction to a toy and a human face. Further, the face outside triggers imitative responses, as can be seen within the first week by observing the baby's changing expressions. Neonates will even stick their tongues out in response to the mother's doing so (Meltzoff and Moore, 1977). At this age this would not be a learned action. Rather, the infant seems to be preprogammed to respond to a visual stimulus in a manner that produces a mirror-image response—the infant's face taking on the physiognomic appearance the infant sees. It is natural that the term "mirroring" has been given to this observation, as well as to the process that psychoanalysts have hypothesized to explain the mysterious link between disturbed mood states shared by mothers and infants. Greenacre's (1941) description is an early effort to conceptualize this process:

> "Mirroring" is a kind of visual and kinesthetic introjection of those around the infant. The child reacts with a puckered, worried or tense expression when people around are cross or gloomy. This may come about through an association of mild discomfort (the restricting, frustrating sensations of being held or handled by a tense and jerky nurse or mother) with the gloomy expression which it sees; nevertheless the infant soon seems to make the connection directly, an anxious nurse being reflected in an anxious baby without the intermediate kinesthetic link. This is an observation of which sensitive nurses are quite aware. This is a kind of centripetal empathy [pp. 49–50].

Thus, even before the experiences with an actual mirror, a long experience of emotional "mirroring" has taken place. In these sender-receiver feedbacks, the infant's looking to the caregiver's expression, especially through eye fixation, builds a communication system of incredible synchronous immediacy (Beebe and Stern, 1977; Beebe and Sloate, 1982).

The toddler's recognition that the mirror conveys information about the self both continues a long maturing behavioral sequence and adds a new discovery. To put the experience in words (which of course the child could not use), the toddler discovers: "That object out there—the mirror—contains an image that is unlike all other images in that it stands for me. Moreover, the image of me has been changed—I don't usually have a label on my forehead or a smudge on my nose." The object (the mirror) is both concrete—it exists on its own—and abstract—it can mirror something else. The image in the mirror also has concrete properties—it exists and conveys information ("It tells me how I look, that there is a label on my forehead or the smudge on my nose I didn't know was there"). More abstractly, the viewer (the "I" implicitly, not reflectively) exists as an image with a known, expectable appearance. ("I can see my image, just as I see those of others around me").

In this way, the capacity to make an objectified visual discrimination is applied to the image of the self. The mirror presents toddlers with an actual image of themselves. The toddlers' reactions suggest that they have an image not simply of those body parts they can see without the mirror, but of the whole body as a unit. The perceived mirror image "stands for" the image of themselves. It can convey a sign (a smudge is on your nose, a label is on your forehead) that will elicit or signal a response, much as a roadsign bicycle conveys the same information as seeing a bicyclist on the road, each signaling—Drive cautiously.

The affective reactions elicited by the mirror experience are also telling. Whereas nine- to 12-month-olds are delighted with the mirror as a source of an exciting spectacle of their own making, toddlers throughout the second year show a range of responses: restrained interest, pensive wariness, coy self-consciousness, strong gaze aversion. I suggest this change in affect marks the shift from a response to the mirror as a source of novel, self-activated stimuli to the challenge posed when the percept in the mirror is construed as a source of information bearing on the developing awareness of self. Yet the ability to use the mirror image as a sign signaling an alteration (smudge or label) in the self image is not accompanied by a more relaxed, pleasure-giving response until the third year of life. There is still, I believe, a further task that is being worked out during the second year—the increasingly discrete awareness of the self as a whole. Amsterdam and Levitt's (1980) observation of frequent responses of painful self-consciousness in the 18- to 24-month-old exposed to the mirror lends support to this premise.

In contrast, children after two respond quite differently (Modarressi, 1981). As we would expect, all children over two notice the label or the smudge and use the mirror to locate it on their faces. These children will remove the label, examine it, and even use the mirror to replace it on their foreheads. The awareness that the mirror image is theirs becomes consciously reflected on recognition, usually accompanied by a smile. At times, there is a sense of surprise, even awe. If the mirror surface is altered to produce a distorted image, these older children will react with a dramatic change from pleasurable interest to acute alarm and distrust. It is as though the concrete, distinct image of self they worked so hard to consolidate conceptually had dissolved before their eyes.

Other Aspects of the Imaging Capacity

I believe these conjectures are supported by other behavior that is concomitant to the mirror discovery. Toddlers in the first half of the second year respond to photographs of their parents—vocalizing and indicating father from his photo and mother from hers a month or so later (Brooks and Lewis, 1974; Brooks-Gunn and Lewis, 1979). The image exists (is objectified) and stands for the person. At this age, the toddler will take mother's hand and lead her to the refrigerator. I suggest that the refrigerator now has an existence as an image that stands for (is a sign of) the contents that will appear when the door is open (like the toy behind the screen). The contents of the refrigerator, in turn, signal the effect that eating them will have. In other words, the toddler can form an image or a series of images placed (oriented) in time and space "out there." The significance of these images lies not in their perceptual input per se but in their meaning in the motivational sequences of the child's life. The refrigerator is one such image, the self moving toward it with mother opening it is another, and the self receiving the food from it is a third. Together, these images allow the child to lead mother to the refrigerator to get food.

Further support for an imaging capacity may be drawn from the toddler's "delayed" imitative play. The infant's imitation of facial expressions and gestures occurs only in the presence of the person being copied. After about 13 months, the toddler is capable of repeating an action after the person has disappeared from view. Piaget and Inhelder (1966) describe "a little girl of sixteen months who sees a playmate become angry, scream, and stamp her foot (new sights for her) and who, an hour or two after the playmate's departure, imitates the scene, laughing" (p. 53). They state that such deferred imitation constitutes the beginning of representation, and the imitative gestures, the beginning of a differentiated signifier. At this same age, the child not only imitates others whose images and actions she has retained, but also imitates herself in some other context. She may play (pretend) that she is asleep, or eating, or going for a ride. Piaget believes that imitation and the action it involves are more important for the completed development of the mental image than perceptual registry itself (see Greenspan, 1979, pp. 155–160). This view underlines the nonstatic nature of the imaging capacity—its occurrence *in* a dynamic situation rather than *as* a photographic "still," held in time.

The imaging capacity at this stage, however, does not yet form a full symbol (Blum, 1978; Greenspan, 1982). That is, the refrigerator is a sign, signaling the image of the self eating the contents of the refrigerator; it signifies an affect-laden *action*. According to Basch (1975), such sign-ordered behavior "is carried out by matching encoded patterns with incoming percepts. Such an organization permits either the reoccurrence of some aspect of past experience to set off very complex behavior patterns or the recognition of some portion of a familiar routine to arouse sensory expectations that delay action or reaction until the next aspect of a familiar pattern registers. . . . Abstraction of perceptual essence or form is an ability that is always involved in complex sign behavior" (p. 507). However, no matter how complex the behavioral response to the sign, the sign does not serve as a symbol. The percept creating the sign may be extremely subtle and abstract (father's raised eyebrow means a temper storm is to come), or there may be numerous displacements in the associative chain from the sign to the gratifying aim (from refrigerator to getting mother, pulling her to the kitchen, opening the door, taking out the ice cream, and eating it). Still, as Basch claims, the sign "does not stand for or represent a situation in such a way that it, rather than the experience it represents, is manipulated intracerebrally or interpersonally. As Susanne Langer (1951) has said, a sign evokes the action appropriate to the object signified, but a symbol arouses the conception of the object symbolized'' (p. 508). Only later in the second year, with the developments I shall describe, are processes set in motion that lead to the image arousing the ''conception'' of the object—food is then generalized as a class and the elements within that class become particularized. The *idea* of food can be distanced from its pragmatic use; it can be incorporated into a game and shifted about from person to person (Piaget, 1945; Nicolich, 1977). With the aid of word symbols, by the end of the second year, the child may be able to play mentally with choices—''I'd like cereal rather than toast''—in the absence of either.

Special Considerations

My use of the term ''imaging capacity'' should be differentiated from the concept of ''imaging'' in states of severe sensory deprivation (Rubinfine, 1961). The imaging capacity is a means of *responding to a perception;* the ''imaging'' Rubinfine refers to *replaces or substitutes for a missing perceptual experience.* The two concepts may be related, in that once both the imaging capacity and the capacity for symbolic representation develop, the individual can respond to a severe stimulus deficit by substituting the imagery of the inner world for the missing perceptual experience. Inner visual and other sensory representations (including whole scenes) built up through the imaging capacity are projected outward to redress the altered balance.

In conceptualizing a capacity to treat optical perceptions as objects of contemplation, as discrete objectified images ''out there,'' I am emphasizing visual functioning, although I believe the image is rarely restricted to the visual.

CONCLUSION

My speculation is that the imaging capacity is brought to bear on different classes of objects at different times. My reasoning is that the toddler's sober, pensive mood response is an indication that a particular group of objects are being "puzzled through" as discrete entities, apart from the actions involved in the toddler's contact with them. If this is so, the timetable would be: persons other than the day-to-day familiar ones (eight to 13 months), the image in the mirror (13 to 15 months), the image in the mirror as self (15 to 24 months), and mother at moments of the "rapprochement" crisis (18 to 24 months). It is suggestive that the toddler recognizes (images) mother from her photograph later than others, even a bit later than father (Brooks and Lewis, 1974; Brooks-Gunn and Lewis, 1979). I believe this indicates the mother's enormous importance as a sustaining presence, leading the toddler to hold her longest *within the action mode*—mother is to have near. To more formally establish her discreteness as an entity would substantiate the painfulness of her disappearance, through the memory of an image of someone not present and not able to be found. In other words, it is because mother functions both as an object of intense *immediate* interest and as the concrete base for a sustained sense of support that the toddler may place mother last in working out the problem of her discreteness as an image, held in memory, to be used in her absence.

What I am trying to describe here is how an affective-cognitive capacity, already present, may be brought to bear on a series of related problems in an inner-ordered sequence. From clinical analysis we are familiar with the inner-directed timetable by which the patient selects specific problem areas for consideration. Returning to the toddler, we might surmise that, on the affective end, the early stages of the effort to objectify the image of the mother become a source of panic because, on the cognitive end, the imaging capacity at first treats mother as a disappearing toy. The distressed toddler no longer obliterates the missing mother from memory in the absence of perceptual cues, but has not yet established an image beyond the recognition stage of one or two displacements. It would seem that a reliable evocative memory of mother must take hold for the toddler's pensive, anxious response to abate.

Mahler et al. (1975) describe the young toddlers of the practicing period as commonly experiencing joy at play in the presence of mother, but becoming "low-keyed" when aware of mother's absence: "At such times, their gestural and performance motility slowed down, their interest in their surroundings diminished, and they appeared to be preoccupied with inwardly concentrated attention, with what Rubinfine (1961) called 'imaging'" (p. 74). Again, let me distinguish this use of "imaging" from the "imaging capacity," which refers to the response to the external percept—the objectification and contemplation of mother when she is there. The "imaging" Mahler et al. are describing entails replacing a missing percept by turning inward. The young toddler's recognition of the physical absence of the mother brings a loss of libidinal investment and "low-keyedness." Whether the contemplative young toddler is able to invoke actual images, however, is difficult to assess. This kind of contemplative state may reflect the toddler's initial attempts to evoke an image of mother from memory to restore the feeling of security lost in her absence. In the older toddler (18 to 24 months), a troubled state may arise in the presence *or* absence of the mother. At this time "imaging," based on the "imaging capacity," may be attempted whether mother is there or not, as the toddler is now moving physically and *emotionally* away. Objectivization and contemplation of the image are complemented by symbolic representation, although this is not yet fully reliable.

The second year is thus marked by a series of developmental steps, occupying (even preoccupying) the toddler. In the toddler's response to the mirror, we can see a particular adaptational sequence. First, there is an establishing of the external world, the "out there" (the mirror becomes an objectified entity having properties of its own). Then, a mode of learning is developed in which the "out there" (the image in the mirror) conveys information in the form of signs that signal responses the developing self can use as guides. Still later, we see an emergent sense of the self as the activator or initiator of action. Eventually, there is a transition from the affective-cognitive mode associated with signs (dependent on the imaging capacity) to a symbolic level, in which two interrelated modes (primary and secondary process) allow for fantasy, metaphor, contingent and causal linkages, and play activity at a higher level of organization.

Chapter Eight

Speculations on the Self-as-a-Whole as an "Emergent Property"

An "emergent property" refers to the occurrence during development of an altered state, the characteristics of which are qualitatively different from the preceding state. The altered state that is to emerge is foreshadowed in the genetic ground plan of the individual's development. The occurrence and timing of its emergence are the result of neurophysiological maturations and psychological developments. Specifically, I employ the term "emergent property" to bridge between the conceptual axes of time (when a development occurs and what its antecedents are) and of experience (whether the occurrence is at the neurophysiological level alone or whether some degree of awareness or consciousness is also involved). The "property" of the sense of the self-as-a-whole that emerges in the second year is an attribute of self qualitatively different from experiential traits of the self-in-action that precede it.

The self-as-a-whole develops as the result of two emergent qualitative gradients: the first at birth, the second during the second year, subsequent to the imaging capacity. At birth (or possibly in intrauterine life), perceptual reactiveness establishes a working system of self-exchange-object (Stern, 1983)—exemplified by the newborn's responding with an alert fixed gaze to the mother's face eight inches away. Each time neonates exercise one of their many capacities for categorical preference (e.g., sound or rhythm), the self (reactor) is differentiated within a system of integration with the environment. Integration with the environment varies depending on the qualities of the system of self-exchange-object. The quality of separateness of the self may differ. The exchange may entail greater or lesser involvement with immediacy and with the source of perceptual input. The object may be more specifically personal (the actual mother holding the awake infant) or more general (the mother-crib-room as environmental holder as the infant drifts into sleep). As significant neurophysiological maturation occurs at 10 to 12 weeks and at six months, the infant's alertness to the interaction brightens and intensifies, and awareness (consciousness)—a level beyond mere neurophysiological reactiveness—becomes more probable.

My thesis is that throughout the first year a focus on the *exchange* between self and other predominates over the awareness of the self as a separate entity and the object as an entity. In the infinity of small interactions during which the infant and caregiver behave in ways that are similar or complementary, the relative synchrony of the exchange places the dominant focus on the interaction. Although those behaviors of the infant characterized by contingency do place greater emphasis on the difference between self and object, they are primarily experienced within the general regulatory matrix of infant-caretaker exchange, prior to the imaging capacity.

The imaging capacity, I suggest, *is decisive in establishing the discreteness and objectivity of both the external object and the self.* At first, this higher level of differentiation of self and object remains in a context of interrelation, but the focus on the exchange itself lessens and shifts to the information being processed intrapsychically. Through the imaging capacity, toddlers become intent readers of signs. They scan their immediate environment for orienting indicators, looking at the parent's face for indications of moment-to-moment responsiveness (a "climate check"), and listening with increasing alertness and comprehension to the spoken word—for both tone and content. At the same time, toddlers become increasingly sophisticated senders of signals, through gestures, facial expressions, and vocalizations.[1] Their signals of physiological needs, and of preferences in the human and nonhuman world of objects, evidence more discrete awareness of how to negotiate their particular environment.

The capacity to treat the self as an object of contemplation and as the origin of contemplation adds to the subjective awareness derived from the self in action in contingent experiences and the self as sender and receiver of signs. The self as the source of contemplation, in comparison to the self in an action response, places a conceptual distance that further differentiates the sense of self. The objectivization that results from the imaging capacity and the shift to a level of sign-signal informational exchange is what I hypothesize creates the self-as-a-whole as a new emergent property toward the middle of the second year. The qualitative alteration in the self then potentiates further developments; in turn, the self is perceptibly altered with the beginning of symbolic representational cognition later, in the second half of the second year.

But what do I mean by "the self-as-a-whole"? I use this cumbersome term to convey a grouping of personal properties, illustrated by the mirror experiment with the smudge on the nose. There is a perceiving "I" behind the perceptual eye and a "self" seen in the mirror. There is a part of self (the nose) that another part of self (the finger) touches, as it would an object. There is a not part of self (the smudge)—a foreign object that is adherent to the self, but outside its bodily boundary as a known image. The imaging capacity, I suggest, comprises and defines all these aspects of self (just as it comprises and defines a not self object). The self-as-a-whole as an emergent property adds to these imagings the experiential mental self, a further extension of the perceiving "I."

---

[1]Possibly the most important information picked up and responded to lies in the realm of affects. Study of this exchange in the first half of the second year may help to explain how certain affects do or don't undergo differentiation, verbalization, and desomatization (Krystal, 1974). The imaging capacity allows the child to read the parent's affective expressiveness, a capacity the parent may welcome or shun. The toddler's response, imitative or oppositional, and the parent's response to this may set in motion complex signals that contribute to the eventual self-recognition and tolerance of affects, or limitation in "reading" and tolerating emotions in one self and others.

THE SENSE OF SELF AS DIRECTOR

The emergent property of self that appears in the middle of the second year is that of the self-as-a-whole as mental "director." Another way of expressing what I mean by "mental self" is to say that a shift occurs from the self as doer in an *action* sense to the self being and doing *subjectively*. If we look at the picture with the caregiver, there is a beginning shift from *interaction* to *intersubjectivity*.

The self-as-a-whole comes into being in children who are already functioning in a complex manner. They lack, however, a way to consistently psychically position their functioning around a "director," to assume ownership of their experiential world as well as relatively greater privacy about their intentions. Three analogies may help to clarify my meaning.

A ship's company without a captain goes through all its activities, its practices and rituals. There are orders on board as to how and where to proceed. The captain arrives and everything changes. At first it is merely that everyone senses his presence. Later, through his actual organizing skills, all the ship's activities become integrated around him.

A person awakens in the morning. She gradually "takes possession" of her body, its movements and its sensations. Then she orients herself and bit by bit pulls together her intentions for the day.

A patient who has been in insulin coma treatment gradually arouses. At first he blinks and rolls his eyes and makes rhythmical movements with his mouth. Then he is able to respond, robotlike, to seeing the glass of sugared juice and to instructions to drink. After a bit, often in baby-talk, he indicates a "me want"—taking increasing control of the coming-to process.

The impetus for the emergence of the whole self as director comes from two sources: (1) an increased appreciation of sequential events, including prediction, and (2) the ability to conceptualize actions in terms of opposites, reversals, or alternatives. When we fully appreciate the interactional matrix of caregiver and infant as the dominant factor in infantile life, we can more clearly assess the relative power of experiencing near-synchrony over experiencing clearly delineated sequential events. The interplay between mother and infant may look like a contingent series to a casual observer, but microkinetic taping may reveal that it is as synchronous as the dance of two well-trained performers (Condon and Sander, 1974; Stern, 1977). For infants, these endlessly repeated mutual entrainments create an experience of having both their initiative and their responses embedded in the matrix of interactions with the mother. Sequential, causal relations can be isolated and appreciated more readily when the infant deals with an inanimate object—"hand pushes, it rolls." The emotion that accompanies the actions initiated by the infant has been referred to as function pleasure (Bühler, 1930), and, when these actions are successful, as efficacy or competence pleasure (Broucek, 1979). This pleasurable experience serves as a powerful reinforcement for the repeating of actions in sequence. (Broucek [1979] regards the sense of efficacy as a foundation of the sense of self.) Sander (1983) suggests that the experiencing of initiative begins in relatively brief spans of time, "open space," during which there is no requirement for interactive regulation by the mother or by physiological pressure. These open spaces for the active exploration of stimuli and the exercise of initiative in action expand if the mother is sensitive enough not to intrude or co-opt the developing infant's attention.

The achievements the growing infant makes during open-space intervals, when mother exists only as supportive background, are the basic experiences around which the toddler's emergent self-as-a-whole builds a sense of ownership of one's images and responses, as well as a sense of privacy of one's mental space (Goldberg, 1983). Piaget's work suggests that the cognitive operations that permit the sense of volitional action require not one causal sequence, but a grouping of a series of sequential actions (Inhelder and Piaget, 1955). Only then will the child's actions and mental operations become "reversible." Reversibility implies that the child can invent an operation first in action and later in the mind, and that one is able to examine a task from two opposite viewpoints. Then as infants modify their imperfect attempts by feedback from previous action, they are capable of a form of regulation in which actions are semi-reversible. Later as a more functional concept of space develops, a toddler can perceive an object to be behind a screen as well as perceive it to be in plain view in front of the screen. In attempting to solve tasks, such as locating a disappearing object, "the child can now distribute his forces, he can direct them, regulate their strength for a given purpose. Hence, he is able to time his action, he can coordinate means with ends. In short, his action becomes *rational* instead of *impulsive*" (Cobliner, 1968, pp. 309–310).

These skills in regulating complex action sequences that the child consolidates, largely in the realm of activities with inanimate objects, provide capacities that the toddler employs to solve the more difficult tasks of sorting out the relation with mother. The satisfactions of dependency—both at an overt level, in the joy of synchronous exchanges, and at a deep level of primitive merger, which hypothetically occurs in regressive moments of passage into sleep (Lewin, 1950; Jacobson, 1964; Pine, 1981)—vie with the pleasures of competence and efficacy. The mother's responsiveness to the infant's indication of need along the path of progression and regression provides the regulatory core for these exchanges. The balance between remaining restrictively involved in interactional sequences with the caregiver and emerging from them seesaws back and forth during the second, third, and even fourth year of life.

The toddler's emergence depends on an appreciation of contingent actions within the dyad and the possibility of the self acting to exert its influence in alternative, even opposite (reversed), directions. This process is fired by the accentuated assertiveness of the second year. For the self to emerge effectively from the interactional matrix requires that the toddler be able to carry out an intention in response to a desire (Lichtenberg and Pao, 1974) and, at the same time, monitor this sequence of events in relation to mother's encouragements and prohibitions. Stechler and Kaplan (1980) state: "If a child is behaving and monitoring her own behavior in the context of an interpersonal relationship, is observ-

ing and recording how the other person reacts to what she is doing
and is then influenced by her perceptions so that she proceeds to
integrate her own acts with social cues, we conclude that there is
self-awareness'' (p. 99). The self-awareness Stechler and Kaplan
describe would correspond to what I am referring to as the mental-
self aspect of the emergent self-as-a-whole.

As I have indicated, this type of monitoring of the child's own
behavior and that of the other person could be considered to be an
outgrowth of the imaging capacity. It involves an appreciation of
the discreteness of the properties of the self and the other person,
and a degree of objectivity about the information being exchanged
through signs and signals. Again, this shift in level might be
characterized as a change from inter*action* to inter*subjectivity*.
This shift is accompanied by the growing capacity for planned intentional sequences in which the toddler checks for the possibility
(or confirmation) of mother's consonance or dissonance with his
or her plan. The toddler will find a mixing spoon, set it down,
search for a mixing bowl, look at mother for approval, and then
play at mixing food. Alternatively, the child may push aside offered toys and purposely open a cupboard and pull out a forbidden object, glancing at mother mischievously, inviting or challeng-
ing her disapproval.

During the first half of the second year, the active, organizing
impact of the mother continues to predominate. Thus, although
cognitive advances are indicated by the originating of sequences
outside the synchronous interactions and by the conceptualizing of
alternatives, they are probably not a strong-enough impetus for
the consolidation of the self-as-a-whole. *The emergent objectiviza-*
tion of the self-as-a-whole acting as director of intentional actions
is an organizing experience of great potential, but, like all new
developments, the sense of self as doer is vulnerable to deflating
and enfeebling reactions. The firm foundation of the toddler's
self-as-a-whole—potent enough to emerge more fully from restric-
tive aspects of the interactional matrix, and powerful enough to
restructure a sustaining relationship with the caretaker—derives, I
believe, from the impetus of a series of maturational and

developmental advances that enrich the toddler's life at about 18 months. As I shall now discuss, these include: (1) an upsurge in assertiveness, with its potential for opposing; (2) an upsurge in awareness of bladder, bowel, and genital sensations that gives greater focus to the inner body, the perineum, and particularly to the genitals, further consolidating the body-self image; and (3) the broad general shift from cognition still somewhat tied to action and to sign-signal informational exchange to a greater employment of symbolic representational thinking.

Chapter Nine

The Effect of Assertiveness and Genital Awareness on the Emergent Self

THE UPSURGE OF ASSERTIVENESS

In his exploration of the significance of the young toddler's head-shaking "no," Spitz (1957) states that having a way to signify opposition gives the child a means to objectify the self, the object opposed, and the act of opposing.[1] The assertiveness of the child in the second year gives a compelling quality to the emergence of the self as director from the mother-child interactional matrix. As walking, climbing toddlers energetically pursue their explorations, they meet the inevitable restrictions of the protective mother. Such momentary frustrations engender angry, often tantrumlike, responses, in which the child attempts to push the mother away, to create a space between—both literally and symbolically. Sometime toward the middle of the second year, the child experiences what Parens (1979b) calls the first ambivalent conflict. It is as though the emergent self as director had an influx of energeticness but experienced a pull between wanting to remain in (or restore) the earlier closeness with mother and wanting to widen the latitude of explorations and play contacts with children and other adults. This

---

[1] The development of aggression in early childhood has been the subject of extensive study and debate (see especially Parens, 1979a). The biological underpinnings of aggression have been related to exposure to androgen-based compounds during gestation. Both exposed males and females evidenced a significantly higher potential for *physical* aggression than their sex-matched unexposed siblings. There were no differences in verbal aggression or IQ between exposed and unexposed siblings (Reinisch, 1981).

irreconcilable pull leads to what the toddler probably experiences as an inexplicable frustration. This frustration tends at first to result in the toddler's reversion to an action mode, with angry attacks often directed against the mother.

The increased assertiveness and reactive aggression of the second year may prove to be a source of conflict, potentially divisive to the sense of unity of the emerging self-as-a-whole. It is certain to be a source of puzzlement to the mother, whose very effort to comfort or reestablish her prior closeness may lead to further angry assaults on her. That infants tend to treat their experience of an internal, irreconcilable pull as a failure in maternal regulation places a great strain on the toddler-mother relationship. When the parents respond to the reactive aggression without being unduly counteraggressive or withdrawn, however, the assertiveness normally provides a resource for the differentiation and integration of new capacities that extend the flexible range of the self.

Parens (1979b) describes the reaction of Mary, a 13-month-old, to her mother physically restraining her. At first Mary tried to extricate herself bodily—crying angrily, kicking, and striking. She then rejected her mother's efforts to comfort her. Instead, she sat rigidly upright on her mother's lap. Finally, after an interval, she relaxed passively into her mother's body. According to Parens, this behavioral sequence suggests that an interpersonal conflict has been transformed into an intrapsychic conflict. Regarded from within the child's experience, it is as if Mary's struggle ceased to be between her pulling body and her mother's restraining arms or between her emerging self's desire to go and her mother's opposing will. Instead, it is as if the struggle were between a wish to be comforted and close, to feel loved, and another wish to assert herself, reacting in anger. Parens suggests that Mary's psychological state of being suspended between her anger and her affection was reflected in her physical immobility as she sat upright on her mother's lap. This degree of conflict constitutes a threat to the sense of unity of the self.

Based on pathology we note later in borderline patients (Lichtenberg and Slap, 1973; Kernberg, 1976), we could consider that the intrapsychic disturbance reflected by Mary's behavior is an impairment in the kind of psychic synthesis that I have attributed to the imaging capacity. I have suggested that the imaging capacity functions, in situations of low tension, to produce increased awareness of both self and object as discrete, unified entities giving and receiving signals, including affects. In the case of Mary, the imaging capacity had to function in a situation in which Mary's strong hostile and loving feelings competed. This placed in jeopardy the developing unity of the image of self (loving or angry) and the unity of the image of her mother (lovable or hateful). Mary's mother, however, did not react adversely to the kicking and striking; she did not introduce her own emotional seesawing. Instead, the mother patiently and sensitively waited with Mary rigidly upright on her lap, giving Mary time to collect herself without intruding. Assisted in this way by her mother, Mary's affection gained the upper hand. What is particularly noteworthy—exemplifying how new capacities may develop at a time when stress exists within limits of possible mastery—is that the same evening Mary, for the first time, "began to communicate with her mother vocally, using preverbal infliction and rhythms that sounded like words" (Parens, 1979b, p. 404). This preverbal vocalizing may be regarded as a component of sign-signal communication, in which sounds are added to gestures. This development reveals another imitative aspect of the image of self as director (vocalizer), for it is modeled after the image of others as speakers. The outcome of Mary's struggle was the further development of her communicative capacities and, with this, a marked increase in her flexibility of response.

These observations place the concept of splitting in a different light. The generally accepted view is that splitting either results from a failure of two separate organizations (based on generalized affects of pleasure and unpleasure) to become integrated or involves a reinstitution of that separation as a defensive measure (see Lichtenberg and Slap, 1973; Mahler et al., 1975; Kernberg, 1976). This view, however, does not fit the data I have presented here. Affects, even in the first year, are differentiated in terms of pleasure (function pleasure, efficacy pleasure, sensual pleasure, all graded from simple interest, through smiling, to joy) and unpleasure (from startle, through fear and shame, to anger or sadness, crying and withdrawal). Through the imaging capacity, the emergent property of self, building on prior, differentiated self-functioning (Stern, 1983), creates a unified self as director. In this view, there are not two organizations of self experience to be unified or split, but *one* generalized, experiential self entity at all moments of low and moderate intensity. At moments of high intensity, unity of the sense of self will usually be retained if the general sense of parental support remains intact. At such moments, fantasy elaboration may express and record in developing memory systems the organizing impact of the high-intensity moments. A different process may occur when moments of high intensity recur with such frequency that the integrative capacity is overwhelmed and the sense of basic protective support is eroded. The unity of the self may become endangered or be sacrificed, giving way to separate (split) organizing of the experience along lines more expressive of strong affective states (angry as opposed to loving, exhibitionistically excited or humiliated and devitalized, etc.). In these instances, persistent dichotomous pathological suborganizations form, seriously limiting the integrity and flexibility of the self (Lichtenberg and Slap, 1972, 1973).[2]

Cindy, a 19-month-old described by Parens (1979b), had rather easily moved away from her mother during earlier periods of play and exploration and back to a closeness with her later, sharing with her mother her current interests. On the day of Parens's observation, Cindy started to leave her mother to join the other children, only to stop and return to her mother. Crying, she

---

[2]In taking this view, I share with Pine (1981) the value of conceptualizing the infant's life in terms of moment-to-moment experiences. I also agree that high-tension experiences provide the sources for fantasies that are significant for psychoanalytic clinical practice. I disagree, however, with the significance Pine assigns to high-intensity moments. In my view, for an account of *general development* in the second year, low- and moderate-intensity moments are the major organizing source. Although I agree that unmastered high-intensity moments are significant origins of splitting and other pathological consequences, they are overemphasized in accounts that place them in the center of normal development.

"twisted her body away from her mother as though she were suddenly experiencing acute pain. Let down gently, she dropped to the floor, crying, twisting, kicking her legs in a mild temper tantrum, an unusual reaction for her. . . . Three times mother and daughter reenacted this same sequence, Cindy's ambivalent behavior winding down with the 6th 'hold me close!' communication'' (p. 411). This incident heralded a period of increased irritability and outward manifestations of aggressive behavior in all areas of Cindy's life—a shift that seemed inexplicable in terms of any situational change.

The challenge of this upsurge of irritability and aggression led a week later to an innovative, self-actuated problem-solving sequence. Caught in what to the observer appeared to be an ambivalent pull between remaining emotionally fixed in mother's orbit and pushing outward toward more autonomy and flexibility, Cindy created an island of calm for herself in the midst of her turbulence. She sat close to her mother and, with much pleasure, engaged in a game of throwing a doll off the sofa—casting it away harshly and recovering possession of it with a seemingly gentle satisfaction. Looked at from the standpoint of the imaging capacity and the developing capacity for signification, Cindy's behavior can be regarded as utilizing a clear conception of the ''out there'' to create a play sequence. In the play, the doll stood for herself. The Cindy-doll-self, with harsh assertiveness, propelled her departure from the sofa, all the while having the certainty of a loving return. Simultaneously, the hitherto stormily irritable Cindy could sit more calmly next to her mother.

Six weeks after this play sequence with the doll, Cindy herself moved away from her mother in a widening arc, while letting other people assist her when she became anxious. On her own, she again used her developing capacity for play—now raised to the level of early symbolic play (Nicolich, 1977)—to create an image of the self as director controlling a scene in which being out of visual contact was the dominant motif. Cindy took a pull-toy, left her mother, and went out of visual contact behind the sofa they used. She took the pull-toy apart and made its parts disappear into a drawer. She opened and closed the drawer, "pushing the pieces out of sight when they became visible—all creating the impression that she was working through the separation from the emotionally invested toy. After a 10-minute separation from mother, Cindy returned to her, and both enjoyed the reunion" (Parens, 1979b, p. 413). This play sequence suggests a further movement—on the one hand, toward the emotional tolerance of the lack of visual contact, in which the child is *aware* of absence, and, on the other hand, toward a level of full symbolic representation, in which a permanent image or representation of the self and of the mother persists despite the emotional state.[3]

THE INCREASED GENITAL AND PERINEAL SENSATION

Along with the opportunities and conflicts that result from the upsurge of assertiveness, a call on the self-as-a-whole to integrate an internal challenge comes from another compelling pressure—that of an increase in genital and perineal awareness and sensation in both boys and girls between 18 and 24 months (Roiphe, 1968; Galenson and Roiphe, 1974; Kleeman, 1975). This increased genital awareness coincides with increased anal and urethral sensation and a greater capacity for sphincter control. Genital and perineal exploration and self-stimulation are thus regularly found during this period. This pleasurable activity "is normally without any great emotional excitement" (Kleeman, 1975, p. 98) and is accompanied by body and genital pride, as well as by an urge to exhibit the genital area. The outcome and long-range effect of this early genital activity varies considerably, depending on the responses it elicits in the parents. Amsterdam and Levitt (1980) speculate that the exchange between the touching and exhibiting child and the responding parent is the core experience for the development of normal and pathological self-consciousness. They

---

[3]See Shopper (1978) for a discussion of the role of the pull-toy in separation-individuation.

postulate that coyness and shyness evolve from the awareness of others looking at the self, and that painful self-consciousness results from the parent's disapproving regard. Tomkins's (1963) proposal that shame is innately triggered by a sudden decrement in mounting pleasure provides a further explanation for infants responding to mother's inhibiting reactions to their fondling or exhibiting their genitals.

Looked at from the standpoint of the emergent self-as-a-whole, the upsurge of genital and perineal awareness and sensation provides the opportunity for developments in a number of crucial areas. It enhances the sense of self through the vitalizing effect that excitement contributes. (This is a first step in the regulation of excitement that eventually leads, on the one hand, to the heightened sense of self in lovemaking and, on the other hand, to the pathological compulsive masturbation of the psychotic, who attempts to induce a temporary sense of awareness and integrity of the body self.) Increased genital awareness and sensation also give toddlers a means to provide comfort and soothing, especially at the exact time they are attempting to move outside the interactional matrix. It increases the scope of imaging of self by intensifying the experience in which one part of the self gains the status of "object," while another retains the status of "agent" in a situation of moderately high emotional tension. The integration of these two aspects of self (excited responder and fondler) into one unit contributes to experiencing the self-as-a-whole as "place," the "container" into which both self as object and self as agent fit.

Possibly the most important effect of increased genital awareness and sensation is its effect on gender differentiation, although this is difficult to specify as yet. It is an undeniable empirical fact that the infant's gender means a great deal to each parent and each reacts differently to boys and girls. By one year, gender differences are demonstrable. Boys will range farther from the mother and make more active problem-solving efforts to return to her when artificially separated. Girls stay closer to the mother and when separated will appeal directly for rescue (Korner, 1974). These differences can be related to observable maternal behaviors. Mothers commonly encourage girls to remain closer than boys and respond more quickly to their rescue appeals. What is surprising is the extent to which the self is imaged by the toddler in gender terms. At the time when the boy toddler responds to his mirror image and differentially to his mother's and father's photograph, he cannot separate his photograph from that of other boys, but looks longer at pictures of boys and more quickly puts aside all pictures of girls. The same preference for photographs of the same-sex children is shown by girls (Brooks and Lewis, 1974). The increased genital awareness and sensation probably fills out the body-self image, giving a value-laden importance to that body part. At what point in development the genitals as such become fully integrated in the preexisting gender categorization requires further study.

The father's role at this time also requires further study. Does it have a gender meaning? Herzog's (1980) study of 12 boys ranging in age from 18 to 28 months whose fathers had left their mothers is highly suggestive. In each instance, the child developed night terrors with rather clear symbolic representations of a phobic nature that appeared in the child's words, dreams, and play. Each "boy perceived his father's presence or return as a vital element in controlling or combatting that fear" (p. 228).

Gary, the youngest child in the series, was 18 months when, one month after his father had left, he began to awaken nightly, screaming uncontrollably, sometimes for 20 minutes. With a look of fear, he called for Daddy. When seen by Herzog, he immediately left his mother and got into the therapist's lap. Staying in constant physical contact with Herzog, Gary began to play with clay. He rolled the clay into long, loglike pieces and then broke them into smaller parts, laughing with pleasure. Herzog entered into the play with a puppet who picked up one of the pieces. Gary looked very frightened and said, "Daddy hurt." Herzog asked, "Who can help?" Gary brightened and said, "Daddy help Gary—please," hugging the therapist hard. In a later session, the little boy puppet was sleeping in the same bed with the mother puppet (as had Gary with his mother since his father left). Gary had the little boy puppet jump up, saying, "Scare me—Daddy hurt, quick get Daddy—Daddy help Gary." The therapist had the Mommy puppet get up and try to comfort the boy puppet. "No, no," shrieked Gary, looking afraid. "Daddy hurt, get Daddy." The therapist introduced the adult man puppet. Gary put him next to the little boy. They he had the man put the little boy in a separate bed and return to his wife's bed. "All better now," Gary said happily (Herzog, 1980, p. 224).

According to Herzog:

> Analysis of the dream and the play material supports the notion that the absence of the father at this time imposes a particular strain on the evolving psychic structure of the boy. . . . Under the regressive and progressive sway of sleep, a phobic transformation emerges in which the child's own aggression impulses are seen as hostilely and mercilessly attacking the self in the guise of monsters, big birds, and so forth. . . . The mother is unable to interrupt this process and may even fuel it by moving closer to her son [p. 229].

He suggests that the father "hunger" demonstrated by these toddlers supports Abelin's (1977) hypothesis that the boy is biologically programmed by androgenization of the fetal brain to turn away from the mother and toward the father at about 18 months. Solnit's (1972) report of a sleep disturbance in a 16-month-old girl after her beloved father lost his temper with her suggests some similarities in the father's gender-determined place for the girl toddler.

It is of interest that Herzog's examples, as well as those of a number of other psychoanalytic authors, reveal toddlers at 18 months or younger communicating at a symbolic level. These cases may represent children with a somewhat atypical precosity of development, selected because of the clarity with which their productions illustrate the influence of conflictual disturbances. In these toddlers, developmental progress may be more advanced than usual because of inborn and environmental factors, or the rate of development may be spurred in response to a challenge presented by circumstances, such as those Herzog describes.

By the middle of the second year, the self has available all the capacities built up throughout the period of learning (Greenspan, 1982) that has taken place in the biological-neurophysiological-behavioral mode of the first year and the imaging, sign-signal mode of the beginning second year. As Décarie (1962) summarizes:

> The distance traveled in these 18 months is immense. . . . At the end of this period, thanks to representation and deduction (which is nothing but the systematic utilization of this representation) we have a world of objects whose permanence, substantiality, identity, and externality are no longer a function of the subject. The solidification and objectification of this universe reach from now on into regions outside the realm of perception and immediate action. As a final and important consequence, the body of the child himself now becomes an object among other objects.
>
> Indeed, due to imitation which is more and more internalized, the child becomes able to have a representation of his own body in analogy to the bodies of others and to conceive of his body as having permanence, substance, identity with itself, etc.
>
> Therefore, the 4-week-old baby differs from the 20-month-old child not only because of a series of tightly interwoven new acquisitions, but also by some kind of remodeling of his primitive "Weltanschauung" [pp. 61–62].

Chapter Ten

Symbolic Representation and Consolidation of Sense of Self

Language plays an increasingly significant role in the remodeling of the *Weltanschauung* in the second half of the second year. Long before 18 months, children use their verbal comprehension and vocal communications, first to fit better into the interactional matrix with the mother, and later to attempt to extract themselves from it. Beginning around the middle of the second year, their reliance on the self-activated use of words becomes so strong that the self as speaker and the self as thinker in words may appear (inaccurately) as synonomous with the total self, with being "human." Language is indeed a potent resource for the child because the developing self can utilize it to integrate so many other functions. Moreover, as Shapiro (1979) points out:

> The simple fact that a naming explosion takes place in children between 18 months and three years of age, coordinated with a syntactic explosion during the same period regardless of languages spoken and cultural setting, is suggestive of a universal human timetable. The emergence of a capacity for understanding and stating relational aspects between things is coordinated with those events. The skill in relating subject, action and object in words occurs in a rather fixed sequential form and evolves into later abilities for stating coordinated relations, subordinate changes, and contingency statements [p. 11].

INFORMATION PROCESSING IN TWO COGNITIVE-AFFECTIVE MODES

The flexibility that characterizes the period after the emergence of the self-as-a-whole, however, is not based on language skills. Rather, language acquisition is a tool employed in the develop-

132

ment of the two modes of symbolic representational thought. Nicolich (1977) indicates that researchers have tended to concentrate more on "linguistic aspects of early language development than on cognitive status of children learning language" (p. 98). The cognitive status of children entering the symbolic level of play and language use is more complex and therefore more adaptable than that of the younger toddler, who depends on the imaging capacity and a sign-signal mode of communication. This new level of mental organization involves the parallel, interlocking development of two general modes of perceptual-cognitive-affective organization, by which symbolic play and language use are ordered. These two modes of organization bear so close a resemblance to Freud's conception of primary and secondary processes that the analogy to pouring old wine into new bottles is not only suggested but accurate, if the difference between a contemporary account of the primary process and the original conception is accepted (see Holt, 1967; Noy, 1979).

The main characteristics of the relationship between the two general modes of perceptual-cognitive-affective organization is that they exist as parallel organizations whose functions are interrelated at all times. That is, they are not stratified, as is suggested by the terms "primary" and "secondary." One organization is built principally around sensory impressions (sights, sounds, tactile sensations, tastes, etc.), and the other is built around the rules of combination and sequencing that characterize syntax, word order, and distancing between signified and signifier, but each organization may use words and each may use imagery in the contents that it forms. A patient vividly portrayed the two organizations at work in an experience he described in an art gallery. Entering a room with a large painting (Frederick Church's *The Aurora Borealis*), he clicked on the earphones provided by the gallery and simultaneously reacted to the visual experience. His perception was of the coldness of the frozen arctic scene, the sense of isolation in the midst of nature's grandeur. The message he was simultaneously apprehending was that this was a painting executed in a specific year by an artist who belonged to a certain group of painters, now called "Luminists." At this point, he noticed a tiny detail of a small ship caught in the midst of the ice flow. He experienced a feeling of anxiety, accompanied by a general physical shudder. The recorded talk was at this time describing the artist's use of perspective lines to draw the viewer's eyes gradually to the small ship with a single light on its bridge.

Although each organization develops simultaneously and separately—that is, the secondary process does not emerge out of the primary process—one or the other will predominate at different moments in the toddler's life. During high-intensity experiences, such as toilet training or genital play, referents are apt to lose the distance from body parts they have at calmer moments. For instance, at times of low intensity, the word "doodoo" for feces may be used in a sentence to denote, in objective fashion, a completed act. In moments of high tension for the child, even speaking the word "doodoo" may be a source of self-actuated excitement, with word, act, and bodily sensation all collapsing together. As stated before, perceptual-action-affect responses during moments of low and moderate tension contribute to the central regulatory core of the infant's life, and psychoanalytic accounts that draw too close an analogy between normal development and pathological disorders tend to downplay this essential finding of infant research. Another factor must also be considered to have a balanced view. The infant's experience is far more body-focused than that of the adult (Lichtenberg, 1975). It is reasonable to assume, therefore, that moments of moderate- and high-tension body-centered experience become the thematic source for a significant proportion of the child's symbolic play. These experiences lend themselves to the organizational properties of the primary process so that this mode of perceptual-cognitive-affective organization will often predominate in the toddler period. Furthermore, words, which in time become flexible signifier vehicles at a great distance from the referent, are generally close to the concrete experience in the toddler period. For example, "boom-boom" for hammer collapses with the sensory response. The word "hammer" does not, although "hammer" may be used equally by either organization. The older child, who has shifted to the name "hammer," molds the schematizing activity so that the new vocal material becomes dynamically-physiognomically organized to fit the event represented . . . [but] it still *portrays* aspects of the referent . . . through the way in which it is apprehended internally by the user" (Werner and Kaplan, 1963, p. 129).

Each perceptual-cognitive-affective organization has its own formal characteristics and undergoes continuous development throughout life. Words strung together in the sequence of a sentence provide a way to order contingencies, both semantically and operationally. When a toddler responds with comprehension to mother's statement: "Give me the spoon and I will feed you the custard," the toddler has coordinated a semantic sequence, an action sequence, and a pleasurable visual-gustatory sequence. The familiar rules of logic apply to each of these sequences, and the rules of causal linkage, to the relationship each has to the other. Alternatively, if a toddler clangs a spoon on the table and mother holds up the custard jar and says, "Yummy! Yummy!," the whole percept coordinates sound, action, a nonsense word, and a gustatory stimulus into a holistic image of exuberant joy. The rules that govern the sequence are those of time collapsing toward synchrony rather than delaying into contingency, of rapid substitutions (displacements) of associational linkage rather than more discrete, stable referents.

What I am calling the secondary-process perceptual-cognitive-affective mode of organization, McKinnon (1979) describes as an Auditory-Sequential (AS) semantic form, in which the psychological elements are arranged "as if they were sequential single units of sound" (p. 54). In the adult, we commonly regard verbal communication, with the rules of sentence sequencing and the formal dialectic of its exchange, as a prime example of secondary process. However, any sensory modality may be arranged in this form of sequence, as evidenced by the organization of some symbolic play sequences in the child. McKinnon explains:

Visual images, abstract concepts, nonphonetic sounds, kinesthetic, olfactory, or gustatory images all may be ordered intelligibly by rules peculiar to this semantic form: nonarticulate sounds become melodies and rhythms, postures become dance, visual images become drama, morphemes become words, words become sentences, propositions become logical arguments, events become history, and mathematical symbols become theorems proved. Some of the rules subordinate to AS semantic form, then, are rules of rhythm and melody, choreography, drama, spelling, linguistic syntax, logic, historical chronology, and mathematics [p. 55].

To McKinnon's list, I would add the rules that apply to human relationships that are characterized by separateness, objectivity, discreteness, social forms, and ritual, and the time interval for building up sequences in which contingent relationships predominate. These are the rules that order the relationship of the individuated self (the "I") to a separate, other person and of the self ("I") to one's body or mind, where one monitors "objectively" the state of one's bodily experience or one's emotions and mental activity.

The perceptual-cognitive-affective mode of organization that coincides with primary process is what McKinnon describes as a Visual-Spatial (VS) semantic form, in which psychological elements are arranged "as if they were parts of a visual image to be composed simultaneously in space" (p. 54). The psychological elements in this form gain their meaning "by contiguity, or by occupying the same locus in virtual space. The significance of such an array does not inhere in its parts, but rather in their simultaneous integration into a complex whole" (p. 56). Simultaneous presence is organized by means of displacement, in which one unit substitutes for another, and condensation, in which there is a spatial collapse of multiple elements. The exemplar of the VS form is metaphor, a figure of speech in which one thing is likened to another, different thing by being spoken of as if it were that other thing. I would add to McKinnon's formulation that this perceptual-cognitive-affective mode organizes relationships between the self and others in which qualities, functions, and feelings of self and others may be treated as shared (easily displaced or condensed), and in which emotions may become generalized into moods or global feeling states. These rules would govern the relations between the self and one's own body when pleasure or pain in one body part engulfs (spreads over) all other perceptual-cognitive modalities. These rules order the dominance of the self by the "mind" in the excitement of the collapse of disparities that characterizes the sudden integrative understanding of the "Aha" experience.

To adopt McKinnon's suggestion of a Visual-Spatial form of organization as a model for substitutions and collapsing of elements may seem to contradict my proposal that a visually centered imaging capacity establishes discreteness and objectivity in the toddler's world. This seeming contradiction can be resolved by considering the properties of visual perception. At the focal point, imaging is discrete and precise. The familiar experiment of holding one's finger before one's eyes attests to the fact that focusing on the finger places it sharply in view. The distant background is visible but fuzzy. Focusing on the background, however, sharpens it, while the finger doubles or fades. All the while images in the peripheral field are mostly indistinct. Normal vision, then, involves the composing of foreground and background and periphery by a shifting scan continuously exposing the possibility of substitutions and condensations, particularly along the lines of what is emotionally attractive or repellent. It is noteworthy that Spiegel's (1959) pioneering effort to account for the sense of self utilized shifting visual frames of reference as the basis for the orientation of the self. In addition, when applied to cognition (not external perception), "imagery representations of relations between thoughts typically exhibited certain features, namely, *condensation of contents, ellipsis of content, indicatory depiction, and implicatory reference*" (Werner and Kaplan, 1963, p. 456).

The relationship between vision and hearing has been described by Shopper (1978) in his paper on the role of audition in early psychic development. He states:

Kleeman (1973) gives several examples of the child not only initiating peek-a-boo or using another form of peek-a-boo, but also walking around the house with head and face blanketed (age sixteen months). I would con-

struct that the child was actively attempting to wean herself from
dependence on vision, visual contact, and visual orientation. Kleeman
notes that peek-a-boo is intimately related to the vicissitudes and structuring of a mental representation of the mother and when a very stable mental
image (of the mother) is established, peek-a-boo play becomes less meaningful and stops (p. 15). To this I would add that the cessation of peek-a-
boo also occurs with the greater reliance and acceptability of an auditory
modality of contact and a correspondingly greater independence from tactile and visual modality of contact—a sort of "weaning from vision"
[Shopper, 1978, p. 293].

I believe this "weaning from vision" represents a shift from the
predominance of the imaging capacity and the sign-signal informational exchange to increasing reliance on verbal exchange and
processing of information at the symbolic level. It is not that visual
processing is replaced by the auditory mode, but that both are
lifted to a new level of interacting, integrated organization.

According to Noy (1979), once organized, "the primary and
secondary processes are two developmental lines whose courses of
development are determined by the same intrinsic maturational
factors. Each new cognitive skill that appears in its appropriate
phase influences both processes to the same degree, and each new
stage of refinement of any of their skills is reflected equally in the
operations of both. This means that each process displays at every
developmental phase, the same ability to categorize, make mental
representations, and operate in all other areas of cognitive functioning" (p. 177). He continues:

A mature, normal self image is . . . based on a combination of primary and
secondary modes. According to the primary process mode, a person
perceives himself as from *within,* as a collage of sensations, wishes, needs,
and experiences. According to the secondary process mode, a person
perceives himself as from *without,* as a group of objective phenomena, an
object among other objects, a collection of physical substances and forces.
. . . This double perception and representation pertain to any part of the
body, to the body self as an overall image and to the subordinate self in all
its dimensions. The all-inclusive self image is an inner representation made
up of the two aspects, which I would call the "experiential self" and the
"conceptual self." A healthy sense of selfness results from a sound
balance and optimal fit between these aspects [p. 188].

The balance may tilt toward one or the other of the two forms of perceptual-cognitive-affective organization and remain within the bounds of adaptive personality qualities. The predominance of one or the other of the two organizations can be illustrated by the contrast between two six-year-olds—James and David. James is a fictional version of the analyst-to-be Adrian Stephen, described by his exquisitely observant sister, Virginia Woolf, in *To the Lighthouse* (1927):

> Since he belonged, even at the age of six, to that great clan which cannot keep this feeling separate from that, but must let future prospects, with their joys and sorrows, cloud what is actually at hand, since to such people even in earliest childhood any turn in the wheel of sensation has the power to crystallize and transfix the moment upon which its gloom or radiance rests, James Ramsay, sitting on the floor cutting out pictures from the illustrated catalogue of the Army and Navy Stores, endowed the picture of a refrigerator, as his mother spoke, with heavenly bliss. It was fringed with joy. The wheelbarrow, the lawnmower, the sound of poplar trees, leaves whitening before rain, rooks cawing, brooms knocking, dresses rustling—all these were so coloured and distinguished in his mind that he had already his private code, his secret language, though he appeared the image of stark and uncompromising severity [pp. 9–10].

David, on the other hand, frequently played alone with his soldiers. He constructed forts for them and had elaborate but distinct battle plans, both offensive and defensive. Although he had a number of friends with whom he played outside games, he only enjoyed playing soldiers with Jack, because Jack alone of his friends shared his passion for accuracy. David, who already at six read at a fourth-grade level, had his soldiers organized in units—foot soldiers, cavalry, and artillery. He knew how far the rifles and the cannons would fire; how large the squads, platoons, companies would be; how fast and how far the cavalry and horses could travel. The floor on which he played was, in his imagination, carefully scaled from inches to miles. When Jack and he argued about the validity of a plan, he would consult one of his books or, if necessary, wait for his father to supply the needed information. Although he enjoyed the fantasied charges and the battles as a whole, his real satisfaction came from the categorizing of information and the simulation of objective reality that his carefully made distinctions gave him. To add a new fact from a book or from his father to his catalogue of knowledge gave him as much joy as the whoop of victory when the walls of the fort were breached in a successful assault.

These vignettes illustrate that the traditional linking of primary process with imagery and fantasy and of secondary process with lexical development is overly restrictive. Imagery and language are used in each perceptual-cognitive-affective organization, but the product of the integration is different, just as James and David were very different boys. David's use of language in his expansion of his secondary-process perceptual-cognitive-affective organization is obvious. But the part language played in James's primary-process organization is less apparent, until we consider the important observation by Bruner and Sherwood (1980):

> . . . most of the early utterances we have observed in the children whom we have studied (and so too for every corpus of early speech I have ever looked at) show one clear-cut characteristic: most of the talking by mother and by child is *not* about hard-nosed reality. It is about games, about imaginary things, about seemingly quite useless make-believe. In fact, what is involved is useful for both conceptual and communicative development—role playing, referring to non-present events, combining elements to exploit their variability, etc.

Another traditional formulation that I question is the one that links one perceptual-cognitive-affective organization with responses to drives and the other with responses to external reality. Each organization works separately and together to respond to what is compelling or disturbing from any source (inner or outer) by activating whatever is available as a resource, either inner or outer. Anna, a 20-month-old, was becoming increasingly comfortable in distancing herself from her mother when her mother instituted an effort to bowel-train her. After an unproductive and irritable episode in the bathroom, Anna grabbed her doll and dragged it roughly across the floor. She vigorously dusted off the doll's soiled skirt, fussing angrily at the "bad dolly." She then threw the doll across the room and stood, looking sad. After a bit, she retrieved the doll and began rocking and soothing her with a dreamy expression on her face.

The mutual work of both organizations can be observed in Anna's behavior. The organizing of the entire play unit—its beginning, middle, and end—has the sequencing and "unity" of a tiny drama, that is, the ordering of secondary process. Within the overall organization, however, there is displacement (soil stands for bowel) and condensation (the strength of the aggressiveness combines the mother's mild admonition with the child's projected anger, and a reversal of role). The relationship between Anna, mother, and doll also shows differing organizational tendencies. At first, the scolded "child" is relatively separate—the target of the "mother's" feelings and actions. This relative psychological separateness is further reflected in the physical casting away. I believe that the separateness and targeting of such causal sequences as "If you get dirty, you are naughty and you will be scolded" reveal secondary-process organization. On the other hand, in the final action (the rocking and soothing and the dreamy look), what is suggested is a loss of boundaries, a collapse in space and time of distinction between Anna–mother and her doll–baby. Their psychological, physical, and emotional selves merge, with the shared cognitive-affective state becoming a gestalt of soothing and comforting. This state, in which the function (soothing) and the functioner (soother) become one, is more likely to be organized along the lines of the primary-process perceptual-cognitive-affective organization than is the type of relationship in which separateness and clear distinctions are maintained.

To return to my general point: The self-as-a-whole of this 20-month-old girl could use highly flexible modes or organizations to deal with a state of tension. Anna organized a sequence of behavior in a way that, in its contingencies and distinctions, evidenced secondary-process regulation. Her play revealed two modes of relating: one that widened the distinction between a self image and an object image, and another that evidenced diminished distinction and distance, even merger. Furthermore, Anna built into the sequence the use of perceptual-cognitive-affective processes for defensive purposes: identification with the aggressor, projection of anger, displacement, reversal, and condensation. Some of the specific means of defense utilize perceptual-cognitive-affective regulations derived from the primary process, others derive from secondary process (Lichtenberg and Slap, 1971, 1972).

Pointing to which element derives from which perceptual-cognitive-affective organization, however, may have the disadvantage of lessening our appreciation of the remarkable way the newly emergent self-as-a-whole utilizes the two organizations in concert. The identification of two distinct organizations is the approach of an external observer, viewing separate components; from the viewpoint of the person's experience, the result of the workings of the organizations is a single entity. Similarly, even if—as some researchers believe—these two modes of organization derive from different cerebral hemispheric neurophysiology (McKinnon, 1979), the brain function that results is never *experienced* as right or left brain. The experience is of a unified entity; it is the observer who states that it has the characteristics or patterns of one or the other hemisphere. The characteristics of the secondary process (representation by discrete signifiers, the logic of temporal sequences, and the explicitness of meanings) are integrated with the characteristics of the primary process (generalized images, the collapsing of time and space, and the holistic synthesis of elements) so that the individual's experience is of the unity that results. The origin of this synthesis can be illustrated by an analogy to the skills developed by artists during the Renaissance. Compared with the relatively flat and stylized figures of medieval painters, Renaissance artists' figures are fully rounded, evidencing an increasing knowledge of anatomical discreteness. If we look at a Madonna and child, the figures are the appropriate ages and the composition depicts the interplay of mother and child while continuing to convey, through recognized signs, their religious significance. Matching the new aesthetic developments artists used with foreground figures were different skills, used to tie in the background. Perspective clarifies the relationship in space, bridging any sharp disjunction. Moreover, in late works from this period, a sense of a shimmering space may extend over soft undulating hills to suggest, through *sfumato,* a generalized comfort and support supplied by nature. In the work of a High Renaissance master, the outcome is that foreground and background are so well integrated that the effect is of a single, unified experience.

THE IMPACT ON THE TODDLER

The "foreground" experiences of the second year may at times resemble to the idyllic image of mother and child in Renaissance art, but more often, especially in the middle and second half, the foreground is occupied by considerable turmoil, by high-intensity, high-tension experiences (Pine, 1981). Toddlers are under pressure from competing high-intensity sensations from the mouth, skin, bowels, bladder, perineum, and genitals. They are under pressure from the upsurge of assertiveness associated with their developing but fragile sense of themselves as directors. They show a heightened responsiveness of reactive aggressiveness and resentment to any frustration or frustrator. The strain on the parental support system from the move toward greater autonomy, body exploration, intentionality, and privacy stirs up confrontations in the foreground, and sometimes threatens the background ambiance of basic support and trust as well. Even at moments of moderate tension, toddlers are still working, through the imaging capacity, to treat mother as a full, discrete object of contemplation, to organize her manifold perceptual input into an ordered, persistent, unitary internal representation. The total effect of the moment-to-moment swings of experience creates the pulling and tugging, dysphoric states Mahler has characterized as the rapprochement crisis (see Mahler et al., 1975). Moreover, another shift is taking place. The toddler's communicative dialogue is moving from the sign-signal exchanges of the first half of the second year, to increased vocalization, with increasing numbers of words.

In all this, sources of sensual stimulation overlap, interchange, and fuse. Toddlers are increasingly responsive to approval-disapproval from their sign-signal alertness, and they experience a mounting push against and reactive resentment toward the loved and needed mother. Language usage conveys the polymorphous ambiguity of these experiences in such words as "nasty" (which can mean dirty and smelly, sexually bad, or ill-mannered and ill-tempered) and "nice" (meaning fine, delicate, sexually pleasurable, well-mannered, or of a sweet disposition). To arrive at the genital-centered, triangle-focused sexuality of the oedipal period, children must, over the next several years, differentiate genital sensations from bowel, bladder, and perineal sensations. They must distinguish genital activity from elimination with its specific cultural overtones of soil and dirt, and they must separate genital activity from overtones of reactive aggressiveness while retaining assertiveness. Toddlers' principal resource in accomplishing this is the organization of the two cognitive-affective modes of the symbolic level. This organization permits them to retain a sensation-near mode of representation while simultaneously having at their disposal an organization for discursive treatment of experiences, employing the subtle differences verbalization allows.

As it develops during the second half of the second year, the newly symbolic representational capacity is heavily occupied in structuring the polymorphous experiences of this period. Indeed, this has been the unique discovery of psychoanalysis—that the turbulent, the conflictual, the "demonic" aspects of infancy (and life in general) receive persistent symbolic representation in dreams, slips, free associations, and spontaneous play. Traumatic events can be ordered in this form of symbolic representation at least as early as 18 months (Solnit, 1972; Renik et al., 1978; Ablon and Mack, 1980; Herzog, 1980).

Although natural science observation is useful in providing confirmatory evidence of the functioning of the two perceptual-cognitive organizations, data gained through the analyst's empathic attunement to the analysand's introspective awareness is required to appreciate the subtle way the two organizations work in concert, each operating from a different vantage point (Noy,

1979). The primary process functions as if its perceptual vantage point were from within, sensing wishes, needs, and sensations; the secondary process functions as if it took the perspective of a more distanced, "objective" outsider. The specific experience of the demonic in any individual derives its potential from both organizations. Displacement, condensation, and symbolization are observable in the formation of the imagery of everyday fantasies of boogey men and witches, as well as in their more permanent representation in symptoms and character traits of fearfulness and distrust. The "objectivity" of the view from outside develops in tune with the perspective of the caregiver, and usually helps to place the demonic in a normal context. The caretaker's way of responding and structuring, however, may fail to supply the needed framework into which to place the boogey man and the witch or indeed contribute to the difficulty by creating an overwhelming predominance of high-intensity experiences. Loss of the presence of support of either parent during this critical time may therefore have a decidely adverse effect. Moreover, the secondary process may contribute to the demonic by taking a form notable for its coldness, its rigidity, its "rationalness" (in the sense of a Kafkaesque world). Under favorable circumstances, however, inside and outside experiences are synthesized and integrated by the two perceptual-cognitive-affective organizations, leading to a consolidation of the self as able to adapt to the demonic—that is, to symbolize it, to be fascinated with it, to "play" it out in creative forms without lasting pathological effect.

Stechler and Kaplan (1980) believe the critical "inside" experience is the continuation of an unfulfilled intention over time. The inner symbolic representation will first contain an image of the self-as-a-whole in problem-solving action. If frustration continues, the image of the self will be associated with a sense of being thwarted and of malevolence (inner anger–outer fear), which requires symbolic representation to be handled adaptively. The equally critical "outside" experience "encompasses a number of steps: (1) the parents have to recognize the child's intention; (2) respond to it in a fairly consistent way; (3) communicate back to the child sufficiently clear, consistent signals so that the child knows what their reaction is; (4) permit the sequence to go far enough so that the child (a) has a sense of intention, (b) carries the act to fruition, and (c) receives some kind of message about the consequences of (her) action'' (Stechler and Kaplan, 1980, p. 102). With favorable inner and outer experiences organized by the two perceptual-cognitive-affective organizations, the child will tend to choose an action that constitutes an alliance with the parent rather than behavior that reflects an oppositional desire. The internal representation will then be of a separate self-as-a-whole in a state of intimacy (and function-building identification [Jacobson, 1964]) with the parent, rather than of a demonic, compulsion-dominated self keyed in opposition or defensive capitulation or idealization with an unempathic other.

This view adds to our understanding of the organizing effect of traumatic events that breach the integrative capacity of the self (Schur, 1966), an understanding of the cumulative effect of the events of daily life. It is these "ordinary" events, and the opportunities they offer the self for integration and expansion or for pathological persistence of earlier modes, that join the observations of infant research with the reconstructions made possible by analysis of adult transferences.

To recapitulate these developments from the standpoint of the self: The self-as-a-whole, once experienced, reflects, as closely as possible at any time, the person as a total entity. At its inception, it comprises the "I" as doer or director of the existing sign-signal cognitive-affective-action patterns and the "self" acted upon by others (or by the "I"). With the development of symbolic representation and reasoning, it includes a "mental" self. (Considerably later than the second year, further developments occur, through which the self-as-a-whole becomes capable of reflective awareness of each of the other aspects of self.) The self-as-a-whole formed during the second year has the quality (at least experientially) of constantly attempting to coordinate patterns of impelling pressures and functional capacities. In other words, the principal function of the self-as-a-whole would seem to be the integration of all existing functioning into an organization that retains the greatest possible flexibility. Each subsequent developmental occurrence provides new compelling urges and new functional challenges and capacities, which potentially allow for an increase in the flexible range of the self-as-a-whole. Alternatively, each developmental occurrence may be regarded as potentially divisive, carrying the possibility of diminished flexibility in order to preserve the self-as-a-whole.

The upsurge in assertiveness and reactive aggression, the increase in perineal and genital awareness, the shifts in cognition, and the acquisition of language in the toddler can all be viewed in the light of their effects on the self-as-a-whole. The toddler's maladjustments can be regarded as both unresolved conflicts and regulatory failures. From the perspective I have taken, conflict can be defined as a self experience (conscious or unconscious) of a persistent divisive pressure, which results when one grouping of compelling urges and functional responses is in opposition to another, similarly constituted grouping. Such conflictual experiences are inevitable outcomes of developmental pressures. Their outcome is commonly determined by the regulatory support provided by an empathically sensitive, adequately structured (disciplined) environment (parenting). When regulatory support is facilitating, the result of the conflict may be that a new organization or pattern of functions forms, with an accompanying expansion of the self-as-a-whole. If the confict transcends the organizing and integrative capacity, and/or if regulatory support is inadequate, some flexibility in the potential for expansion of self may have to be sacrificed. Pathology can then be defined as the persistent reduction of autoplastic and alloplastic flexibility, ranging from the relatively moderate limitation of toddlers whose play with peers is overly restricted to toddlers so locked into an aversion response to an equally restricted mother that they are permitted neither the joy of playfulness nor the self-defining assertion of argument. Conflict and incomplete regulatory support will be experienced and remembered by toddlers in the form of intrapsychic tensions they can't resolve. Failures in parenting may be reprojected onto the external world. It is these situations that give rise to the transference phenomena observed in psychoanalysis.

PART IV:

Applications

Chapter 11

Erotogenic Zones Versus Alternative Organizational Models of Infancy

In Chapter 1, I indicated that some might place the findings of infant research outside the realm of psychoanalysis proper, with the argument that psychic representation is a linchpin of psychoanalytic theory and that, no matter how complex the neonate's activity is, psychic representation in the infant cannot be demonstrated. So far, throughout this book, my premise has been a refutation of the argument for exclusion. Now I would like to address the issue from the opposite end—the relative exclusion in many current models of infancy of the findings and hypotheses based on data derived from the psychoanalytic setting. I propose to demonstrate that concepts derived from Freud's theory of erotogenic zones and libidinal phases (1905) must be accorded a place in a general theory of infantile development, but in a markedly modified form. Erikson's (1950, 1959) concept of organ *modes* provides a basis for comparison with both the traditional psychosexual model and general systems models of infant research.

HOW DO WE INTERPRET MEANING?

Let me start with a young man in his third year of analysis. This man reports a dream in which he coughed up a particle that seemed unexpectedly large—about the size of a nut. He states that it looked like a peanut in that it opened easily into two parts. The patient's spontaneous association is that the dream reminds him of a physical experience he has from time to time—coughs up particles of what he believes to be diseased tonsils. This experience, however, did not occur on the day of the dream.

As a result of the exchange between analyst and analysand, the dream is interpreted as follows: Coughing up refers to speaking in the analysis. The patient is often silent for extended periods and rarely speaks freely. Yet, on the day of the dream, after two sessions in which he had been especially silent, the patient was much more forthcoming, recalling a dream and giving associations to it. What he "coughed up" through his verbalizing was thus unexpectedly large. "A nut" is the colloquial expression for someone who is crazy. This connection touches on an area of great embarrassment, the source of his desire to disavow troubled aspects of himself. He generally does not like to open his mind to consider dreams for fear of the nuttiness they might reveal in him. He is reluctant to be responsible for the content of his dreams or his associations. Whenever he speaks more actively, as on the day of the dream, it has the involuntary, uncontrollable expulsive feeling of a cough. All of this is in contrast to the "ease" with which the nut in the dream opened, revealing its inner surfaces. It was like a peanut in which the outer shell had been removed and only the thin husk remained. The dream, then, represents a wish (and possible belief) that he is no longer the "hard nut to crack" that his referring physician told him he would be; rather, he is opening up what is inside him more easily.

Beyond the level of meaning immediately available to understanding within the particular analytic hour in which the dream was reported, other probable meanings exist. Although the dream is couched in terms centered on the mouth—coughing up and food regurgitation—there are strong indications that this condenses body imagery from other sources. A violent involuntary expulsion also suggests rectal-anal activity and the *pea* of "peanut" suggests urethral activity, especially as the patient's most frequently used colloquialism for anger is "pissed off." Moreover, "nut" is slang for testicles; tonsils are also associated with testicles. The fantasy of coughing up diseased particles of tonsils implies fears of body damage that come under the general heading of "castration anxiety."

Historically, the ability to interpret the meaning of dream images in this manner is intimately entwined with Freud's observations about erotogenic zones. The capacity to make similar metaphoric translations from symptoms, slips, jokes, character traits, myths, and aesthetic themes is so powerful a means of unraveling mysteries of the human condition that it has been incorporated into the intellectual lore of the public at large. Indeed, every practicing psychoanalyst receives reinvigoration from the use of this powerful tool—of being an interpreter of dreams, like the Biblical Joseph—only with a body of scientific data added.

We are confronted with a problem: Many of the assumptions of Freud's theory of libidinal zones and their central significance for development are contradicted by the data and assumptions I have presented from infant research. Yet no alternative conception is proposed (or for the most part sought) by the researchers on whose organizing principles I have leaned. I shall contrast the two approaches and raise several hypotheses about resolutions of these difficulties. It is well for the reader to keep in mind one fundamental distinction: Freud's theory emphasizes the significance of moments of high tension (see Pine [1981] for a defense of this position, especially as it is employed in the developmental scheme espoused by Mahler). Heightened tension may either be zonal (bodily erotic) excitement, or it may be the result of a traumatic event. In either case, the specific experience of heightened tension is believed to have a profound generalizing effect, similar to that of a rock thrown into a quiet pond. Infant research, on the other hand, emphasizes the significance for development of low- and moderate-tension state experiences—those in which "redundancies," repetitious action patternings of infant and caretaker, take place. Infant researchers would argue that the analogy of the effect of the rock in the quiet pond is false—that in fact the pond is not quiet at all; it is an extremely complex ecological system with continuous change occurring in multiple subsystems (chemical, biological, diurnal, and evolutionary). The cumulative background effect of subsystem changes will determine the significant or lasting effect of the rock. It is the cumulative background factors that will persist in their impact on the pond after the momentary effect of the rock has passed (see Peterfreund [1978] for a critique of the traditional constructs).

UNDERSTANDING DEVELOPMENT

Freud's Conceptualization

The explanation Freud offered that unlocked the mystery of dreams was an ingenious set of postulates about energic transformations, the primary process, topographic and structural relationships, and developmental reconstructions. Let me now briefly summarize Freud's (1905) theory of development: Freud based his proposal on the idea that all sexual experience involves libido, a special form of energy at the border between the physical-biological realm and the psychological. Looking backward from adult sexuality, genital contact and its pleasure has its precursors in other bodily pleasures derived from other especially sensitive areas of the body, all of which involve discharge of the same energy. In the adult, these zonal pleasures—directly, as in kissing (oral zone), or indirectly, as in holding back (anal retention)—become aspects of foreplay. Alternatively, these zonal pleasures may be organized as central functions of the adult's sexual life in the form of perversions (fellatio, anal intercourse).

The timing of the occurrence of sexual experiences in infancy is determined by the point at which a zone provides particularly heightened sensations. The sensual body sensations achieve psychological significance as a result of representation of memory traces of the buildup and discharge of libidinal drive urges. The physical sensation of the zone is signified psychologically by the existence of a high energic placement (libidinal cathexis) of the representational image of the body part. With the omission of the complex epigenetic relationship between phases, a rough analogy would be a neon sign flashing the words "oral," "anal," and "phallic-oedipal."[1] First, "oral" would light up, with the others dark; then, "oral" would remain lit, but "anal" would be more brightly lit; finally, "phallic-oedipal" would become the most brightly lit, with the other two evening out in intensity. The time sequence is roughly: oral, birth to 18 months; anal, 18 months to 36 months; and phallic-oedipal, three to six years—with considerable overlap, as well as alternative datings.

In Freud's conceptualization, the heightening of libidinal energy produces tension and unpleasure; its reduction produces quiescence and pleasure. Thus, the properties of libido bear the same profile as the buildup and release of sexual orgasm. Each libidinal zone—oral, anal, and phallic-oedipal—in turn exerts a powerful pull on unconscious, preconscious, and conscious awareness and the self and object representations that form as a result. The vicissitudes of libidinal urgency, then, constitute an intrapsychic dimension that influences the child's orientation to the surroundings and their record in the child's psyche. On the one hand, a difficult-to-assess biological factor—the infant's genetic constitution—affects the intrapsychic dimension; oral, anal, or phallic-oedipal proclivities may be stronger or weaker. On the other hand, the manner in which the needs of the oral, anal, or phallic-oedipal phases are responded to by the caretaker influence both their strength (id urgency) and the strength and resilience of the ego functions attempting to mediate, channel, or defend against their dominance of preconscious and conscious awareness. The economic factors in the libidinal phases (drive strength and ego resilience) have a long-range, lasting influence on the individual and character development. If fixations occur, the potential for symptoms and neurosis is laid down, like a time bomb ticking away. But even if no specific pathology arises, the individual's personality traits, fantasy life, and preferences will be influenced

---

[1] These terms are used as general headings with traditional meanings, without my filling in the specifics of subphase activities or of gender differences. For a contemporary account, see Tyson (1982).

by the relative strength of each libidinal phase. Further, even if no specific pathology arises, the individual's personality traits, fantasy life, and preferences in love and hate relationships will bear the marks of the inevitable conflicts based on the restraints civilization (culture) imposes on the demand for immediate gratification (tension reduction) inherent in the urgencies of each libidinal phase.

Freud's libidinal phase theory has undergone extensive elaboration, with each phase being further subdivided and with different sequencing for boys and girls, centering on castration anxiety. The qualities of object relations—dyadic and triadic—have been examined in depth, and the theory has been challenged from within psychoanalysis on the basis of the relative significance of libidinal and aggressive drive development, the relative significance of drive and ego development, the relative significance of drive and object relations, and the timetable for the phases. For a considerable number of psychoanalysts, however, the libidinal phase concept provides five important explanations: (1) Activity at the specific erotogenic zone is a specific central organizer for the infant's and toddler's experience. (2) In states of zonally determined drive urgency, all other perceptions are distorted by virtue of the specific need (hunger, dependence, biting, retention, expulsion, thrusting). (3) The qualities derived from these conscious and unconscious experiences become generalized into influential character traits (dependency, receptiveness, withholding, aggressiveness, etc.). (4) Occurrences in each libidinal phase receive symbolic representation, ranging from the most primitive imagery of unconscious fantasy (primary process) to more remote, language-organized modes (secondary process). (5) Finally, important qualities of object relations subsequent to the libidinal phases are determined by representations formed during these phases.

The View from Infant Research

The broad developmental schema derived from contemporary infant research offers a far different approach. It begins with the assumption that the human, like all living systems, begins life in an organized state (Sander, 1980a). Because the human is an extremely complex living organism, at birth the neonate already possesses integrating mechanisms at multiple levels—biological, neurophysiological, and behavioral. In fact some of these integrating systems function already *in utero* (Graves, 1980). Each of the neonate's levels of integration is simultaneously integrated with response patterns and potentialities of the surrounding environment, as mediated through the caregiver. Infant researchers study these integrations by means of around-the-clock monitoring. Observed in this way, neonates are both self-regulating in the sequence of states through which they pass (alert wakefulness, quiescent wakefulness, crying, REM sleep, and NREM sleep) and exquisitely sensitive to the regulatory effect of the caregiver in the temporal organization of these states. Hunger satisfaction and mouth zonal pleasure are but one feature of the exchanges between the neonate's endogenous regulatory cycle and the caregiver's regulatory efforts. Even if we focus on the feeding experience itself, infants appear to be far more broadly stimulus seeking than is suggested by an oral-zone focus. They look, hear, smell, and grasp in remarkably discriminating fashion within the first few weeks. They seek visual, auditory, olfactory, and tactile patterns for which they have both preprogrammed and rapidly acquired preferences—and they avoid those stimuli which are aversive.

Based on an appreciation of the give-and-take between infant and caretaker in the sharing and dosing of stimuli, Bowlby's (1969) premise that a bond of attachment is building between mother and neonate within the first month has been substantiated. The initial attachment derives from *all* the exchanges between infant and caretaker that affect the 24-hour regulation of states—adjustments involving biorhythmicity, synchronization to state, and entrainment of contact. This theory of how attachment occurs is at considerable variance with the theory that states that, subsequent to biological caretaking, the infant only gradually awakens psychologically to the existence of mother as an oral-need-satisfying "part-object." In the view of contemporary infant research, attachment is a continuous process, from the first few minutes of postnatal experience. It extends throughout life, taking different forms at different times.

The interesting parallel to the pattern of attachment is the pattern of disengagement, which also begins very early in life. For a few minutes, infants who have been fed, when placed in their cribs, will "play" on their own—that is, they will respond to such immediate stimuli as a mobile or the sight of their hands. The increasingly complex action patterns in response to stimuli when the infant is "alone" in the presence of the caretaker form one path toward disengagement during the first year. Disengagement is also seen in the first year in the shift from patterns of action responses that in their repetition appear obligatory, toward a range of reactions more indicative of initiative, as the infant organizes behavior in accord with more complex conditions. Another shift occurs during the second year, when more or less automatic action reactions to stimuli are replaced by new cognitive organizational possibilities, facilitating increasingly independent choices. The process of disengagement becomes particularly important at this time (in the first year it tends to be overshadowed by the caretaker-infant interchange).

Much research focuses on the *infant's* capacities—and the yield of this research has been dramatic. Yet a particularly fruitful approach at the theoretical level has been to explore the nature of the *exchange* between infant and caretaker. According to Brazelton (1980a), as the neonate becomes able to organize preprogrammed and learned responses "in order to reach out for and respond appropriately to an external stimulus or toward a whole adult behavioral set, he gets energized in such a powerful way that one can easily see the base for his entrainment. The matching of his responses to those in the external world must feel so rewarding that he quickly becomes available to entrain with them, and he becomes energized to work toward inner controls and toward states of attention which maintain his availability to those external sequences. In this way, 'entrainment' becomes a larger feedback system which adds a regulating and encompassing dimension to the two feedback systems of internalized control and of external-ized stimulus-response. Hence, entrainment becomes an envelope within which he can test out and learn about both of his feed-back systems" (p. 224). The attention of formulations such as Brazelton's falls on the nature of "redundancy," that is, on the repetitious pattern of small interactions within each state and especially the management of transition between states. Ex-periments that violate the infant's expectancies provide an exam-ple (Call, 1980). If a mother approaches a six-week-old who is lying quietly and places her face in the child's visual field, the in-fant responds with mounting excitement all over his body. If the mother, following instructions, holds her face expressionless, the infant at first increases his part of their previous routine of syn-chronous gestures. When the mother fails to respond, the infant's efforts become more hectic and disorganized, until finally he lapses into a pained immobility. This reaction is explainable only by taking into account the repetitious interactional exchanges that have preceded it. The specificity of matching the pattern that begins with the mother's face entering the infant's visual field and the cooing, clucking, smiling exchanges that follow must be seen against the background of a structured interaction, built out of repetition and expectancy.

Pattern establishment through redundancy also provides the background for observations of phase transformation in infancy. The transformations at 10 to 12 weeks and at about six months are characterized by a heightening and broadening of sensorial responses in general. It is believed that these transformations are primarily the result of integrations at the neurophysiological level. Often, just before their occurrence, there is a temporary disorgani-zation of patterns established through the repetition of mother-infant exchange; after the transformation, new integrations become possible. For example, after the marked heightening of alertness at six months (what Mahler et al. [1975] have called "hatching"), the infant-mother exchange is characterized by a wider range of more subtly employed affect-expressional signaling.

None of these accounts of development by infant researchers, however, mentions intrapsychic representation. In presenting this research, I have characterized the infant's psychic functioning as existing solely in a perceptual-affective-action mode. I have argued that this mode is a complex organizational system, present at birth. Throughout the first year the increasingly complex integrations at the biological level (sleep-awake diurnal patterning, hunger-satiety cycles, etc.), the neurophysiological level (increasing alertness, affect differentiations, control of motility, etc.), and the behavioral level can all be conceptualized as taking place within the perceptual-affective-action mode. At the beginning of the second year there is a shift from action as the dominant mode of informational exchange to a mode in which discrete, "objectified" signs and signals are used. Then, in the second half of the second year, there is a further shift—to a mode of experiencing through symbolic formation, in which organized representations of self and of others build up a cognitive field.

TOWARD A NEW THEORY OF LEARNING

If the perceptual-affective-action mode characterizes the first year of life, this calls for a major revision in a theory of learning implicit in psychoanalysis (Greenspan, 1981, 1982). The psychoanalytic conception that derives from the theory of libidinal phase development holds that repeated absence of immediate oral gratification (hunger and mouth zonal pleasure) leads the infant to awake to the absence of an expected state of pleasure. The infant then activates a memory image of the prior gratification—a hallucinatory wish fulfillment. As the unpleasure state continues, the infant is forced to attend to the external world, where the presence of the offered breast (or bottle) and the offerer (mother) exists as a perceptual match for the memory image. In this way part-object and, later, whole-object representations are established and then elaborated with further experience.

This conception not only provides the model for the origin of psychic representations but also implies a psychoanalytic learning theory. Knowledge of the mother's existence (and activation of the reality principle that guides the infant away from fantasy toward external reality) occurs as the result of unpleasure. The degree of unpleasure stems from the match between the constitutional drive urgency and the timing of the feeding by the mother. In this theory, no delay (only a hypothetical possibility) would result in "perfect" gratification and therefore no learning would take place, with the child remaining in a state of narcissistic bliss. Optimal delay would lead to optimal learning, and prolonged delay would constitute a traumatic state, leading to organismic panic and fragmentation of functioning. This theory has been transposed into the clinical psychoanalytic situation, where the incentive to seek insight is believed to derive from optimal frustration and the resulting nontraumatic level of unpleasure. Although analysts conduct analyses with an awareness of the multiple aspects of both frustration and gratification, a model emphasizing frustration has nonetheless been maintained as central.

The conception of learning that derives from infant research is far more complex than that derived from the theory of libidinal phase development.[2] In the first place, the research data indicate that a remarkably broad spectrum of response patterns does not have to be learned at all. Neonates do not have to learn to acclimate themselves to a female voice—they are neurophysiologically preprogrammed to respond maximally to voices within the female tonal range. Learning to recognize the particular mother's voice is therefore extremely rapid. And infants do not have to be urged by necessity to look at the mother's face—they are preprogrammed to respond to the stimulus of a face at the eight-inch gaze focal point. Nor do they have to learn to connect mother's voice with her face—this and a number of other linkages across sensory modalities are seemingly "pre-wired." If, for exam-

---

[2]Ego psychology, with its focus on adaptation, has modified the conception of learning to include responses to task-defined activities. Thus, the learning theory implicit in ego psychology is more compatible with that of infant research, but less precise in its specifics and more reliant on energic transformations (neutralization) for its explanatory conceptions.

ple, an object having a discrete shape is placed in the infant's mouth and the infant is then exposed to an image having the same shape and another image having a different shape, the infant will respond visually to the image with the shape of the object in his or her mouth (Meltzoff and Borton, 1979). Moreover, many of the activity patterns that guarantee attunement between infant and mother do not require deprivation to spur learning. Infants are preprogrammed to respond with whole-body rhythm to the tempo and intensity gradient of mother's voice (Condon and Sander, 1974; Stern, 1977). Infants also have a built-in response pattern that allows them to imitate the caretaker's affective expressions, including sticking their tongues out before they could possibly learn by experimentation "where" the tongue is (Meltzoff and Moore, 1977; Field et al., 1982). Thus, a set of preprogrammed "preferences" for patterns that coordinate with the caretaker and the infant's environment exists to promote an initial interactional state of synchrony between infant and caretaker.

Learning in the sense of action-schema assimilation and accommodation also takes place at an early age. Within a few months, this learning leads to much greater complexity in the patterns of preprogrammed connections across sensory modalities. This trial-and-error learning, based on action sequence recognition, is most productive in states of low to moderate tension. Experimental evidence strongly indicates that sensorimotor learning is guided by a preprogrammed affective capacity for interest, plus pleasure in functioning and pleasure in achieving competence. Once again, the concept that learning occurs primarily in response to an optimal high-tension deprivational state does not seem borne out by these findings. In reference to the clinical psychoanalytic situation, this suggests the likelihood that a great deal of learning (insight) comes about on the basis of motives of interest, exploratory curiosity, and a desire to use a method (tool) "playfully" (see London, 1981). In other words, such insight is gained during moments of low and moderate intensity, against a stable setting of redundancy of time, place, and person; insight is not restricted to states of high intensity—of marked anxiety, depression, guilt, or need deprivation.

All of this leads to three questions: What is the effect of high-tension experiences on learning? Are high-tension experiences disruptive to general mental functioning? Does learning that takes place in settings of high tension differ in quality or long-range impact from learning that occurs during low- and moderate-tension states? I shall address these questions first by considering the high-tension experiences of maternal departure and fear-induced physical risk. Then, via an excursion into Erikson's (1950, 1959) theory of organ modes, I shall consider high-tension erotogenic zone experiences directly.

The Impact of High-Tension Experiences

Two experiments on children one year of age may help in understanding the impact of high-tension experiences. In one experiment, mentioned earlier, children were exposed to three episodes of brief separations from mother (Ainsworth, 1979; Sroufe, 1979). To recapitulate: The largest group of the infants tolerated the first leaving without distress. By the third leaving, however, they reacted to the mother's return by crying and signaling a desire to be held and soothed. Another group of children showed greater ambitendency in their reactions: They wanted to approach and to be held, but angrily protested both being held and being put down. Observers of the mothers of this group described them as insensitive to the infant's signals and inconsistent in their responses—at times the mother ignored the child; at other times she made contact without regard for the child's indications. A third group responded to the returning mother with visual, bodily, and communicative avoidance. The mothers of these infants were observed to be manifestly angry with their children, and insensitive to their signals. These mothers were generally emotionally unexpressive and unable to establish physical contact in a manner that was not jarring or overstimulating.

The second experiment looked at year-old children who were exposed to a situation of fear-arousing ambiguity (Emde, 1981b). The children were placed on a table that gave an optical illusion of a drop in depth in the middle (a visual cliff). The mother was placed at the far end of the table, with an attractive toy near her. The children started out eagerly for the end of the table with mother and the toy. When they reached the middle of the table and observed the illusory decline, however, they stopped and looked at mother's face. If mother, following instructions, smiled, they would proceed, after an effort to solve the problem. Some children backed over the imagined crevice line as though backing down steps; others proceeded cautiously forward. If mother, again following instructions, gave a look of anxiety and alarm, the children did not proceed. They stopped, looked troubled, and cried.

The two experimental situations constitute high-tension experiences of danger, but ones that are titered not to mount to traumatic proportions. In response to departure, a common "naturalistic" occurrence, the three groups have each learned a different response pattern. For one group it is that when a breach in contact with mother occurs, it can be restored by a direct appeal of distress and physical clinging. The second group has learned that responses to distress are inconsistent, and the third group has learned to avoid a reparative reunion effort because their expectation is that contact will increase rather than reduce distress. In the experiment with the illusory slope, the one-year-olds had learned that in states of doubt, alarm, and ambiguity about danger the mother's facial expression served as a sign signaling information useful in resolving the ambiguity and guiding their behavior.

Similar responses to high-tension situations are familiar in clinical psychoanalysis of both children and adults and the nature of the patient's problems bring them to the fore. Absences lead to a variety of responses based on prior experiences. Ambiguity as to perceived danger triggers a search for reassuring orienting responses—in fact the analytic experience with adults is one in which tension between analyst and analysand is heightened by virtue of the restriction of orienting visual cues that the use of the couch entails. Yet the patient in analysis, by acceptance of the basic rule, is committed to communication by symbolic representation, a form of communication infants are incapable of, despite all their sophisticated learning. It is this difference that lies at the core of the distinction between the accounts of infancy provided by libidinal phase theory and the infant researcher's models. Clinical analysis repeatedly and conclusively indicates that high-tension states exist, that these states are based on regulatory difficulties (such as in adaptively modulating sexual or exhibitionistic excitement or frustration states of hurt, anger, and rage), and that the consequence of the regulatory failure is commonly manifest in the existence of conflicting tendencies. The existence of a high-tension state is indicated by representations of the self and others symbolically signified in bodily metaphors of an oral, anal, or phallic-oedipal nature—as in the dream of coughing up the peanut.

Infant researchers also recognize the existence of high-tension states. They conceptualize these as creating potential disturbances in integrations at the biological, neurophysiological, and behavioral levels. These disturbances are manifest in the exchange between infant and caregiver and in the infant's experiences in the perceptual-affective-action mode. All this, as I have argued, occurs without representation and symbolic formation. In other words, in the first 18 months of life, the infant functions in all ranges of tension through a perceptual-affective-action mode *without* using symbolic signification to represent mouth and breast, anal activity, and the products of excretion. How, then, can we reconcile this view with the analytic one, which places the high-tension experiences from this same period at the core of the organization of significant conflictual configurations?

Erikson's Concept of Organ Modes

An early attempt to expand the erotogenic zone model was made by Erikson (1950, 1959). It had been commonly appreciated that the activity associated with the pleasure inherent in each zone (mouth, anus, and genitals) provides the basis for psychological modalities, such as dependency and oral aggression, and for specific mechanisms, such as incorporation and projection.

Erikson describes how organ modes, such as incorporation (mouth), retention and elimination (anus and urethra), intrusion (penis) and inclusion (vagina), become generalized to organs and zones other than the original erotogenic body part and eventually are separated from the zone of origin to form the individual's characteristic behavioral patterns and psychic functions. As Erikson describes it: "in addition to the overwhelming need for food, a baby is, or soon becomes receptive in many other respects. As he is willing and able to suck on appropriate objects and to swallow whatever appropriate fluids they emit, he is soon also willing and able to 'take in' with his eyes whatever enters his visual field. His tactile senses, too, seem to 'take in' what feels good" (1959, p. 57). "With all of this a number of interpersonal patterns are established which center in the social modality of *taking* and *holding onto* things—things which are more or less freely offered and given, and things which have more or less of a tendency to slip away" (1950, p. 104). The totality of these occurrences leads to the *"firm establishment of enduring patterns for the balance of basic trust over basic mistrust.* . . . [The] *amount of trust* derived from earliest infantile experience does not seem to depend on absolute *quantities of food or demonstrations of love* but rather on the *quality* of the maternal relationship" (1959, p. 63).

Expanding on these ideas, Erikson stipulates:

> The anal zone lends itself more than any other to the expression of stubborn insistence on conflicting impulses because . . . it is the model zone for two contradictory modes which must become alternating; namely, *retention* and *elimination*. Furthermore, the sphincters are only part of the muscle system with its general ambiguity of rigidity and relaxations of flexion and extension. This whole stage, then, becomes a battle for *autonomy*. . . . Every mother knows how astonishingly pliable a child may be at this stage, if and when he has made the decision that he *wants* to do what he is supposed to do. It is impossible, however, to find a reliable formula for making him want to do just that. . . . The matter of mutual regulation between adult and child now faces its severest test. . . .

> As is the case with all of these modalities, their basic conflicts can lead in the end to hostile or to benign expectations and attitudes. Thus, "to hold" can become a destructive and cruel retaining or restraining, and it can

become a pattern of care: "to have and to hold." To "let go," too, can turn into an inimical letting loose of destructive forces, or it can become a relaxed "to let pass" and "to let be" [1959, pp. 67–68, 69–70].

In both spirit and particulars, Erikson's theory is in line with the emphasis placed by contemporary infant research on the infant-caregiver exchange and its interactive focus. For example, Erikson remarks: "It is as true to say that babies control and bring up their families as it is to say the converse. A family can bring up a baby only by being brought up by him" (1959, p. 55). With regard to the psychoanalytic view, however, in his emphasis on the interactional (psycho*social*) aspects of development, Erikson alters the central position assigned to excitement (high-tension pleasure) of the erotogenic zone itself in Freud's theory of psycho*sexual* development. Moreover, Erikson's epigenetic sequence of phases of psychosocial development describes which behavioral modes are generalized from their organ of origin but *not how*. The issues of how and when intrapsychic representations are formed and the timing of symbolic formation are not addressed. Erikson accepts the libidinal phase model and its timing as a basic given. His theory therefore covers the middle ground between the perspective of infant research and that of Freud's psychosexual theory, but it cannot serve to reconcile the problem of the disparities between the two models.

What Is Needed for a Reconciliation?

Let me restate the problem. A mother looks at her three-month-old infant and states: "My baby wants me to feed him." The infant researcher, on the other hand, states that the three-month-old has an expectation that a match will occur between a known (remembered) tension state (hunger) and a series of perceptions, actions, and affects (mother approaching with breast or bottle, sucking, and a change in state from hunger to pleasure and satiation). The infant's participation is thus limited to a perceptual-affective-action mode. Outside of that mode there is no intrapsychic self (me) wanting an internally represented object (mother) to perform an objectified action able to be specified ("to feed"). From still another perspective, an onlooker, observing an infant being fed, may empathically (as if from within the state of mind of the infant) savor the mouth pleasure and conjur up a image of breasts, pleasant tastes, and blissful intimacies. The position I have suggested is that the infant's experience is similar to that of the empathic onlooker with respect to mouth pleasure—that is, the infant experiences a pleasurable level of stimulation to the mucous membranes, a taste that coordinates with an inborn, preprogrammed preference, and a pleasurable diminution of rising tension from hunger. But the three-month-old does *not* conjure up an image of a breast; the infant experiences a perception of a total unit of sensory continuity across visual, tactile, olfactory, and gustatory modalities, a continuous action sequence largely characterized as a series of synchronous interactional coordinations. Moreover, the infant does not have a symbolic representation of passive intimacy. What the infant has is an interactional body-movement pattern. This pattern is probably holistic rather than discretely mouth-centered, and during feeding, it is probably an expression of *active* competence (coordinated head movement, body turning, finger grasping, and mouth sucking with patterns of stopping and starting, breathing, etc.) rather than "passive bliss." The body-movement pattern of generalized relaxation, passive pleasure, and an interactional component is more likely to arise in presleep rocking.

Let me state the problem yet another way. Lewin's (1950) idea of an oral trend—the wish to devour, the wish to be devoured, and the wish to sleep, as well as its associative links to claustrophobia and claustrophilia, agoraphobia and agoraphilia—can be repeatedly confirmed in analytic patients—that is, in individuals who are expressing their wishes and fears in the form of symbolic representation, either in symptoms, dreams, or words. If infants do not have this capacity to represent their oral experiences in this symbolic form, how and when does this come about and what connection do these symbolic forms have to the experiences that occur during the "oral phase" (the first 12 to 18 months)? I suggest that the toddler of about 18 to 24 months is in a position similar to Pirandello's six characters in search of an author: The infant has memories, affects, organized states (with transitions between them), preferences, and complex interactional patterns, all in search of a form of symbolic representation.

What this broad metaphoric statement indicates is an across-the-board transformation from an action mode to a symbolic representational mode; it does not spell out the specifics of the representations associated with erotogenic zone stimulation. Yet the erotogenic zone experiences *do* receive important psychic representation during the second half of the second year, when symbol formation, accompanied by a vocabulary explosion, occurs. Language is from this time forth forever "impregnated" with metaphors of body origin (Sharpe, 1940; Lichtenberg, 1978a). In my opinion, the key to understanding the special significance of oral, anal, and phallic-oedipal[3] experiences lies in an understanding of affects.

THE IMPACT OF AFFECTS

From the beginning of neonatal life (and possible *in utero*), varied densities of neural firing trigger such affects as interest, enjoyment, startle, and distress (Tomkins, 1962, 1963; Demos, 1982). The sensation-rich erotogenic zones are very active sources of different patterns of neural firing. The triggered affects give the perceptual-action patterns involved with the zones (feeding, sucking, defecating, penile erections, and vulvo-clitoral engorgement)

---

[3]In referring to "phallic-oedipal" experiences, I am employing traditional terminology. By "phallic" I subsume the boy's experience of sensation with his penis and the girl's with her clitoral-vulvo-vaginal area. By "oedipal" I refer to a rich complex of sensual and social relationships. These can only occur after the level of symbolic formation has been reached. As Basch (1981) indicates: "only then does it become possible to play with situations mentally and imagine them to be different than they are. At this point, and not before, forbidden wishes can potentially be entertained in which the father is removed in imagination from barring the way to a boy's exclusive possession of his mother. To avoid anxiety, defences against such thinking must be developed" (p. 167).

the experiential amplification that renders them so meaningful both during infancy and later. The other source of their significance lies in the repetitiveness of their biorhythmicity; that is, hunger and elimination, and to a lesser degree, genital excitement, have an endogenously cyclic nature. Moreover, the neural firing is not restricted to an inner trigger; it is also coordinated with external "objects" (food, feces, urine, and clothing that rubs the genitals) and with persistent regulatory interactions with the caretaker (feeding, diapering, washing). This view of affects indicates that it is not a special form of energy—"libido"—that marks the high-tension experiences of the mouth, anus, urethra, and genitals. Rather, the experiences associated with erotogenic zones arise from the affective amplification triggered by dense neural firing. It is this affect and not some special sexual energy that fits Freud's concept of "cathexis" as a marker of significant experience.

Are these the only experiences that regularly receive intense affective amplification in the first year? Freud noted two sets of "component instincts," which are similar to the drives that arise from the erotogenic zones: voyeurism and exhibitionism, sadism and masochism. Each is rooted in a bodily experience. Voyeurism involves the eyes in a state of excited attentiveness. Exhibitionism involves the whole-body skin surface in an aroused state. Sadism and masochism are built around experiences of bodily pain. The aspect I would emphasize is that in both erotogenic zone and component instinct experiences there is a potential for rapid fluctuations between rising and falling tension involving bodily sensation. These high-intensity fluctuations range between interest increasing to excitement and enjoyment mounting to joy. The same is true for motion-equilibrium excitement, which can provide an enormously pleasurable sense of thrill and risk (as when a father holds a baby or toddler high in the air, tosses the child free for a second, giving a momentary sense of falling, and then catches the child, with a shared glee) (Lichtenberg, 1982b).

It is quite possible that the infant does not experience these different body-centered sensations as discrete in their zonal location, as they might be for an observer (see Greenacre, 1954). That is, if a baby is engaged with mother in a conversational game of rising and falling synchronous gradients, the sense of excitement may involve all the body excitement-sensitive modalities—mouth, anus, genitals, eyes, skin, and motion equilibrium, rather than one specific body locus. Thus, the specificity given in the sequence of libidinal phases (first oral, then anal, etc.) may be a function of later differentiation during the period of reorganization during symbol formation—or it may be an incorrect assumption of analytic theory. Infant researchers increasingly find that genital excitement exists much earlier than previously recognized. I would suggest that the type of ready displacement of imagery among mouth, anus, urethra, and genitals observed in the dream of coughing up the peanut may reflect that, for the child, sensation crosses modalities more than has been previously thought. What is discrete about erotogenic zone experiences would not be the physical locus but the specific combination of a body sensation and an affective amplification of excitement or joy.

To return to the main point: Analysts, looking backward from stages of development after symbolic representation has occurred, note that experiences centering on body sensation stand out as organizers for the individual's love-hate relationships, neurotic symptoms, and creative tendencies. Infant research, as I have understood its findings, states that these experiences do not receive intrapsychic representations because that level of psychic functioning is not possible until the later half of the second year. Basch (1981), who would put the timing of representational symbolic processing still later, states: "The relatively late onset of associational thought suggests that so-called infantile fantasies may represent the working over of earlier experiences and their interpretation by the more mature mind of the child" (p. 162).

Furthermore, during infancy, the high-tension body sensations appear not as the discrete entities psychoanalysts regard them to be, but as elements in a regulatory challenge between infant and caretaker—states of excitement that may persist as moments of body pleasure associated with an intimate exchange or may lead to disorganized functioning. If the psychoanalytic premise is correct and these experiences of heightened body sensation have an organizing effect on the content and intensity of fantasy life, the marker for them lies in the episodic memory of a perceptual-affective-action pattern involving their stimulation. The marker, I believe, lies especially in the affective amplification that results when fluctuations occur between rising and falling, controlled gradients of intense sensation. By taking the view that, in infancy, emotion exists as a phenomenon independent of cognitive processes, it becomes possible to conceptualize an early source of motivation akin to the "system" unconscious, in that the affect acts as a marker that is unlabeled and unsymbolized (Lester, 1982). The special affective marker that we come to call sensual excitement and pleasure becomes associated with a grouping of perceptions and actions—for example, the mother's approaching to feed and the entire motor behavioral pattern of salivating, sucking, swallowing, looking, grasping, etc. Later, when symbol formation comes into being during the second year, this unit of perception, affect, and action receives representation according to both the primary- and secondary-process modes. The secondary-process mode tends to differentiate the sensual from the nonsensual elements, whereas the primary-process mode tends to condense and collapse all elements. That representation will occur is assured by the inevitable repetition of an associated instance of oral, anal, or genital heightened sensation, of visual and general skin exhibitory excitement, of motion-equilibrium, thrill, and of pain. Freud's (1915) theory of the part attraction plays in repression suggests a parallel mechanism. He hypothesized that a current incident was not only pushed out of awareness, but also pulled into the unconscious by an association it bore to a previously repressed, analogous element (see Lichtenberg and Slap, 1972, p. 784). An occurrence of oral, anal, or genital excitement will be associated with (attracted by) the previously unsymbolized and unlabeled affect and gain sensory image representation (especially primary process) and labeling (especially secondary process).

This formulation casts a doubt on the assumption that as adults we regularly make empathic contact with infants and young toddlers. If we define "empathy" as entering into the state of mind of the other person, then an adult has a very difficult, almost impossible, task to empathize with the infant. As adults, in the very attempt to enter the infant's state of mind, we use, at least in part, an adult symbolic mode of cognition; that is, to the extent that we put thoughts in the head of the baby in order to understand him or her, we miss the nonsymbolic nature of the infant's state of mind. The suggestion that the empathic mode of perception is based on two steps—receptivity and understanding (Agosta, 1983)—provides a way to conceptualize what occurs in the adult's empathic response to a baby. The receptivity to an affect that arises in conjunction with a perception and a behavioral reaction triggers in the adult a sensitive resonating response—one that may be in tune with the adult's own deep affective markers of this early period. The second step—that of "understanding"—is an automatic cognitive effort by which the empathizer attempts to give meaning to what he or she has been receptive to. This second step—the cognitive search for meaning—has become an inseparable component of any complex affective sequence after the transition to the symbolic level.

To appreciate the significance I am giving to affect as the amplifier and memory marker of the infant's activity in the presymbolic period, it is useful to consider several other aspects of affects. From birth on, the expressional physiognomic aspects of affect play an important role in the intercommunication between infant and family. For the infant, affects are felt; for the parents, affects are both felt and labeled. In the infant, affects become integrated into more complex contexts within perceptual-action modes. In the adult, affects are integrated into contexts of representations of self and others, with complex cognitive modes having definable coordinates of space and time. The empathic link between infant and adult is the shared feeling, combined with the inferences the parent draws from the behavioral context present at the time of the affective exchange. Thus, in states of moderate tension, the caretaker can, from the infant's affective expressions, easily pick up and respond to indications that the baby wants social contact, or is in physical distress, or is in need of soothing for a transition into sleep. Titering stimulus intensity and providing the needed stimulus response require an appraisal of the affective state plus a sharing of aim. For example, a mother who wants to share in the social aspects of the feeding experience will titer the stimuli to provide a shifting gradient appropriate to the needs for hunger satiation, sucking pleasure, and visual and auditory synchronous social exchanges. A mother who wants to get the feeding over with and get on to other things will not respond to the cues her baby may give for greater social interaction. A mother who herself craves social interaction may do all she can to elicit responsiveness in a relatively quiet, passive infant, or, in frustration, she may turn off, thus complicating their mutual problem. The repetition of exchanges guided by affect expression builds up a series of expectancies in mother and infant.

When we consider situations of high-amplitude affective experience associated with erotogenic zone stimulation of mouth, anus, and genitals, it is easy to infer the trends that occur in the affective-communication exchange. In these instances, the infant has an endogenous source of stimulation, a rapid rise–rapid decline intensity gradient that triggers an amplified affective experience. The expressional side of this reaction establishes a communicative exchange—the parent sees the infant's pleasure in thumb sucking, inward directed attentiveness in defecating, or state of bodily excitement at stroking the penis or vulvo-clitoral area, and the parent communicates back his or her affective response. It is at this exact moment, as psychoanalysis has noted, that culture (mediated through the individual parent) and the pressure of development within the infant meet. Infant research on facial configurations of the small infant (Izard, 1977) indicates the probability that distress, disgust, shame, and contempt are early, preprogrammed affects—providing negatively toned alternatives to joy and interest in even the young infant. Repetitive sequences of intercommunication between infant and mother in which the infant's autogenous erotogenic pleasure is responded to by shared pleasure, or by cool, businesslike indifference; or by distress, disgust, shame, or contempt will leave episodic memory markers. Moreover, these repeated early episodes of erotogenic pleasure expression and parental response will provide a context of expectancies for match or mismatch reactions. If, for instance, the mother's repeated initial response to her infant's signs of pleasure in defecating or urinating or touching the genital is comfortable pleasure, a response of shaming or contempt at an older age will be more noteworthy as a mismatch signal. In this way, a history may be laid down before it can be "written," that is, before it is given symbolic representation.

The sequence of affective intercommunication can at first be appreciated by the infant only as an action exchange, as an event or happening that in itself influences the infant's affective state. The affective exchange that occurs ranges from synchronous to sequential. Later, toward the end of the first year, the infant's active monitoring of affect appears to be at a different level of organization, with a heightened level of awareness. The mother's affective expression is sought, and the whole experience appears more objectified, more a property of an orderly sequence. The exchange of emotion between infant and caretaker provides information that guides the infant's behavioral choices. Affects now may be thought of as preverbal, presymbolic signs signaling "go on" or "stop," "faster" or "slower," "come here" or "go away."

Monitoring is a two-way street—monitoring the affect of both the other and the self. The monitoring of the mother's face is well documented in the illusory cliff experiment (Emde, 1981b). Stechler and Kaplan (1980) write of nine-month-old Nancy:

> . . . she could differentiate between her father's "spanking" her with a smile on his face and enter the game with smiles and sounds of delight, and a similar spanking accompanied by his frown. Furthermore, when she was presented with the frown, her state of upset was followed by active efforts to engage him and to get him to smile—at which point she relaxed and joined the game. We see here early evidence of her awareness of different affects and her active searching for ways to influence events so that she would end with a pleasurable affect [p. 96].

We are less knowledgeable about infants' monitoring of their own affects than about their monitoring of the caretaker's affects. Emde (1980) suggests that *"at 9 months, affect provides a signal to the inside not just to the outside"* (p. 101). He regards the fearfulness of this period as an initial example of an affect being involved in an evaluation or appraisal in a cause-effect sense, with a subsequent phase of distress and physical avoidance. Whereas Emde speaks of this sequence in cognitive terms, I regard it as an increasingly differentiated example of functioning within the perceptual-affective-action mode. A central thesis of Freud's structural hypothesis is the guidance provided by "signal affects" to the functioning of the ego. The concept of affects such as anxiety signaling a danger situation is, I believe, only possible at a level of organization in which full symbolic representation can be given to the contextual unit of experience of self and object, time and place, affect and cognition. What the transition steps are between infants' and toddlers' monitoring of their own affects and the integration of affects into a symbolic system is an area in need of further study. The suggestion that such affects as signal anxiety, depression, and guilt represent complex affective-cognitive assemblies rather than simple affects seems supported by the available evidence (see Brenner, 1974; Emde, 1980).

Another aspect of affect is its relation to cognition. Cognitive theory has often emphasized the disorganizing effect of affects. Crying clearly limits the informational receptivity of the infant, whereas alert wakefulness, a state in which interest is easily triggered, is optimal for sensorimotor schema building. Throughout this chapter I have emphasized the organizing aspect of affects—the amplification of perceptual-action modes that gives significance to the infant's experiences. Analytic theory, on the other hand, usually addresses the problem of interference with optimally adaptive thought caused by anger, sexual excitement, anxiety, depression, shame, or humiliation. It is in this sense that affects are regarded as "primitive," infantile, and in need of taming. Infant research takes the view that affects are fundamental components of all mental functioning. In any given instance of mental functioning, the total effect may be organizing or disorganizing. In a one-year-old, anger may be helpful in communicating to the caretaker the need for regulatory intervention to find the source of frustration. If anger interferes with adaptive perception and action in the one-year-old, the source of disorganization should not be regarded as anger per se, but as a combination of the affect and the frustration (to which the anger is an affective amplifier). The situation would have to be studied to assess the particular infant's tolerance for the frustration, on the one hand, and for the specific affect (anger), on the other.

Further Considerations on Regulation

With regard to the excitement experiences associated with the erotogenic zones, the psychoanalytic view is that they have an inherently disorganizing effect on perception and cognition. That experiences derived from erotogenic zone stimulation can result in major disruptions is clear. What is less certain, however, is that the excitement in itself is the source of the disruption, unless the excitement has become mixed with a dystonic affect such as distress, fear, or shame (V. Demos, personal communication). In thumb sucking, for example, is there a level of excitement that is disorganizing; or, if disruption occurs, is the source not more likely to be a combination of excitement and distress induced by parental response? Is the basis for disruption in an instance of intense, prolonged tickling, the increasing excitement or a mixture of excitement with the feeling of being helpless to stop the stimulus input? Chronic understimulation, as may occur with infants raised in an institution or by a depressed, cold, or self-preoccupied caretaker, will also lead to lowered functional levels of activity, and, if not reversed in time, to disruptions in the organization of many functional systems.

To return to the question: Are the stimuli arising from the erotogenic zones inherently disorganizing (distorting) to perception and to cognition? Infant research, as far as I know, does not address this question directly. However, its general theory of regulation would not single out any experience of infancy as inherently disorganizing. It would agree with the view of self psychology that each phase may present polarities (biological pulls and contradictory behavioral inclinations) to be coped with through the mother-infant interaction (Kohut, 1983). Success in regulating the strain inherent in these polarities is based on communication of the specific needs of the moment against a background of successful overall regulatory efforts. Although these polarities may be adequately responded to within the range of needs of the infancy period, persisting polarities may receive symbolic representation in the form psychoanalysis calls intrapsychic "conflict." These persisting polarities, encoded as intrapsychic conflict, are not necessarily a source of disorganization but may give a dynamic intensity to life. From this standpoint, the high-intensity experiences associated with erotogenic zones, by virtue of their recurrent bodily source of stimulation and interactional significance, persist as polarities calling for regulation—first largely administered by the caretaker, and later increasingly monitored by the developing child. The affects involved are key, providing signals for both regulation and monitoring. Interest and excitement, pleasure and sensual joy, alternate with distress, disgust, shame, and contempt and provide alternating signals between parents and infant, calling forth these regulations by which universal polarities are handled in an individualized fashion within the particular family group. Regarded in this way, erotogenic zone stimulation is not inherently disorganizing to other functions; rather, like all stimulation sources in infancy, it provides a call for regulation and learning. Moreover, what is learned by virtue of the interactional regulation of erotogenic zone stimulation provides the vitalization of life through sensuality.

   Whereas it is reasonably easy to recognize successful regulation as a positive basis for integration of all psychic systems, infant research indicates that it is more difficult to assess the specific continuities over time of less-than-optimal regulation. From his review of the literature on infant's self-righting tendencies and resiliency, Emde (1981a) concludes: "We probably need to tone down the attitude of irreversibility of adverse effects from early experience, even when it involves major deprivations of mothering. . . . There are many features we do not understand about the processes by means of which people develop competence in situations of deprivation and environmental handicap" (p. 218). Greenspan (1981) reports on infants at risk, who were either globally over- or understimulated, or in other ways were not afforded the minimal "experiential nutrients" essential to development because their mothers were schizophrenic or depressed. He reveals that in the first year babies are remarkably responsive to corrective interventions. Infants with badly diverted development could be restored from aversive, sad, or disorganized responses to normal receptivity to human contact. Some of these infants, through their positive affects and seeking behavior, "assisted" in the therapeutic program by activating responsiveness in their mothers. Greenspan's program, sensitively constructed in terms of the findings of contemporary infant research, has been able to reverse developmental blockages without hospitalization or other disruptions of family life.

THE MODIFICATION OF EARLY EXPERIENCE

Emde concludes his essay on changing models of infancy by stating: "we have probably placed far too much emphasis on early experience itself as opposed to the process by which it is modified or made use of by subsequent experience" (1981a, p. 219). I have suggested that the second half of the second year is the time of significant modification of prior experience. At that time major developments occur: (1) new intense experiences of bodily sensation involving all the erotogenic zones and "component instincts"; (2) new tensions in relation to the newly emergent self, particularly with respect to autonomy and separateness; and (3) new organizational capacities—the primary- and secondary-process modes of perceptual-cognitive-affective organization, which integrate linguistic and nonlinguistic skills into a symbolic level of processing information. It is during this transformational period that the developing child creates his or her own "history" in the dual language of primary- and secondary-process symbolization. There may well be an inherent attraction between a primary-process mode of representation and high-intensity experiences such as those of the erotogenic zones. In intense experiences of excitement and sensual pleasure or of distress, shame, disgust, and embarrassment, the perceptual-cognitive-affective state tends to generalize, radiating to broad associational pathways (displacement), on the one hand, and drawing in disparate associational elements into a holistic experience (condensation), on the other hand. The 20-month-old rubbing a "transitional object" blanket against mouth, nose, and cheek may spread the sensation to broad sensual areas of the body and to a generalized feeling state of security, while drawing in images of maternal cuddling—all in one experience of holistic pleasure. Alternatively, a 20-month-old who has been shamed for soiling may spread the sense of dirty badness from the act of defecating to the sensations of bowel passage in the rectum and anus, to feces and all substances with a similar smell or appearance, to the whole body and the general sense of self, while drawing in images of approved activities such as finger painting or even touching the potty seat with the buttocks—all in one general sense of "yuck!"

Psychoanalysis has studied extensively the fate of these representations organized in the primary-process mode—their relationship to defensive activities, to unconscious memory, and to creativity. The question that remains unanswered is: To what extent does what is reconstructed from decoding these representations deal with events from the presymbolic period of the first 18 months, or is it a new creation "written" in the psychic record by later events? Emde (1981a) points out: *"Discontinuities,* with major organizational shifts, are prominent in development. It would seem the synthetic ego . . . may construct from modes of experience and aspects of reality we would never have been aware of if we were there or on the spot" (p. 217). Arlow (1963) has suggested that at the end of the oedipal phase a transformation takes place which reorganizes all the elements of preoedipal experience. This thesis is supported by the logical assumption that when a major change, such as the systematic internal assumption of moral and ethical self-regulation occurs, the subsequent integration constitutes a reorganization (Jacobson, 1964). The changes with adolescence and transition to adulthood provide another instance in which the individual will "redo" his or her biography, current and past (Lichtenberg, 1982b). To what extent the form of each new organization is determined by experiences that occur prior to each major transformation remains a subject for careful investigation. For example, the timing and impact of the bodily changes at puberty may be a relatively independent factor, neither predictable nor explainable by earlier genital or other erotogenic zone experiences (Lichtenberg, 1982b).

CONCLUSION

To return to the proposition that representation is the sine qua non for a psychoanalytic psychology: I believe that only that which has been encoded through the primary- and secondary-process modes of organization can be known through the analytic method of free association. Therefore, using the psychoanalytic method, we cannot expect to reconstruct the events of the first 18 months. We can find out only how these events have been organized, first in the second half of the second year, and later through major transformations. Experiences in the first year may cast their shadow, but the recognition of discrete patterns of perceptual-affective-action modes that have not received symbolic representation is "beyond interpretation" (Gedo, 1979) via the verbal communication of psychoanalysis. Such reconstructions must be inferred from observation of nonverbally communicated behavior, in the same way that researchers make inferences from observing the perceptual-affective-action modes of the infant. Empathic receptivity alone, rather than empathic receptivity and empathic understanding, is the analyst's primary means of apprehending a patient's earliest experiences. How often this may be necessary in the therapeutic endeavor is a subject for debate (see Silver, 1981).

What we have learned from infant research and the theory of erotogenic zones contributes extremely valuable information for child-rearing and for preventive intervention in infancy. Nevertheless, for the analytic treatment of adults, I believe Emde is correct when he states: "Perhaps it makes sense for the psychoanalyst to place renewed emphasis on recent and current experiences—first, as a context for interpreting early experience and second, because it contains within it the ingredients for potential amelioration" (1981a, p. 217). Certainly, there are exceptions —some experiences of the first year may not receive symbolic representation and yet may be crucial in understanding the individual's pathology (see Chapter 12). More than that, analysts have much to gain from an as accurate as possible developmental model of the organization of the infant's life experience in the perceptual-affective-action mode and how these experiences contribute to the subjectivity of later life and its organization in the symbolic mode. The significance psychoanalysis has given to erotogenic zones and early libidinal phases must give way to a broader organizational model, closer in spirit to Hartmann's attempt to address early undifferentiated ego functioning. In addition, questions about the impact of high-tension experiences and how these affect-amplified perceptual-action events receive representation need to receive greater research focus.

Chapter Twelve

The Psychoanalytic Situation
and Infancy

CHANGING PROGRAMS FOR INTERPRETATION

The late 1950s marked something of a turning point in psycho-analysis. In the flush of a great wave of popularity and the confidence born of 20 years of experience with ego psychology—with the second phase of psychoanalytic technique, that is—analysts were emboldened to widen the scope of their therapeutic endeavor. The debate over the advisability of widening the scope led to a reappraisal of what constituted the essential elements of psychoanalysis. A work that stands out in this multifaceted attempt to place the techniques of classical analysis on a firmer conceptual footing is Leo Stone's *The Psychoanalytic Situation* (1961). To quote Janet Malcolm: "Stone's plea for humaneness and flexibility and common sense is encased in the most subtly reasoned, profoundly erudite, and awesomely 'difficult' of meditations on a complex subject" (1981, p. 44). Stone makes two central points. First, it is an essential requirement for analytic success that the analyst convey a sense of his or her physicianly commitment since "the intrinsic formal stringencies of the [analytic] situation . . . contraindicate superfluous deprivations in the analyst's personal attitude" (1961, p. 22). Stone's second point is that the primary unconscious meaning of the psychoanalytic situation lies in the reverberations it stirs of tensions that exist for the young child. I shall not detail Stone's rich argument but merely note that these two central issues form the basis for debates that persist to this day: (1) How best do analysts convey their humanity

183

and physicianly intention, while establishing and preserving a therapeutic regimen aimed at increased self-awareness and understanding? (2) What are the anlagen from critical early (preoedipal) periods of development that constitute the underpinnings for all transference relationships?

Stone indicates that most writings on technique, with regard to the psychoanalytic situation itself, contain more warnings of what *not* to do than positive indications of what to do. Stone's own main point occupies a middle position: Humanness is described against the background of what Stone believes to be a major deterent to analytic success—"arbitrary authoritarianism," the refusal to answer questions and the mechanization of the analyst's functioning by "superfluously remote and depriving attitudes" (pp. 52, 54). But Stone's own "positive" recommendations refer mostly to attitude—and, although I believe this is a powerful statement in itself, it has a somewhat nebulous quality in practice (see Lichtenberg and Slap, 1977). One of his most positive directive statements refers to interpretation having value beyond insight: "the interpretive function . . . has a tremendous primary transference valence, but only when linked by compelling unconscious associations, via recognition of the impulse to help, to relieve suffering, with the primary caretaking attitudes which give all early teaching its affirmative infantile significance" (1961, p. 63). Stone's emphasis throughout his book is on explicating the "primary transference valence"—how all the elements of the psychoanalytic situation (the use of speech, normal and excessive deprivations, the recumbent position, etc.) link with infantile experience. Interpretation as such he takes essentially as a given—the communicating to the patient of intrapsychic conflicts of a sexual and aggressive nature construed within an id-ego-superego conception of the mind. Stone's point, then, is not to question what is interpreted, but to give greater depth to an understanding of how and why it works. To do so, he gives greater weight to the dyadic relationship between mother and child. In his account of the child's early life, Stone relies on traditional views combined with some of Spitz's infant observations. Although Stone points toward two areas of recent reconceptualization—what is interpreted and what residuals from infancy remain in the grownup—his book breaks little new ground in either. Nevertheless, his reassessment of the relative value of insight as such, in comparison with all the other elements of the psychoanalytic situation, provides, I believe, a most elegant revision of the elements at work in the curative process.

The first effect, then, of this reappraisal of classical analysis was to refocus analytic attention temporally and structurally, backwards from the oedipal phase into the early life of the developing infant and toddler. Stone astutely links "the states of relative physical and emotional 'deprivation-in-intimacy'" (p. 105) of the psychoanalytic situation with a crucial point in infancy, with the series of basic separation experiences in the child's relation to the mother (the point Mahler was later to call the phase of separation-individuation). Stone states: "the psychoanalytic setting in its general and primary transference impact tends to reproduce, from the outset, the repetitive phases of the state of relative *separation* from early objects, and most crucially . . . that period of life where all the modalities of bodily intimacy and direct dependence on the mother are being relinquished or attentuated, pari passu with the rapid development of the great vehicle of communication of speech" (p. 86). For Stone, the transference represents, at its base, a dialectic between "the insistent irredentist craving for union with the original object" and "the craving for understanding, instruction, and facilitation of the displacement of interest to the environment" (p. 94), Stone is describing a way to formulate the transference as it occurs in the ordinary psychoanalytic experience. He is not proposing a program for interpretation itself; nor even, as Kohut was later to do, an investigation of the precise dynamic interplay of the craving for union and the craving for understanding as they appear in analysis.

I shall stop here and indicate what I mean by "a program for interpretation." All analysts would concur that what is interpreted derives from the data of the patient's communications (verbal and nonverbal). But as we all agree when we pay homage to Freud and

his discoveries, we do not approach each encounter with the unconscious as *terra incognita.* Although we suspend prejudgments,
we are guided by the knowledge of prior analytic discoveries. This
and that association cue us to the possibility of a primal scene experience. This and that, to a fear of anal penetration. And so on.
These sets of cues constitute, I suggest, a program or schema that
aids us in recognizing conscious, preconscious, and unconscious
configurations regardless of the disguises (defense mechanisms)
that hide them. At the same time they restrict us to the continuous
rediscovery of the, by now, familiar. The daily work of analysis
consists of applying a learned, and deeply appreciated, schema as
the communications of the analysand point to an appropriate
match. New discoveries are made within the general context of the
schema, or they are made on a scale large enough to challenge the
value of the existing schema, thus leading to the proposal of a new
one.

Freud's own discovery of ego psychology and the signal theory
of anxiety is an example of a proposal so broad in scale that it
called for the development of a new schema to replace id
psychology. A new program for interpretation was gradually
developed, based on knowing what to look for by virtue of the
schema—a drive derivative, a defense against it, a compromise
formulation, a conflict involving a prohibition, and a quantity of
affect signaling the effectiveness or ineffectiveness of the ego's
response to the demands made on it. This was essentially the program for psychoanalytic interpretation that Stone took for
granted.[1] What he saw as requiring explanation was what made interpretations based on this schema effective or ineffective. In his
opinion, effectiveness lay in the dynamism of the analytic situation
as it resonated with the analysand's early life experiences. As I
have indicated, Stone's pointing to infancy was not at all to demand a new program for interpretation. Nonetheless, new

---

[1]Stone states that the beneficial effects of insight gained from interpretation are "the
neutralizing of instinctual energies, the conversion of primary-process elements into
directed thought, the extension of the integrating scope of the ego" (1961, pp. 100–101).

schemata for listening, conceptualizing, and interpreting did result from the widening scope. These new schemata have in common new, albeit very different, interpretations of the preoedipal phases.

The Kleinian Program

Even before Stone's work, the Kleinians articulated a fully developed schema for interpretation that focused on preoedipal phases. American analysts tend to underestimate the powerful hold of this Kleinian program in terms of the number of direct adherents and the indirect effects on theory making. The Kleinian schema derived from analytic work with relatively disturbed children, and in that sense is related to the widening scope. It was not developed to deal with a special group of patients with preoedipal problems. Rather, all patients are seen as developing their basic structure from the outcome of these conficts, and so its program of interpretations covers the whole spectrum of cases.

The Kleinian analyst engages a patient of whatever type problem in a discourse that translates relatively inchoate awareness of unrest into symbolically coded statements for the unrest. Good breasts and poisonous milk, the loving self and the hateful other, and the reverse—the envy that would destroy the good, the reparation that would restore the harmed, the gratitude that would repay the effort to help—all are highly evocative images with which to transact business between a troubled person in a state of regression and a conscientious, intelligent, physicianly oriented psychoanalyst. Moreover, although most of the Kleinian conceptions of infantile life are not confirmed by the recent explosion of information about the first two years of life, impressive fragments are. For example, the mother-infant interaction does begin at birth, and it is a highly dynamic interplay, with mother and infant participating in a two-way exchange involving affect. The principal dynamic of this exchange, however, is to lay down a matrix of regulatory transactions about schedules of active alertness, feeding, crying, and sleep, and it is normally characterized by a great deal of pleasurable exchange. Except in highly pathological situations, I do not find observational support for the Kleinian "Star Wars" imagery of destruction projected onto breasts and introjected via poisoned milk. Nor do I find any evidence for a primal form of envy, or even the capacity to conceptualize or experience the earliest exchange with the mother in such cognitively organized terms as fantasy, no matter how primitive. Although direct observation can't provide decisive evidence to disprove a premise about the inner life of the psyche, the findings of infant research and clinical premises demand some degree of confirmatory integration to convincingly support such a conception about the very young infant.

Kernberg's Perspective

A second program for interpretation, one specifically related to the widening scope, is Otto Kernberg's (1975, 1976) schema for the treatment of borderline personality disorders. At the Menninger Foundation, Kernberg observed that many of the formulations of Melanie Klein and of the British Object Relations School fit the discourse and behavior of these patients. Previously, therapists had been baffled by the manner in which these patients conveyed obviously dependent neediness mixed with inexplicable states of antagonism. Whatever tack the therapist took might seem to work for a while, but then would paradoxically lead to negativism—often in in extreme forms. Kernberg reasoned that these patients had internalized a state of seesawing modes of relating based on essentially negative experiences. They had built their characters around the expression, and defenses against the expression, of these aggression-dominated infantile relationships. With this formulation, Kernberg developed a theory that welded more or less effectively the conflict theory of ego psychology, Jacobson's theory of internalized representations of self and object, and the aggression-dominated motifs of infancy from the Kleinian schema. The program for interpretation that he evolved enabled therapists and analysts to "read," for the first time, the text of patients' puzzling inclinations to pull toward and push away, to praise and denounce, to worship and hate, to envy and appreciate. What therapists could read, they could confront, and what they could confront, they could care about, and what they cared about they could treat (and be perceived by the patient as treating).

What of Kernberg's premises about infancy? Kernberg's theory conforms nicely with the concept of a matrix of mother-infant interaction out of which the shape of the infant's inclinations develops. At the neurophysiological level, what happens experientially is regarded by some researchers as affecting such basic organic phenomena as the rate of myelinization and the formation and strength of inhibiting and feedback loops. At the behavioral level of organization, regulation of hunger, alertness, sleep, and elimination derives from patterning in the interactional exchange; thus, those manifestations that psychoanalysis labels drive derivatives can be conceptualized as developing secondarily to object relations. But there are, I believe, many differences between the nature of the observed interactions and those construed by Kernberg. The most important of these deals with splitting. Although Kernberg does not hold with the Kleinian developmental timetable or with the death instinct concept, he leans heavily on oral envy and other primary manifestations of the aggressive drive as explanatory concepts. Key to his conception is "splitting," which he regards as the basic means of organizing experience in infancy. In this formulation, the infant is biologically primed to organize all experience into good-pleasurable or bad-painful groupings. The task, then, is to integrate these divergent groupings, a task presumably made difficult or impossible by an excess of unpleasurable experiences resulting from or connected with primary aggression.

Here again the evidence from infant observation lends little support. First, it fails to confirm that early psychic experience is organized in broad categories of pleasure/unpleasure or good/bad. Instead, it indicates that from the earliest days there are a number of affects, with *ranges of intensity* within each. Moreover, it fails to support the idea that splitting inevitably arises from an innate inclination for aggression; most if not all manifestations of anger or rage in the infant appear to be reactions to frustration (Parens, 1979a). Nor does infant research confirm the premise that the sense of self is pieced together from disparate images or representations. Rather, most researchers take a holistic view of the infant's organization, suggesting that the sense of self derives as a unitary experience (see Chapter 8). Infant observation indicates that the 24-hour cycle of the infant's life is dominated more by moments of low or moderate intensity than by the moments of high intensity (the conflictual experiences that analytic theory has emphasized). Accordingly, it is conjectured that the infant generally experiences the world more as unified than as discontinuous or split. Even in moments of high tension, the unity of experience may persist if the stress is not too intense or prolonged. Commonly cited examples of high-tension experiences include states of sensual excitement from erotogenic zone activity and moments when the toddler is pulled between an urge to remain within the security of mother's orbit or broaden his or her exploratory range. What might be observed as splitting—the toddler's psychological designation of a pairing of self and caretaker as "bad" with another pairing designated as "good"—takes place only in the second year, under the severe stress of a failure of adequate empathic support—sometimes, of course, of an unavoidable nature. In sum, the clinical phenomenon of splitting found in adult patients points to a broad-based failure in regulation. It is not a normal vicissitude of development.

Mahler's and Kohut's Schemas

Two of the most intriguing schemas available to the psychoanalyst today come at the problem from opposite directions. Margaret Mahler (1968; Mahler et al., 1975) begins with infant observation and provides a schema rich in new perspectives. She does not, however, offer a specific program for interpretation as such. In contrast, Heinz Kohut (1971, 1977) begins with clinical data and provides a radically different program for interpretation. He expresses skepticism about reliance on direct observation, on what he sees as belonging "to the conceptual realm of a psychoanalytic interactionalism" (1971, p. 219n). Yet Mahler's schema has been used by others to develop a program for interpretation (one that comes close in certain ways to that of Kernberg), and Kohut's program for interpretation and his theory have been used by others to provide a basis for viewing infantile experience. For instance, Marian Tolpin (1980) has, metaphorically speaking, created "Kohut's baby"—a smiling, joyful infant, giving and receiving eye contact, coos and giggles. Indeed, this hypothetical creature conforms to the baby of observation, replacing the cocoon neonate of the theory of primary narcissism. But by confining the source of his data to empathic reconstructions in adult analysis, Kohut has overlooked the opportunity provided by infant researchers, especially those who look to adaptive rather than pathological principles for guides to development.[2] Without being tied in to a detailed developmental schema based both on observation and reconstruction, self psychology's core concept of self cohesion lends itself to concretization or murkiness as to its level of abstraction.

On the other hand, Kohut's assertion of the primacy of assertiveness, with aggression seen as a consequence of frustration, provides a clear postulate for direct observation and for comparison with Klein's, Kernberg's, and Mahler's postulates of primary aggression. As I read the evidence (Lichtenberg, 1982a), it points to assertiveness, with its regulatory affects of functional and efficacy pleasure, as primary. In fact it is commonly interference with the gratification of functional and efficacy pleasure that provides the stimulus for reactive aggression. These two ways of viewing events in the infant's and toddler's sequencing of reaching, crawling, pushing, hitting, crying, etc., lead to different programs for inter-

---

[2]Kohut's parenthetical statement, "I should like to mention here that Sander's work in particular . . . promises to enrich self psychology, and, in turn, to be enriched by it," points in this direction (1980, p. 475).

pretation. A theory of a primary aggressive drive, with derivatives becoming defended against and tamed, points to one interpretive approach; a theory of primary assertiveness that with support leads to functional and efficacy pleasure, and with frustration leads to reactive anger, points to a different interpretive approach.

Another difference centers on the formulation of separateness and individuation as partial goals (Kohut's view), or end-points of a developmental sequence (Mahler's view). As a partial goal, separateness means the taking over of functions from the caretaker (such as responding internally to anxiety), while retaining a need for the general support of others (the mature forms of mirroring and idealization). As an end-point of preoedipal development, separation and individuation (object constancy) mean that the older child's and adult's search for various forms of mirroring or alter-ego experiences, or for idealization, is defensive. How this issue is viewed will make a considerable difference on what is interpreted as pathological in analysis and what criteria for termination are followed.[3]

Further Questions for Our Clinical Approach

The universe of concepts that is opening up to us from infant research is indeed so complex that it is understandable that analysts might wish to remain distant and skeptical. Moreover, skepticism is inevitable when so many formulations of what are cornerstones of our theories have come up for questioning. A stage of primary narcissism, for instance, is contradicted by the infant-mother and infant-father relatedness at birth. The theory of symbiosis is contested by the active role of the infant as behavioral initiator of interaction. But most of all, psychoanalytic theory is challenged by how the experiences of the infant are registered. Psychoanalysis has a variety of theories of internalized representations, but infant researchers tell us of what I have termed in Chapters 1 and 2 a biological-neurophysiological-behavioral level

---

[3]Brody (1982) has surveyed the broad terrain of psychoanalytic theories of infant development—evaluating each against the background of infant research findings.

of organization. Then, in time (during the second year), there is a level of organization in which communication is based on a sign-signal interchange, and a discrete sense of self and the other is increasingly established. Shortly thereafter a full level of symbolic representation is reached and sealed forever as the human's unique affective-cognitive experience through the use of language. This view is somewhat mind-boggling at first and requires a great deal of rethinking. We need to ask what it means for our clinical approach.

To play the devil's advocate, I might argue here that ordinarily the psychoanalysis of an adult patient can be conducted without resort to information gained from infant research. Information is exchanged between analyst and analysand via a symbolic process (language). Moreover, the pertinent subjective data to which the analysand gains increasing access is encoded in symbolic representations. Thus, if we are attempting to understand the analysand's subjective experience and the past only as it consciously and unconsciously influences the present, we have little need for the infant researcher's veridical view of presymbolic development. This is especially true if the past influences we are concerned with are experiences that occurred in the third year or later, after they received full symbolic representation. From a scientific perspective, we might want to know what happened as it would be viewed by an "outside" observer, but, as analysts, our concern is to empathically perceive from within the analysand's total state of experiencing. When this can be done (as it can be argued it regularly is done in the analysis of a psychoneurosis), then the adult can be analyzed without knowledge of his or her presymbolic experience.

But, you may ask, is this contention more hypothetical than actual? It can also be argued that in every analysis the communication between analyst and analysand involves informational exchanges at both symbolic and presymbolic levels. From this perspective, an appreciation of affective and motor patterns, drawing on continuities of experience from the early mother-infant interaction, will enrich the analysis. Independent of current infant research, analysts have described monitoring of motor patterns (McLaughlin, 1982) and manifestations of affects (the so-called body language) that are believed to have direct links to the presymbolic phase. I suggest that what has been referred to as the analyst's using "his unconscious to decipher the patient's unconscious" (Major and Miller, 1981, p. 459) may in part reflect the analyst's preconscious monitoring of motor and affect expressions. At times the analyst's attention may drift off from the symbolically organized communication, with its discursive, even defensive quality, and tune into the analysand's more general state of mind, which, especially in a regressive transference, may communicate the early presymbolic experience of the baby with the caregiver.

Gedo (1979) has specifically addressed the question of how presymbolic experience affects a program for interpretation. Essentially, he asks: If behavior receives its first regulation in a presymbolic form, do some of these behaviors—especially maladaptive ones—persist? If so, then must we not encounter them in analysis? Since these would be without mental representation in the usual sense of symbolic registry, do we not need to broaden our means of observing and interpreting to effect change in behaviors as basic as these?

I believe questions such as these are indeed mind-twisters. To make them easier to comprehend, I shall give some clinical examples. But even at the outset a contradiction must be struggled with. The tool we have at hand for comprehending the very proposal I am making about an absence of symbolic representation is symbolic representation and symbolic logic. How to imagine not having what each of us manifestly has and uses all the time is no easy matter—particularly when I suggest that fairly complicated problem solving can and does take place without symbolic representation (see also Basch, 1975). A simple explanation may give the flavor of my meaning: The infant is the *first* year, who learns to roll the ball back and forth with mother, needs only the perceptual actuality of the situation—no permanent representation of a ball, of mother or of self. I can't prove the infant doesn't have these representations, but it can be argued effectively that it isn't necessary. For operations the toddler performs at the end of the *second* year, symbolic representation *is* necessary.

CLINICAL ILLUSTRATIONS

I shall present three clinical vignettes from completed analyses of adults. The first illustrates the persistence of a basic regulatory deficit; the second, residua from an early experience in the form of a bodily symptom; and the third, problems of a primary cognitive deficiency. The findings in the first two cases are suggestive of pathology that develops prior to and independently of memory coding via symbolic representation. The findings in the third are indicative of problems that lie outside the realm of trauma or interpersonal conflict and that in turn contribute, as independent sources, to disturbances in symbolic representation and to intrapsychic and relational problems.

Case 1

Mr. K entered analysis at a point of great indecision in his life. He had doubts about his career choice, his recent marriage, and his relationship to his family. I shall deal here with only one facet of his long and, for the most part, successful treatment. During the analysis, he gained a lot of weight. The weight gain occurred in stages, roughly parallel to periods of intense resistance as one or another problem area was worked with. One of Mr. K's fears, which he initially stated as a threat and a prediction, was that he would become like his obese mother. The meanings of his body image and his fear of identification with his mother were a major concern of the analysis. Being identified with his mother meant not being identified with his father, whom he saw as powerful but ethically flawed. But not being identified with father meant giving up a form of regulating food intake. (His father, who had been an overweight child, had developed a way of remaining thin by following bouts of sudden gorging with extreme food restriction.

During his abstinent periods, the father tyrannized everyone else about eating.) Being identified with his obese mother, on the other hand, was an idiosyncratic source of fantasied strength—he conceptualized bulk as a form of armor that would allow him to resist penetration, or he envisioned the penetrator's phallus becoming encased in his fat. Yet being identified with mother was also a source of weakness, in that it meant that he would be a depressed martyr whose general insensitivity to children's feelings made him unloved but easily exploited (a form of parenting Mr. K feared he was following with his child).

My point in giving these examples is to illustrate the rich "find" of symbolic representations that surrounded a nuclear symptom. Analytic progress resulted from these discoveries—technically achieved through a complex tapestry of transference experiences centering on my presumed and often actual failure to empathically perceive the seesawing waves of his sexual and career ambition swings. Career decisions were made, parenting improved, gender identity confusion disappeared, the marriage consolidated, and his depressive tendencies were markedly reduced. But Mr. K's moderately severe obesity persisted.

Throughout the analysis, whenever possible, I tried to ask about the details of his eating. This inquiry met with the greatest resistance, as if he were a concealed gorger like his mother, eating salads in public and bags full of cookies in private. Yet, in time, another possibility emerged from the smallest of nuances. A question I asked about hunger led to anger and denial. Somehow on that particular occasion I sensed so positive a feeling about my helpfulness that the resistance struck me as repetitive *pro forma,* and I detected a slight indication of a wistful wish to give an answer. I suggested this and, to our mutual relief, Mr. K agreed, but he said he really couldn't give an answer about hunger. Usually Mr. K was a man full of answers, a bright student, to whom not knowing something was a source of embarrassment. His flat statement puzzled me, but it occurred to me to take it at face value. With this as a starting point, we were able to construct (not reconstruct) a notion of his infancy that suggested a major deficit in the regulation of food intake.

Mr. K literally did not know when he was hungry. "Hunger" was a word he used without meaningful connection to a perceived physiological state. Only during the late stages of the analysis, if he restricted his food intake, did he begin to experience a body sensation that from his description seemed to both of us to be hunger. He also did not experience satiation. He would eat foods he labeled as desirable as long as he could, to the point of nausea. Taste as a discriminator seemed very underdeveloped—a particular food was considered desirable because of some external factor (e.g., father hated it or his best friend in adolescence loved it). A further construction, based on our knowledge of later interactions, was that mother and father, rather than being attentive to their baby in a normal manner, had been preoccupied with their fights over eating. Caught up in their fears about their son's food intake, they both failed in the sensitive mirroring of the child's basic inner state that permits the pattern of hunger and satiation to achieve consensual validation in the infant-caretaker exchange. Consequently, the regulation of hunger and satiation through responsiveness to internal physiological cues could not be taken over from the infant-caretaker exchange, internalized, and given later appropriate symbolic representation. The highest level this reached for Mr. K was the internalization of the sign-signal communication of *eat–don't eat* as a part of a dominance-submission-rebellion interchange. Subsequently, eating received multiple symbolic representations connected to body image and anxiety regulation, but these overlay the basic regulatory deficit.

On termination, Mr. K felt freer of the stresses of the conflicts and other self-destructiveness that overlay the basic regulatory problems. He hoped, by careful attentiveness of a self-educative nature, to handle his eating more adaptively and pleasurably. His case calls to mind my previous report of the analysis of a 27-year-old man who had had a milk allergy and a celiac-like syndrome in infancy (Lichtenberg, 1978a). This man "would sometimes gorge himself, other times neglect eating; he would retain feces and urine until painfully distended before he became aware of his need; he would sleep irregularly and would be fatigued without any awareness of cause, or would play tennis to the point of exhaustion without recognition of limit" (p. 374).

Discussion

Mr. K represents a group of patients who appear to have specific regulatory deficits involving the monitoring of internal bodily processes, such as eating, sleeping, bowel functioning or tiredness. These patients do not attend or monitor the necessary internal bodily signals to determine hunger or satiety, physical exhaustion, or bowel and bladder urgency. In some, a regular day-night sleep-awake cycle appears to be poorly established. Whatever seemingly normal regulatory functioning these patients have is acquired by imitation. In these instances, knowledge of normal and pathological infant development makes it possible to recognize a basic deficit underlying the conflicts in this specific area. Only with a comprehensive understanding of *both* the conflicts and the regulatory dysfunction can real progress occur.

Regulatory deficits may affect other functions besides vegetative activities. At this point it is only conjectural, but I believe that some of the so-called alexithymic patients, described as unable to label, recognize, monitor, and experience affects (Nemiah, 1975; Krystal, 1974), have a regulatory disturbance that originates in early presymbolic experience. Their perceptual-action and perceptual-cognitive experiences do not become amplified by the full experience of some or many affects—leaving a flatness or impoverishment to their life. Analysis or exploratory psychotherapy is often a puzzling disappointment to both participants without the cause being appreciated. A study of these clinical problems from the standpoint of early regulatory development of affects may provide us with new, clinically relevant understanding.

We can consider the problems of regulation of hunger and sleep (regulating vulnerabilities I suggest analysts need to pay more attention to) with the problem of regulating sexual stimulation. With respect to sexuality, psychoanalytic theory has long included richly elaborate concepts about the dangers of sexual overstimulation and the factors responsible for it. Freud wondered to what degree this problem was constitutional. Experiences of primal scene exposure, overt or covert seduction, castration fears, penis envy and penis awe fantasies, all have been detailed in investigating this area of childhood. Infant research, however, indicates that regulation of stimulation is a significant feature of the neonate-caretaker interaction in *all* areas of the infant's functioning from birth on. The pattern of the neonate's responsiveness to stimuli normally ranges from highly active, through average, to quietly active. On the abnormal end, we find infants who fall apart in the effort to process ordinary stimulation and underreactive infants, who make attachment and engagement extremely difficult. Looking at the normal range, it is highly suggestive that an infant's "basic core" (Weil, 1970) with respect to stimulus processing in general may be a precondition of the way the developing child will respond to the ranges of sensual excitation that he or she is confronted with. As I discussed in Chapter 9, infant research pinpoints a stage in development (at about 18 months) when there is an upsurge of genital sensation and exploration (Roiphe, 1968; Kleeman, 1975). Amsterdam and Levitt (1980) suggest the way this is responded to has consequences for embarrassment, shame, and anxiety responses. Similarly, at the same age an upsurge of assertiveness occurs and this calls for a different regulation effort. These findings for the 18-month-old stand at the interface between the earlier mode of organization and symbolic representation. It is at this point that symptom formation involving intrapsychic conflictual tendencies can first be recognized. When regulatory disturbances become coded through the symbolic process, the conflictual configurations that result take the symptomatic and characterological forms familiar to psychoanalysis. Our technique is designed to recognize and work with these conflicts. It may be that we can benefit from a heightened awareness of various regulatory difficulties that do not receive complete-enough symbolic encoding to be recognized through our traditional approach.

Case 2

Mrs. G's analysis centered on her phobic symptoms, her depression, and her hypersensitivity to anxiety. Early in her analysis she described a symptom that was unique in my experience. Her mouth would be held open as if to yawn but, unlike a yawn, she would not inspire air. Instead, she would try to get her mouth to close. We spoke of this as a yawn for lack of a better designation and related it to a response to mounting anxiety. Yet this coupling with anxiety struck me as unsatisfactory because I couldn't determine why this particular response should occur rather than any of her other responses to anxiety.

During the long working through of the middle phase of her analysis, Mrs. G became generally more able to associate to and master anxiety. Her "yawn" disappeared—or more accurately did not occur (neither of us being aware of its absence). Then, during the final months of her analysis, Mrs. G was telling me an anecdote about her new baby and her five-year-old daughter. She seemed rather comfortable about it, and I was listening with my attention easily placed within her state of mind. She described feeding the baby a bottle, with her daughter looking on and asking if she could help. Somewhat reluctantly, Mrs. G answered "yes" and gave her the baby and the bottle. After turning away for a moment, she looked back to see the baby having a bit of distress because the five-year-old feeder had let the bottle press too deeply into the baby's mouth. Mrs. G proceeded to describe her reason for bringing up this anecdote—initially she had been ready to react with a panicky yell, but was able to get control of herself and simply help her daughter reposition the bottle properly. As she talked, I basked somewhat in her pride in her mastery of her inclination to panic and her implied appreciation of me as the parent-analyst who had helped her to do so. Involuntarily, without conscious thought, I found myself opening my mouth and feeling the sensation of a nipple thrust into it too far to suck in or push out. I repeated to her this aspect of her description before asking her about my conjecture that her so-called yawning symptom was a somatic memory of a nipple thrust too far into her mouth. Before

I could verbalize my question, she reproduced the symptom for the first time in several years.

The construction we made was based on a great deal of information about her early life. A premature baby, she had spent two months in an incubator before coming home. This gap probably interfered with the attachment between mother and infant, which was also attenuated by the mother's general anxiety and preoccupation with her own mother's chronic physical illness. We postulated that her mother, pulled by this concern, had at times turned over aspects of Mrs. G's care to Mrs. G's older sister. Whatever difficulties arose, especially mechanical ones of a too-intrusive nipple, may have been aggravated by the mouth sensitivity of this premature child, plus a degree of weakness in thrusting the bottle away. What was most fascinating to me was that dream material that seemed related to this experience appeared *after* the analytic work. Work with this material led to associative links to conflicts over impingement. Yet dreams prior to this construction, viewed retrospectively, did not reveal that the bodily registery had received a symbolic representation, as far as I could discern.

Discussion

Examples of this type of physical or body residue of early experiences are part of the folklore of analysis. Keiser (1977) describes a strange manifestation of an analytic patient, who held her hands in a particularly rigid manner. Keiser deduced that during infancy the patient had had her hands tied. The patient was unable to recall this event but was able to confirm it by direct investigation. The knowledge played a useful role in her analysis.

I suggest the experiences of Mrs. G and Keiser's patient were coded only in the perceptual-affective-action mode and did not receive later recoding into symbolic representation. They can thus only be appreciated analytically by the analyst's empathically entering (as much as possible) into the manner in which physical states, actions, and affects are experienced by the infant. By employing deductive reasoning, and guided by knowledge of infant development and the patient's overall sensitivities, the analyst can then formulate a mutually convincing interpretation.

Well-documented instances of this sort are indeed rare, but they raise a question about the persistence of memory from the presymbolic stage, as reactions from this period may have pathological consequences. Engel (1979), for instance, reports on his follow-up of Monica, who was born with esophageal atresia but recovered very nicely from the consequences of this deprivation state, with its absence of mouth feeding and all the interrelations that go with it. Monica managed to marry and to handle her pregnancy well. To the surprise of the investigators, however, she fed her baby the bottle in the same distant, cramped way that she had been fed in the stomach opening. I have reported another case in which an otherwise warm and caring mother automatically fed her babies at arm's length—the strange practice of her mother (Lichtenberg, 1982c). One of the children had a brief psychotic episode; the other became a distinctly schizoid personality, with difficulty in establishing eye contact.

Infant researchers have identified a number of behavioral manifestations that warrant consideration as early residues of the normal or abnormal infant-caretaker interaction—for instance, eye contact as engagement and gaze avoidance as aversion responses. In addition, the relationship between physiognomic expression and affect has been studied in depth. The neonate's capacity to mimic the facial expressions of the caretaker has been demonstrated. This observation opens questions about the nature of infant-mother empathy, as well as the modes of picking up disturbed affect states of depression, hatred, etc.[4] If these ex-

---

[4]Dowling (1982) suggests that specific traumatic experiences tend to overwhelm the infant's developing capacity for symbolic representation and force the child into an affective-action mode. Of interest in this regard is McLaughlin's (1982) report on the recoding into a symbolic process of a perceptual-affective experience, which took the form of Isakower phenomena. For years the three analysands he describes had had vivid presleep experiences of an amorphous mass consolidating and moving toward them in a rhythmic, enveloping fashion. For two of the patients, this was accompanied by affects of distress and fear; for the other, the affect was a mild sensation of anticipating pleasure. All had sensations in their mouths of fullness and a feeling of finding it hard to breathe. "All had initially well-concealed and highly conflicted early relationships with mother, and with severe process- and shock-trauma, such as maternal illness or death in the first two years of life. In all three instances, as analytic work in the mother transference was accomplished over time, the vividness of the Isakower experience gradually faded" (p. 233). What I find striking is that with the fading of the perceptual-affective experience itself, similar imagery appeared in dreams and fantasies, where it was more accessible to an associative symbolic process.

changes of affect states as physiognomic "behavior" strongly code early experience—say, in the first year—we may need to question certain aspects of our analytic technique. I have already mentioned Gedo's (1979) remarks on the possibility that early experiential residues exist "beyond interpretation" based on verbal free association alone. As a general rule, do we force analysands to communicate via the symbolic representation of speech and thus lift the level of the discourse? If so, does this restrict the messages that some patients could and need to give about their earlier experiences? Do these come out in different behaviors, outside or even inside the consulting room? Is it advantageous for the analyst to keep the patient's face in view and use this information, or not? (See Jacobs, 1973.)

Case 3

Mr. N, a patient I have described in detail elsewhere (Lichtenberg, 1983), was able to establish a strong working relationship. Despite considerable transference resistance to accepting interpretations, he participated in a working-through process. The aspect of his analysis I wish to focus on here is a limitation in his use of metaphor and analogy. For a long time I regarded this as a manifestation of his obsessional "style" and assumed that dynamically it served as a form of character resistance against primary-process material. Thus, I expected that as Mr. N became less anxious and more able to be introspective, his compulsive adherence to secondary-process cognition would relax and he would be better able to work with metaphor and analogy. However, as the analysis progressed, I revised this assessment. As Mr. N became less anxious, he was in fact freer in reporting dreams and, more important, spontaneous fantasies—indicating a freeing up of primary-process cognition. But this freeing up occurred without any change in his inability to process the material of these fantasies and dreams through the active use of analogy and metaphor. On the other hand, when I worked with him actively, using analogy mixed with a more detailed explanation, he readily and appreciatively utilized the information. This indicated to me that his own failure to employ analogy and metaphor was not a pseudo-deficit, in the service of resistance. Moreover, he himself gave examples of conversations with other people in which he could recognize this deficit. We could recognize similar instances in the analysis, when he experienced painful feelings of embarrassment and humiliation at not "catching on" to some suggestion I made based on metaphoric bridging.

Looking back, I could see that his sensitivity to this impairment played a part in his reluctance to work "analytically" (symbolically) with transference material—a problem that had produced a puzzling barrier to progress. His frustration could be seen, retrospectively, as one of the meanings of his frequent appeals to me for help—he wished me to be the empathic caregiver, sensing his cognitive constriction and the deleterious effect it had on his self-confidence. He wanted me to come to his aid to bridge his difficulty—to "uncramp" his mind—rather than ask him ordinary analytic questions. The ordinary questions, designed to guide him to form linkages, exposed him to feeling inadequate, without helping him to identify the source of the problem. As his limitation in appreciating and working with analogy and metaphor was recognized and his sense of failure understood, he became more adventurous in his attempts to associate symbolically.

Discussion

Mr. N's limitation in the use of metaphor and analogy is a specific, although minor, example of a class of cognitive deficiencies, which encompass a wide variety of learning disturbances (e.g., dyslexia). Another example, from my current practice, is a professional man with a very high IQ who can amass incredible numbers of facts but who has considerable difficulty in appreciating hierarchical arrangements. His academic career seemed inexplicably checkered because neither he nor his teachers recognized the disparity in his abilities. His facility at fact assembly led him to be a whiz in some courses, but the deficit in hierarchical structuring caused him to be borderline in others.

This whole area of cognitive-processing disturbances is becoming increasingly appreciated in educational circles and in the field of child psychiatry (Weil, 1977). The number of individuals with such difficulties is not inconsiderable (statistics range anywhere from 2 to 10% [A. Lichtenberg, 1981]). Thus, the likelihood is high of an analyst encountering a certain number of analysands with these difficulties. The problem of recognition is made difficult because the learning disability will interact with intrapsychic and interpersonal problems, which may then overshadow the primary deficit.

Since dyslexia, dysgraphia, dyscalculia, disturbances in sequencing, in hierarchical arranging, and in symbol manipulation are disorders in processing symbolic modes of organization, it might be argued they have no place in citing the relevance of infant research to the analytic situation. These findings, like those of deficiencies in the use of metaphor, which occur after the period of the first two years, illustrate the need for our heightened appreciation of the neurophysiological level of functioning. Normal developments that depend on this substrate level of both perceptual-action-affect responses and symbolically organized responses has been illuminated by infant research. In the neonate, the linking of functional modes—such as vision with hearing and both with grasping—calls the attention of the psychoanalyst to the means by which fundamental emergent activities governed by neurophysiological maturation dovetail with developments in human relations. Each such development adds flexibility to functioning and raises the level of regulation. The failure of each such development establishes the potential for disturbances in human interrelatedness and self-regulation. The disturbances may appear in analysis organized in the form of conflict or as perceptual-cognitive deficits. Their recognition may call for both analytic understanding and remedial intervention.[5]

---

[5]Glauber (1982) makes a similar suggestion about stuttering: "Classical psychoanalytic technique may succeed in resolving the neurotic elements. Successful treatment of the primary fixation requires reeducational methods" (p. 168).

APPLICATIONS TO THE
PSYCHOANALYTIC SITUATION

I predict that the new knowledge from infant research will have a profound but subtle effect on psychoanalytic practice. The most significant feature of its findings lies in the turnabout of its approach, in its focus on normal development. It starts with the question: How does the unexpectedly complex level of organization of the neonate, operating in an interactional matrix with a caregiver, undergo transformations into the levels of organization of later stages? It does not move backward from the neuroses or psychoses to hypothesize "normal" early stages from the distortions in these disturbances. The current infant research does not tilt toward a "demonic" imagery of infancy. But it does tilt away from an appreciation of psychic awareness, of fantasy, and of the unconscious, that is, from the vicissitudes of conflictual experience (what Sander [1980a] calls the inevitable polarities). Psychoanalysis will not and should not surrender its ground on many of these points. Nonetheless, I believe that when infant research is seen as leading toward a useful new conception of normal infant organization, and a useful new conception of problem areas such as I have described in my clinical vignettes, analysis will benefit, without losing any of its capacity to penetrate the depths of our unconscious.

How can we apply what is known now about infancy to the psychoanalytic situation? Stone (1961) has described both a framework that permits analysis to take place and the formal operations that represent its main task. The framework is the relationship between the reliable adult physician of good will and the mature responsible patient, which reverberates with the relationship of the mother, who both gratifies and separates, and the infant, who must come to terms with deprivation in intimacy. The formal operations are the interpretations that take place within this context. Stone refers to the controversy about manipulating the framework, a debate that persists to this day. Is the medium the message? Is the psychoanalytic situation itself—the physicianly concern and care, the empathic ambiance—the curative agent? Certainly some analysts perceive a focus on deficits in early development, whether regulatory, relational, or cognitive, as implying a cure by replacement, a second version of child-rearing. In fact, given the transformations between infancy and adulthood, this is both impossible and unnecessary. It is impossible because the experiential world of the infant of the first year is so different—and unnecessary because the adult has achieved symbolic representation and can bring this problem-solving mode to bear on his or her difficulties through the regular means of verbal interpretation.

The question we are left with, then, is: Interpretation of what? The answer I would give is: Interpretation of whatever analysands communicate that they have responded and reverberated to within the analytic situation. This response might be to the analyst as a discrete, separate person, in relation to whom the analysand has a sexual wish, or a wish to relieve loneliness, or a wish to assert superiority. Or it may be to the analytic situation, which the analysand feels is helpful or not in some way. In other words, the medium is not the message. The medium is a person (the analyst) and a milieu (the analytic situation), which serve as a wonderfully ambiguous stimulus for reverberations of specific desires and regulatory needs, past and present. The message is the communication back to the analysand of interpretations that facilitate his or her introspective understanding of the meaning of what he or she has communicated.

Foreground-Background Communication

I have suggested that analysts form their constructions by having their perception shift between what analysands are experiencing in what I term the "foreground" and the "background." In the foreground is the immediate context and meaning of the associations the patient is relating. Here the analyst might be the recipient of well-organized wishes, the analyst might be needed to serve some suspended, unavailable or underdeveloped function. In the background is a general sense of the receptivity that the analysand presumes will come from the analyst as a transference person or milieu. At any given moment, patients may or may not have a conscious, or even preconscious, awareness of the psychic reality they perceive as coloring the background. For example, a patient may have come habitually to experience his masculinity or his competence as under question; as a result, he may be unaware he lives his life and even the analysis as though in a state of siege. By and large, the transferences that characterize the background communication in analysis tend to be centered on the broadened sense of "support systems" that succeed or fail to form and sustain self cohesion and basic trust, optimism and a capacity for joy. The analyst's listening focus and interpretive stance must shift back and forth between foreground and background, gradually assisting the analysand to increase awareness of both. This should include as much as possible a systematic exploration of both success and failure of present and past "support systems."

Conceptualizing the analytic situation in terms of the patient's communications as responses to foreground and background stimuli provides a key analogy to infant experience. Sander has stated: "We traditionally rely on a linear cause-effect model—one thing leading to another. . . . This we need to replace with . . . a model . . . where there can be a background and a foreground" (1980b, p. 195). Foreground events, such as making eye contact in infancy and providing associations in analysis, are given meaning in the framework of the background of a shared organization of expectancies constructed from the infant-mother regulatory efforts in development and from the operational consistencies of the psychoanalytic situation. In infancy and in analysis, foreground and background should be thought of as experiential rather than concrete entities. Each of these aspects of psychic reality develops because an individual who has achieved the level of symbolic representation shifts in the experience of self and others between a tendency to generalize and a tendency to particularize (Lichtenberg, 1979). The tendency to generalize builds up the background. The tendency to particularize leads to a foreground focus. The tendency to shift back and forth between the two constitutes perceptual and conceptual roots for the associative sequencing in analysis.

A qualification seems necessary here. Just as the repetitions between mother and baby form the patterns of the background in infancy, repetitions in the analyst-analysand exchange build background expectancies. Yet there is a difference in how this effect is responded to. In infancy, the mother alters her patterns to promote growth, relaxing some controls and rules to facilitate more independence. In contrast, the analyst does not seek to change the basic patterns of the analytic exchange to achieve progress. Rather, the analyst tries to examine the effect of the repetitions and expectancies in order to explore their meaning.

The Place of Empathy

At this point I should like to comment about empathy. If the medium is not the message, what about empathy? If generalized empathic failures in caretaking have created a disturbance in shared expectancies, giving rise to distrust in the background, or if particular empathic failures have created traumatic overloads around which pathological fantasy systems have formed, giving rise to affective-cognitive disturbances in the foreground, then is empathy the means to repair the damage?

I believe empathy is the means to the means to repair the damage. First, empathy as a general ambiance is an ingredient of the "physicianly" warmth and commitment of the analyst; it is thus, as Stone (1961) indicates, the means to create the analytic situation. But empathy in a technical sense is a specific mode of analytic listening (Schwaber, 1981) and perceiving (Lichtenberg, 1981a). It is the means to apprehend and comprehend the affective and cognitive experiential sense of the analysand's state of mind, thereby providing the data on which interpretation is based. The empathic mode of perception in analysis is a form of attunement that, for the most part, entails the analyst's apprehending, through the symbolic level of representation, information communicated by the analysand, also through symbolic representation.

Thus, the empathic attunement of infant and mother of the first year is not the usual mode of communicative interchange in analysis. It may indeed exist, and many analysts, including Freud, have placed great significance on unconscious intercommunication—penetrating to the navel of the unknown (Major and Miller, 1981). As indicated in my second vignette, the analyst can use his or her bodily responses to reverberate with unconscious communications of the patient and this may be "related to the use of the body as a prime conveyor of affect between mother and child" (Jacobs, 1973, p. 87). Nonetheless, in the ordinary conduct of analysis, the empathic mode of listening is commonly based on perceiving at a symbolic level of communication, and, if derived from a bodily level, it is then apprehended symbolically. Thus, an effort to understand at the symbolic level should be exhausted before the analyst concludes that residua from before its formation have remained outside its mode of coding. I conjecture—with a readiness to be convinced otherwise—that, with the exception of rare instances of bodily listening, what we perceive outside the empathic mode of listening via symbolic representation, we achieve through exclusion, deduction, and a grasp of intuitive inference within a background of considerable empathic attunement.

The distinction I am making about analytic empathy does not eliminate the analogy of the early mother-infant exchange. Stern (1982) describes moments of empathic communion that "appear to establish a *springboard* from which the mother or baby can expand their interactive repertoire." In formulating a sequence of increasingly penetrating interpretations, I find it useful to begin with interpretations that follow the pattern of: "So is what you're saying or feeling or thinking . . .?" That is, when the analyst, through empathic perception, is able to construct a verbally communicable understanding of the patient's immediate state of mind, the analyst may offer an initial bridging interpretation as a way to affirm that a shared state of emotion-laden comprehension exists. This initial interpretation may refer to the analysand's overt or somewhat covert attempt at direct expression, or to a state of resistance and the motive for it. Especially with patients who maintain a persistent, often automatic conviction that their attempts to share will be met with disappointment, such an initial affirmation of successful communication can prevent a chronic resistance to discussion of more sensitive material. In addition, it offers the patient an opportunity to share for a moment an *"observation platform,"* looking at the data available to the analyst's empathic perception and the analysand's introspection. This observation platform for analyst and analysand differs from Stern's springboard for mother and infant in one respect. Stern speaks of communion (attunements of affective states) in distinction to communication (exchanges of information intended to alter the other's beliefs or actions). What I am suggesting is a working closeness (or momentary sense of communion) that results from the success of communication.

The Mother-Infant Interaction as Metaphor

From what I have said so far, it should be clear that the main value I perceive in a new understanding of the mother-infant interaction lies not in the analyst's imitating good mothering, but in the metaphors this new understanding contributes to conceptualizing the analytic exchange.[6] Contributing metaphors may sound like a thin benefit until we recall the explanatory leverage Freud derived from metaphors borrowed from physics and archaeology. In addition to the aspects of foreground-background communication and empathy mentioned above, an important concept I have borrowed from infant research is the concept of regulation. One application

---

[6]It is important to note that the analyst's goal is *not* to do the caregiving of a parent. The analyst attempts to understand the conscious and unconscious wishes that influence the analysand's present experiences and their antecedents as they appear in the transference. Thus, the analyst will neither try to do what the mother did, nor try to make up for what she may have failed to do. While many activities of the analyst—reliability, physicianly concern, tact, and attentiveness—coincide with positive parenting, the analyst will direct his or her primary effort *only* to conceptualizing experience, present and past, in terms of its unique individual meaning to the patient.

of this idea can be seen in Stern's (1982) remarks on the positive regulatory effect of the mother's being in a dialogue with an infant as she imagines, guesses, wishes he or she will become, and his imaginative analogy to the analyst's alignment with the analysand's potential state of being (a point made by Friedman, 1982).

Taking her cues from the child, what the mother attempts to regulate are the many behavioral ambitendencies of the developing infant. The strength of these ambitendencies and the mother's success or failure in regulating them contribute to either success or failure in self-regulation by the child. When the results of these interactive and self-regulatory efforts receive symbolic representation, they may take the form of normative or pathological conflicts—an area that psychoanalytic theory has brought to light. There is then a complex relationship between regulatory efforts and intrapsychic conflict. Exploring this complex relationship may enrich analysts' understanding of their patients. And it may help to bring to the fore many regulatory concepts that I believe are implicit in traditional analytic theory. Exploring the relationship between regulation and conflict may also help to reconcile valuable observations of self psychology, in which concepts based on regulation of the state of the self are presented without an adequate account of the intrapsychic conflicts that inevitably accompany regulatory disturbances.

To recapitulate: Stone (1961) assigns major significance to infant development in his explication of the analytic situation. He asks: What mileage from critical early periods of development constitute the underpinnings for transferences? Infant research provides answers to Stone's question by defining with greater precision the nature of the infant-mother interaction and the patterns of attachment and disengagement that are its dynamic force. But infant research raises new questions. By highlighting the different organization of experience in the infant prior to 18 months, infant research points to a problem in establishing the relevance of its findings for clinical analytic work. Analytic therapy is based on data processed via symbolic representation. If a presymbolic mode of organization, what I have termed the mode of perceptual-action-affective responses, persists in some clinical conditions, then an understanding of observations from this early period has direct immediate application. By presenting cases that spur this possibility to clinical investigation, I have attempted to broaden the manner in which we draw on Stone's inferences.

Stone also drew an implicit distinction between infancy as the foundation for the deprivation-in-intimacy analytic relationship and the content of the interpretive effort. I have attempted to illustrate that new research findings challenge this distinction. They raise questions about schema on which interpretations are based, and on the modes of experience that characterize the interactions between analyst and analysand.

It might be argued that the harvest for clinical work—the specific case illustrations I have cited, the critique of programs for interpretations, and the gains by analogy and metaphor—is limited. I would advise that we consider the relatively short time we clinicians have had to absorb into our experience the data of these findings. I don't feel we are yet in a position to appraise the full potential of current and future infant research for psychoanalysis.

Chapter Thirteen

An Experiential Conception of What Is Curative in Psychoanalysis

My plan is to follow the traditional approach to discussing what is curative—that is, to analyze (segment) this enormously complex subject, and then build up a synthesis of the parts. My overview is that an invaluable perspective for conceptualizing psychoanalysis is the experiential (encompassing conscious, preconscious, and unconscious experience). From this perspective, the success of an analysis derives from the total experience two people have as a result of the combined, but differently focused, effort of each. The one person, the analyst, tries physically and mentally to use his or her skill, sensitivity, and experience to help the other person, the analysand, to come to terms with his or her problems. The analysand, in turn, tries physically and mentally to provide the introspective information both need to succeed in their joint effort. Within the total experience many things happen—unconscious resistances are understood, transferences form and shift and dissolve, apparent understandings turn into misunderstandings, seemingly disastrous misunderstandings provide the key information for later understandings, and so on. In teaching technique, we may emphasize how to recognize and analyze resistances, transferences, conflicts, regulatory deficits, therapeutic impasses, and the like. Without an understanding of each of these, we can't get the total experience. But, in our ardor to teach a particular facet of analysis that we believe to be crucial, we may sometimes lose sight of the total ongoing nature of the whole.

It can be argued that an experiential focus allows only for a description of what takes place in an analysis—that it will not provide a causal explanation. This argument is irrefutable in the terms in which it is stated. My description of what has been and is regarded as curative will provide, at best, an explication of what facilitates cure. An underlying nonexperiential process, parallel to or coexistent with the inherent tendency of the human to grow, must be called upon to answer beyond the experiential. Nevertheless, if it is possible to conceptualize descriptively what is experienced as curative in an analysis, this will convey understanding, in the sense of *meaning*: "Meaning can only be measured in terms of dispositional power, the intent or behavior to which it gives rise in a particular individual at a given time" (Basch, 1981, p. 166). I shall endeavor to demonstrate that ultimately the dispositional power in analysis comes from the unique interaction between analysand and analyst, with strain at its junction and a joint search for insight through empathy and introspection as its working basis.

VARIOUS CONCEPTS OF CURE

What has traditionally been regarded as curative derives from the answers to three questions: How does the mind work? What needs curing or what is responsible for pathology? And what comprises a therapeutic exchange? For example, if the mind and the body are regarded as an enclosed unit, then something foreign to normal functioning (such as evil spirits or bad humors) can get into or be manufactured within the enclosure. A cure would then result from the removal of the destructive foreign agent by an exorcist or doctor, whose authority and power would be so fully accepted by the sufferer that the rituals imposed—whether prayer, purging, or leeching (in or out of a trance state)—would create the conditions for an experience of a changed state.

Early Views

Bringing this perspective closer to psychoanalysis, we again encounter a model of the mind as an enclosure, with compartments of conscious, preconscious, and unconscious. In the unconscious, according to early theory, rest excitation cathexes representing strangulated affects from past traumas, and, according to later theory, unacceptable wishes that are incompatible with the dominant mass of ideas. If strangulated affects are the symptom source, then they and the traumas responsible must be reexperienced, undergo catharsis, and be abreacted, under the persuasive sway of an analyst-hypnotist. If incompatible wishes are the basis for the problem, then, by means of free association, these unconscious wishes must be moved from the unconscious, through the preconscious, to the conscious. This shift is accomplished with the help of an analyst who recognizes the derivatives of the wishes in the associations, and interprets their true character to the patient. In the case of the cathartic method, the why of the cure is self-evident experientially: If you have an undesired content in you, be it a splinter, excrement, or troubling secret, it feels good to get it out; if you "get out" your fears, your anger, or your sexual desires in conversation with someone who is sympathetic, you feel relieved. In the case of the revelation of the incompatible wishes, the why of the cure is subtler. For the symptomatic individual, unmasking the true nature of one's disguised sexual or aggressive wishes provides one with information hitherto unavailable to conscious awareness and therefore to the dominant mass of ideas (the ego). The conflict between the two may now be fought out in the open. The ego can recognize the childish nature of the wish, its impracticality or moral reprehensibleness. These undesirable aspects of the wish become particularly apparent in their current form as they adhere to the person of the analyst as transference. The motivation to resolve the conflict on the side of the dominant mass of ideas comes from the desire both to be free of symptomatic suffering and to rid oneself of shame, embarrassment, and guilt about the persistence of now conscious wishes that are recognized as childish, unachievable, and against one's morals and ideals. The cure then results when most remnants of the previously unconscious infantile wishes are renounced and the remainder sublimated.

The Structural Model

The full articulation of the structural hypothesis has added layers and layers of complex reasoning to a consideration of what is curative. In this model, the mind is construed as working through the differentiation and integration of three separate psychic organizations—id, ego, and superego. Each organization is defined in terms of its functions: the id, as drive peremptoriness; the ego, as a group of regulatory, channeling, and executive functions as well as functions of more persistent delay and distortion, in the form of defenses; the superego, as a guidance system incorporating moral and ethical prohibitions, as well as ideals and standards. Each organization interacts with the others and with the external world. Each interaction involves tension and potential conflict. Tension and conflict may also occur between components of each of the organizations. In this formulation, it becomes easier to state what needs curing or what is the source of pathology—it is unresolved conflict.

What comprises a therapeutic exchange can be stated equally clearly: The analyst takes a position equidistant from the patient's id, ego, and superego. The neutrality of this positioning guarantees the analyst's nonintrusiveness; at the same time, the analyst's general demeanor of physicianliness establishes a therapeutic or working alliance. Although the analyst is in the position of an "outside" observer, he or she can utilize moments of trial identification with the patient to guarantee emotional closeness to the patient's state of mind.

I believe that there is general agreement that the curative agent derived from the perspective of the structural hypothesis is insight. But insight into what? Insight into the complex transactions among the three psychic organizations (intersystemic conflict) and between components within the structures (intrasystemic conflict) and between each organization and external reality. The strength of this way of conceptualizing cure lies in its remarkable inclusiveness. Through the abstraction of interrelating organizations, an analyst who has mastered the theoretical constructs of ego psychology (e.g., Rapaport, 1960; Hartmann, 1964; Hartmann et al., 1964) can both account for and appreciate the most intricate aspects of the determinants of psychic multiple functioning. The limitation of this way of conceptualizing is that in each instance in which one attempts to state what the conflict is for which insight proved curative, it is necessary to move away from the abstract level of the theory to the experiential level.[1] This limitation has led to major criticisms of this remarkably comprehensive theory, and there have been a number of attempts to revise or discard it.

The structural hypothesis is built around an experience-near theoretical construct. It states that, in each instance in which an individual has a motivating urge, a representation of a wish, its aim, and its object will be subjected to an intrapsychic "trial" by the ego. If there is a memory of a past danger situation associated with the urge and its gratification, then a signal of anxiety will be automatically elaborated and defensive measures will be instituted, with more or less success. In this formulation, the wish is represented by a potentially recoverable fantasy, the past danger situation by a memory of a seemingly threatening experience (also recoverable or able to be reconstructed), and the defense by an identifiable mode of cognitive manipulation. The flicker of anxiety may even be recognized. Insight, then, refers to bringing this pattern of response into conscious awareness, with the identification and recognition of each component. For the analysand, this process constitutes a very impressive experience of learning about how one's mind works. But insight into how one's mind works constitutes a conceptual tilt that, with all its considerable value, pulls one away from where one experiences much of one's world— that is, in the context of human relations, those currently active and those remembered consciously and unconsciously. In clinical

---

[1] I agree with the appraisal of L. Friedman (personal communication) that, despite the experience-distant language employed, "the underlying thrust of the work of Hartmann and Rapaport was to open up the field to experience-near meanings that had not been previously elaborated."

practice, such a conceptual tilt is more apparent than real when the focus is on the transference. Thus, it can be argued that some of the objections to and revisions of this formulation have been directed more at a theoretical than at a clinical imbalance.

The Focus on Self and Object Relations

Numerous attempts have been made to correct this seeming imbalance while preserving some form of a structural hypothesis. Jacobson (1964) emphasizes intrapsychic representations of the self and object. Sandler and Rosenblatt (1962) propose a representational world. Melanie Klein (1952) describes an inner world of fantasy involving exchanges between self and good or bad part- or whole-objects. Mahler (1968) suggests the sequence of a practicing self moving to a separating and individuating self, and a cognitively impermanent object developing into an emotionally constant object. Kohut (1971) formulates a developmental sequence leading to cohesion of the self and internalization of idealized parental imagoes. Each of these proposals is at some variance with the others in terms of how much weight is given to the influence of constitutional factors (such as the strength of aggression or libido), to the impact of the child-parent interchange, and to the effect of perceptual-cognitive distortions resulting from developmental vicissitudes of drive strength and ego functions. Some of the theories derive object relations from drive-ego vicissitudes; some derive drive-ego vicissitudes from the outcome of the earliest object relations (Loewald, 1971; Kernberg, 1975). These issues have provided a valuable stimulus for an attempt to conceptualize and weigh causal factors in emotional illness.

Yet what the theoretician regards as the more important etiological factor in a given disturbance loses its immediate significance in the analytic setting. There, the analyst enters the experiential world of the patient, the patient's *subjective* state of mind. In the analysand's subjective state of mind, the analyst discovers only the record of the individual's attempts to adapt and adjust to positive and negative influences. It is a record that, through reconstruction, tells an individual developmental story, organized and reorganized in successive phases. In formulating causal explanations, the analytic theoretician makes inferences about data from many sources. In contrast, the analytic clinician, giving evenly hovering attention solely to the analysand's associations, perceives only the effect of the causal factors, in the analysand's subjective "readings" of his or her past and present experiential world. Within the treatment setting, the analyst of course attends to, as part of the meaningful communication of the patient's subjectivity, the analysand's own assessment and conviction of "actuality" and "objectivity" about what has influenced his or her development.

Clinical practice has always dealt straightforwardly with interactions between people, centering on the phenomenon of transference. Thus, the tilt in the theories of Jacobson, Sandler and Rosenblatt, Klein, Mahler, Kernberg, and Kohut, toward a self and object relations focus and away from a central focus on interactions between hypothetical structural organizations, in itself does not call for a redefinition of the curative agent. But, because each theory offers a different perspective on what is to be cured, each influences method profoundly. For the purposes of contrast and discussion, the differences in method can be characterized by *hypothetical* polar positions, designated as a confrontational approach and an empathic approach.

Confrontational Versus Empathic Approach

Roughly speaking, the theories that derive the source of pathology from the infant's presumed imperative need to cope with his or her own destructiveness (such as those of Klein, Kernberg, and, to a lesser degree, Mahler) channel the analyst toward a more confrontational approach. The theories that derive the source of pathology from presumed failures to master the challenges of libidinal development (such as those of A. Freud [1965] and Sandler and Rosenblatt [1962], as well as the theory of self psychology) channel the analyst toward a more empathic approach.

If the analyst's theoretical stance leads him or her to conceptualize the unfolding of the transference in terms of unresolved primitive envy, murderous rage, devaluating inclinations, or defensive idealization, then the analyst will quite logically attempt to convey to patients the nature of their aggressive urgency. This view in general holds that these manifestations of destructiveness unfold in layered modes, one used defensively to cover another. Under this stance, since the analyst must interpret to patients that they are making the analyst the inevitable target of their heightened aggression, it does not matter how neutral the analyst's actual emotional and ideological position—the analyst is, to the patients, a confronter. From the patients' point of view, having their communications labeled as expressing hostility, by someone with whom they already may regard as being in a struggle, may temporarily add presumed insult to injury. At the least, it will give a sense of lively actuality to the transferred world of a troubled past. According to proponents of this technical stance, however, the basic constructive communication between analyst and analysand is such that the correct distancing for interpretive work is assured. Through the interpretive confrontation, insight will be gained in each present analytic exchange about the nature of the struggle with aggression at the moment as well as its position in the layered defensive structure. An important basis for the curative effect, then, is the belief that, with insight into the nature of their aggressive inclinations and their distortions of the intentions of others, analysands will be able to recognize the inner signals of anger and rage—and take full personal responsibility for their failures and successes in this area. The flexible assertiveness and the ability to negotiate disagreements that a mature human requires are the anticipated results of the analysis.

Alternatively, if the analysand's pathology is believed to arise, not primarily from permutations of primitive aggression, but from a faulty attempt on the analysand's part to seek or give *love*, the analyst's neutrality may tilt toward a more sympathetic, less confrontational, trial identification with the analysand's wishes and their source in unfortunate infantile fixations. From this perspective, analysts see themselves as the inevitable target for the analysands' wishes for eroticized gratifications. Consequently, although they may respond with a distancing challenge, for the most part they will use nondistancing interpretations, which are easier to formulate for failures to love effectively than for continued destructiveness. For example, an interpretation that the patient's previously unconscious sexual desire toward his analyst is a rekindling of his boyhood desire to enjoy with his beloved mother what his excited little body craved, and what he envied his father for being able to enjoy, carries a wistful yearning. An affect of wistful yearning or some similar emotional sharing arises more easily in interpreting a frustrated effort to receive or give sensual affection than in interpreting a murderous impulse, and this affect may help to bridge the gap between the adult position of the appropriately nongratifying analyst and the infantile "demanding" of the analysand.

Neither widening nor lessening the gap between analyst and analysand is itself the goal of either approach, whether the focus is on aggressive-destructive or libidinal conflicts. Accuracy of analytic inference and interpretation is the aim. From both theoretical positions, the analyst through empathy in the form of intermittent trial identifications attempts to facilitate comprehension of oedipal and preoedipal conflicts. Insight into distortions that result from the unresolved conflicts is seen as the means for increasing the analysand's objectivity. Freed of such distortions, the analysand arrives at lasting change by using his or her understanding to modify previously inflexible patterns.

From a self-psychology perspective: If the analyst's theoretical stance emphasizes self pathology, resulting from failures of parental empathy, and regards the transference as primarily toward someone whose active responsiveness is felt as needed to bring forward retarded development, the understanding of this state *must be* from within the analysand's subjective reality of the moment-to-moment exchange (Lichtenberg, 1981a, 1983). This theoretical viewpoint makes it imperative that the analyst adopt a *consistently* empathic mode of perception from within the subjective world of the analysand rather than shifting between intermittent trial identifications and "outside" observation of distortions in "objectivity" and reality. The cure becomes inseparably interwoven with this mode of listening,[2] and with an ambiance marked by sympathetic understanding and responsiveness. The analysand's sense of being understood is seen as an essential foundation for the state of self cohesion that permits analytic progress and functional change. Interpretations formulated from the way the patient subjectively experiences the world may or, more often, may not be pleasing to the patient, but the sting is usually taken out by the reduced distance that results from the analyst's staying within the patient's immediate focus of affective and ideational interest.

In self psychology, which views pathological deficits in self structures as the result of empathic failures, the role of empathy has been ambiguous. Despite specific efforts to restrict the function of empathy in analysis to being a means to facilitate change by way of *information gathering,* empathy seems, from some of the clinical descriptions, to have become itself the *agent of change,* through "being empathic" (giving empathic responses). Self psychology has noted that it is precisely where the parent was perceived to have failed to mirror achievements or respond with closeness, that the analysand calls for the analyst to respond. A perceived failure of the analyst to respond leads to disturbances of the optimal cohesive intactness of the analysand's self state. In order to distinguish between giving empathic responses as such and interpreting the patient's experience of needing such responses, a theory of cure has been advanced, based on the building of structure through transmuting internalizations. According to this theory, brief, not-too-severe perceived failures of the analyst to provide a mirroring or confirming response allow precise recognition of the function called for by the patient from the analyst. The theory holds that this functioning of the analyst is required

---

[2]Schwaber (1981) has demonstrated that the empathic mode of listening is a technical approach that is applicable to analysis regardless of the theoretical stance employed to organize the data.

because, due to parental empathic failures, essential self structures did not form and the regulation of self-worth and the idealization of others remain at an archaic level. In the moment-to-moment analytic work, as the function called for from the analyst is recognized in shared, affectively meaningful words, but not directly provided by the analyst, it is then internalized by the patient as part of his or her psychic fabric.

I shall not enter into the arguments for and against this proposal, except to say that I am skeptical about it. I do not believe that analysands as a general rule build new basic structures in the course of analysis—whether by empathy or by insight. In those instances in which regulatory disturbances from early infancy persist (see Chapter 12 for examples), adult analysands develop compensatory means to adapt through relearned responses. I believe that in precisely those small moments that Kohut (1971, 1977) singled out, a significant past troubled *relationship* is reactivated (Lichtenberg, 1978b). The disturbance in this relationship (whether traumatic or, more commonly, extended over time) interfered with the consolidation of capacities at their optimal level of functioning. In other words, the individual has the capacity but lacks consistent access to its use. During analysis, the troubled relationship is reactivated. Because the tension this reactivation arouses occurs in a setting in which the painful alteration of the sense of self and the nuances of its meanings are being explored, regression to archaic need states is less likely to occur in response to the reactivated deprivation. Instead, a new balance in the expectation of assistance from others can be struck. The current empathic failure, when subjected to analysis in depth, often simply puts into a whole new perspective the meanings and motivations of the subjectively viewed disappointing parental person—now the analyst. In this way, the analysand may now regard people and circumstances with understanding and compassion, whereas previously his or her perspective was inflexibly restricted by the persistence of an infantile solipsistic viewpoint. This changed view allows for a readjustment of unconsciously determined, charged human interaction. As a consequence of these changed expectations in human interactions, the analysand's suspended or inaccessible functioning capacity becomes restored to fuller regulatory control. The data of analytic observation, I believe, support this view rather than the one that holds that a nonexistent functional capacity has been built *de novo*.

The moments in analysis of shared viewing of empathic failures and their effects constitute for the analysand a safe exposure of an authentic sense of self in a context of empathic intercommunication. In a more recent consideration of the therapeutic action of those moments of deep understanding that constitute empathic communication, Kohut has proposed that the analysand not only experiences the resonance between analyst and patient, but also learns to recognize these reassuring occurrences of optimal (incentive-stimulating) gratifications inside and outside the analysis. In this way, the analysand can alter his or her wariness and defensiveness, gaining considerably more flexibility in all his or her relations (E. Wolf, personal communication).

Before readdressing the questions about mental functioning, pathogenesis, and the therapeutic exchange, I should like to add a final comment on the dichotomy between a confrontational and an empathic approach. Although I believe my hypothesis of a polarization along the lines of an emphasis on confrontation or on empathy represents actual technical distinctions, the clinical differences may not be as exaggerated as might be inferred from the theories themselves or from clinical examples in the literature offered to illustrate the theories. Certainly, in confronting a patient about evidence of oral envy, an analyst can claim he or she is being empathic to the patient's state of mind and needs. On the other hand, any analytic interpretation of defense can be seen as confrontational from the patient's point of view. Moreover, the issue of empathy can be shifted in its focus from trial identifications to the way interpretations are phrased or the manner of the analyst's overall relating to the patient. In this regard, I believe that a false note may have entered a needed consideration of significant technical differences. Unfortunately, value judgments have equated empathy with kindness and confrontation with insensitivity. In addition, conceptual confusions have bedeviled the use of the very term "empathy."

As an example of this confusion, I will take the concept of "empathic mothering." A 20-month-old is called to eat by his mother. He continues to play with his blocks. A second, more imperative call leads to an active refusal. His mother takes the block out of his hand. In fury he hits his mother and knocks over the blocks he has assembled. After a heated moment between them, the boy's opposition wilts and he breaks into tears. His mother pulls him to her, soothing him against her breast. She then carries him to dinner, jollying him out of his sadness and sulkiness. Has she been empathic? The boy may well remember, possibly in the form of a merger fantasy, her breast, her soothing, and her jollying as providing a degree of satisfaction—a satisfaction that he will again seek from her and others. But what of the early confrontative moments? Will they be largely unconnected in his experience, separated off as bad moments from the later soothing—with the transition lost? If so, this would leave, as an unconnected memory, a sense of a relatively unresolved state of struggle, which, if repeated over and over, might leave a regulatory deficit in the ability assertively to negotiate disagreements. Was the mother, then, being empathic? The answer could be "yes," if a full understanding of the child's state of mind indicated that what that child needed at that moment was soothing into passivity and a sense of merger. The answer would be more "no" than "yes" if a full understanding of the child's state of mind indicated that what the child needed was only enough soothing to make the transition into a renewed, negotiating contact, followed by a verbal exchange about the regulation needed at dinner time. Such an interaction might provide an autonomy-building moment or two of refusal before compliance was expected.

To place this in an analytic context, let me first state again that, in analysis, the analyst's goal is not to act as an empathic mother, but to *understand* the wishes that characterize the revivals of such experiences in the transference. So the analyst would not try to do what the mother didn't do. The analyst would try to conceptualize the experience in terms of its meaning to the patient. On a microcosmic level, the analyst's tone and manner will inevitably move a bit toward responding in a way that the patient experiences as either soothing or confrontative—and either might be felt as correctly empathic. But the analysis is not the result of these microcosmic tilts of the analyst, whether experienced as empathically correct or not. The *analysis* lies in *understanding* their meaning and effect. Nevertheless, as I shall indicate, careful attention to the patient's way of perceiving the analyst does provide a unique source for understanding. The confusion here lies in the use of the term to mean "being empathic." In my approach, the term "empathy" has only one proper usage with respect to analytic technique: Empathy is a mode of perceiving the analysand's state of mind (Lichtenberg, 1981a; see also Schwaber, 1981). It is solely a means of acquiring information. The empathic mode of perception refers specifically to the analyst's *systematic* (rather than intermittent) attempt to listen and to discern conscious and unconscious configurations as though from within the mental state and perspective of the analysand.

A REVISED VIEW OF THE THERAPEUTIC PROCESS

I shall now wrestle with the perplexing questions of how the mind works, what is to be cured, and what the analyst-analysand exchange consists of. I regard the analysand (as well as the analyst) as an individual whose mind functions through a complex symbolic process involving two distinct perceptual-cognitive-affective organizations (McKinnon, 1979). One organization corresponds to what psychoanalysis has called secondary process; the other, to primary process. Each organization contributes a different cast to the individual's conscious, preconscious, and unconscious experience.

As I explained in Chapter 10, the *secondary-process* mode of organization applies the rules of linguistic syntax and logic. It governs human relationships that are characterized by separateness, objectivity, discreteness, social forms, and ritual. In analysis, the secondary-process organization governs those experiences in which the analysand's sense of self is of an individuated person dealing with a distinctly separated other person—the analyst. It operates in introspective associations based on monitoring, as objectively as possible, the state of one's bodily experience, or one's emotions and mental activity.

The *primary-process* mode of organization is characterized by the simultaneous integration of parts into a complex whole. Simultaneous presence is organized by means of displacement, in which one unit substitutes for another, and by means of condensation, in which there is a spatial collapse of multiple elements. In analysis, the primary-process mode governs situations in which the analysand experiences qualities, functions, and feelings of self and analyst as fluid and sharable (easily displaced or condensed), as well as situations in which emotions are experienced as generalized moods or global feeling states. It governs experiences in which pain or pleasure in one body part engulfs the whole sense of self. It is the source of those rare but memorable occasions when distinctions that produce puzzling disparities suddenly collapse into the integrative comprehension of the "Aha" experience.

Pointing to which type of experience reveals the working of each perceptual-cognitive-affective organization may have the disadvantage of lessening our appreciation of the remarkable way the two organizations function in concert. As I noted earlier, the approach by which the primary- and secondary-process organizations are identified is that of an external observer cataloguing separate components; from the viewpoint of the person's experience, the result of the workings of the organizations is a single entity. The integration of the two organizations permits us to retain from infancy a sensation-near mode of representation (the primary process), aided by the ambiguous and metaphoric properties of language, while simultaneously having at our disposal an organization for discursive treatment of experience (the secondary process), employing the subtle differences that denotative linguistic usage allows.

I regard what needs curing in analysis to be disturbances in one or another of three broadly defined experiential states (Lichtenberg, 1975). In one state, analysands experience themselves as separate and distinct from others (actual and intrapsychic). In this state, the disturbances center on the analysands' conscious and unconscious love and hate relationships, especially those characterized by peremptoriness, which have become rigidified, inflexible, and stereotyped. In a second state, analysands experience themselves as interacting with another person (actual or intrapsychic) whose responses are construed as so important to the regulation of a positive sense of self that the other person is experienced as an extension of the self. In this state, the disturbances center on the sense of self in relation to experiences of expansiveness, power, display, and idealization. In the third state, the central focus is on the analysands' bodily experiences. People and inanimate objects are experienced primarily as contributing to the successful regulation of bodily needs or as the source of relief of physical discomfort. These experiences range from the physiological appetitive, through the body-centeredness of the athlete or ballerina, to bodily experiences that are symbolic representatives of current or prior interpersonal interactions.

My concept of analytic therapy centers on the recognition and interpretation of the changing conscious and unconscious experiential states of the analysand. I therefore emphasize the systematic employment of the empathic mode of listening as the perceptual means by which the analyst attempts continuously to be in touch with the analysand's total state of mind. Using an empathic mode of perception, the analyst forms constructions by having his or her perceptions shift between what the analysand's associations reveal the analysand is experiencing in the foreground and in the background (Lichtenberg, 1981a, 1983). Again, by foreground, I mean the *immediate* content and meaning of the associations that the patient is relating. By background, I mean the more general status of the receptivity that the patient expects to receive from the analyst as a transference person or milieu. I give particular attention to symptomatic alterations in the analysand's sense of self and to his or her intentions, especially contradictory ones, as seen from the analysand's perspective. I try to follow patterns in each hour and in each sequence of hours that indicate subtle and gross fluctuations of the patient's way of sensing the analyst and the analytic milieu.

In speaking of an empathic mode of perception, it is useful to recognize that all perception is informed by positive and negative expectations: "Love looks not with the eyes, but with the mind" (Shakespeare, *A Midsummer Night's Dream,* Act 1, Scene 1). Freud (1909) took this factor into account when he noted that the analyst must "suspend" any prior judgment of the meaning of a symptom and instead give "impartial attention to everything that there is to observe" (p. 23; see also 1912, p. 112). Total impartial attention is, to my way of thinking, neither possible nor desirable. Rather, I believe the analyst's flexibly hovering attentiveness should be guided by two goals: (1) to remain as close as possible to the analysand's total state of mind, and (2) to use his or her knowledge of how to follow associations and how to recognize configurations of the unconscious in order to penetrate ever more deeply into the analysand's experiential world. The derivatives of the unconscious experiential realm that orient and guide the analyst may involve oedipal relationships; primal scene imagery; oral, anal, or phallic fantasy elaborations; self-state alterations; or separation-individuation crises. Whatever the form of these configurations of the unconscious, the analyst will view them as nearly as possible in close attunement to the analysand's own subjective way of sensing them. These familiar configurations should not be viewed from the perspective of a diagnostician making a relatively abstract assessment, or an analyst attending a case conference. Rather, they are to be regarded in the limited, immediate sense of the clinical setting. There an unconscious configuration is meaningfully empathically appreciated, and cognitively integrated, in the specific individual form in which it appears *within* the subjective feelings and thoughts of the analysand as he or she responds to the dynamic interchange of the analysis.

The theoretical position that underlies my approach is that, as the gateway to the patient's introspective awareness is gradually opened, what has been deeply unavailable, comes closer to preconscious and conscious awareness, and to empathic recognition and sharing by the analyst. In a successful analysis, one can anticipate an expanding awareness, over time, which will assure that the deeper unconscious moves continuously into greater availability. It is thus only what is relatively accessible to preconscious and conscious awareness that must be attended to by the analyst in each hour. From this perspective, awareness and interpretation of defenses have to do with expanding the realm of the analysand's intrapsychic communication, that is, the freedom of the analysand's inner observation and inner speech. The analysis of resistance has to do with expanding the realm of the analysand-analyst communication.

Using a focus on experience points toward a sequence for the interpretive effort of the analyst. Regarded overall, the aim of this sequence is to enable analysts to construct for themselves and their analysands an "observation platform" on which both can stand and perceive the data of the analyst's empathy and the analysand's introspection (Lichtenberg, 1981a, 1983). Interpretation itself occurs in stages back and forth between analyst and analysand. When the analyst, through empathic perception, is able to construct a verbally communicable understanding of the patient's immediate general state of mind, the analyst offers this initial bridging interpretation as a way of affirming and confirming the shared state of emotion-laden comprehension. This initial interpretation may refer to the analysand's overt or somewhat covert attempt at direct expression, or to a state of resistance and the motive for it. Especially with patients who maintain a persistent, often automatic conviction that their attempts to share will be met with disappointment, this initial interpretation can prevent chronic resistance against entry into more sensitive, personally invested material. Analysands who feel they have been successful in communicating a state of mind, and who experience the ambiance of the analysis as a sustaining alliance, may be more forthright in their observations about themselves. Rather than defensively disavowing aspects of a problem, they may assume and assert a higher degree of personal responsibility for it. Once able to recognize and communicate that their symptoms, behavioral disturbances, pathological wishes, etc., originate from their own choices (conscious or unconscious), analysands will often provide evidence in their associations of an alternative or variant (often potentially more normal) disavowed self—the loving, or tender, or energetic, or ambitious, or shy little child they once were. The analyst's discovery of this nascent alternative aspect of the self often opens the way to an understanding of a conflictual struggle-in-depth (current or developmental), which for the patient is often subjectively embedded in a perceived analyst-analysand or parent-child failure.

During those moments when analysands respond to feeling understood and to having their experiences articulated, they will provide associations from a perspective of working within a dialogue, with a shared aim of analyzing or exploring a feeling state, symptom, dream, or puzzling transaction. At these times, the analyst often has a rather unique experience, involving rapid shifts in vantage point. The analyst may fleetingly establish a mental scene in which, like an outside observer, he or she visualizes an affectively charged experience, fantasy, dream, or sensation the patient is describing. The analyst's empathy may shift between the patient and the others involved. The analyst's attention may then fall on how the analysand is experiencing the analyst, even though the patient's focus does not seem to be on the transference. The analyst's quickly oscillating attentiveness may again shift to his or her own response to the shared closeness. At times the analyst may move away from the more emotional side of empathy or introspection and suddenly see, from the shared platform, a whole vista of the experience of the hour, the prior hours, and the already-made reconstructions of the past. From this sudden coming together, the analyst may construct a new set of integrations. This new formulation will facilitate the analyst's ability to subject the problem to a deeper, more penetrating inquiry. This process illustrates the optimal unity of the analyst's primary- and secondary-process functioning. The analyst may then be prepared to offer the new formulation to the patient. To do so, however, the analyst will first return to a state of intuneness with the patient's state of mind, in order to get clues as to the optimal timing and phrasing of the interpretation.

A description of this technical approach requires detailed clinical illustration (see Lichtenberg, 1981b, 1983). Rather than a step-by-step illustration of the successful application of empathic perception, I shall offer a brief vignette involving a disturbance in my listening stance. This description of my effort to understand analytically the meaning of my altered empathic attentiveness may be suggestive of my approach.

Mr. A was a patient with whom I'd perceived unusual difficulty in carrying out my intent to systematically utilize an empathic mode of perception. In the middle phase of his analysis, I felt reasonably able to follow his associations from within his perspective for the first 10 or 15 minutes of the hour, during which he would report significant events or dreams. Then my attention would drift off. My attempts to analyze this persistent loss of resonating attentiveness failed to relate it to any conflictual response on my part to the content of his associations or to him personally. During one hour, I associated my attentional drift to how I felt when I sat with my children watching a TV show in which I had only a distant interest—I would attend to it enough to talk about it with them, but otherwise I would think my own thoughts. Within a few moments, Mr. A mentioned (as he had previously) that when he came home after work he turned the TV on, made dinner, and the evening drifted away without his getting to work on his long overdue tax-refund claim. Cued by my association, I asked him about his reference to turning on the TV. He described a state of mind in which he would begin to listen to the news and then the TV would become a general background blur, which he would tune in and out of his awareness. His girlfriend had complained about it but had become used to it.

Once this drifting state of mind came into focus for us, we were able to relate it to his use of drinking and pot smoking—not to enhance his experience (as he had claimed), but to produce this sense of being with another in a state of remoteness and drift. Stimulated by dream images of furniture placement in his childhood apartment, he began to recall a seemingly innocuous scene, which served as a nodal point for the reconstruction of significant relationships and their intrapsychic effect on him. In this scene, he was sprawled out on the floor with the TV on in front of him. His mother was sitting behind him, on the other side of the room, knitting or reading. His father had gone to work, leaving him, as he saw it, to keep his lonely, depressed mother company. In desultory fashion, he was watching TV while flipping a rope, imagined to be a cowboy's lariat, over a chair. There was no conversation between himself and his mother; the only sounds were the TV. His attention was dominated by anger-filled fantasies of heroic battles. A mood of depressed remoteness, irritability, and mutual withholding characterized the exchange. The analysis of this scene provided welcome entry into the transference relationship that had developed in such a puzzling fashion. This analytic work then provided the leverage for change in many of his conflictual pulls.

This vignette illustrates, I believe, the value for the analyst of a systematic attempt to maintain an empathic mode of perception and to monitor any disturbance in the use of the analyst's listening instrument. It also reveals the by-play of the analyst and analysand's primary- and secondary-process modes of perceptual-cognitive-affective organization, and the search for configurations that permit matching and the establishment of a common observational platform and field. Finally, it shows the movement into the foreground of a background state of mind—in this case, the sense of interactional remoteness that in the background acted as an unconscious resistance, but in the foreground provided key associational material. What it does not illustrate is the systematic, moment-by-moment application of the empathic mode of perception for information gathering, and the use of this information in an expanding pattern of interpretation.

A CONCLUDING VIEW

Now I shall attempt to pull together the strands of my presentation and sketch in the outline of an experiential conception of what is curative in psychoanalysis. As it has been traditionally portrayed, the total experience that constitutes a successful psychoanalysis derives from the relationship between analyst and analysand, and the insight that evolves from it. Many accounts give greater or lesser importance to the relationship or to insight; others regard the two as equally important, clearly distinguishable components. Although it is generally agreed that neither the relationship nor insight alone can be curative, I believe their curative power evolves from their unique experiential interaction, rather than being the simple sum of the parts.

The partners in the relationship do not gather to have a relationship; they gather to effect a positive change in the analysand through understanding in depth the nature of some problem (or problems). But to conclude simply that this shared goal to work on, with, and "through" a problem via understanding makes cure possible through insight alone would miss the nature of the unique interaction that characterizes the analysis. However much at any particular moment analyst and analysand share a goal of understanding the nature of a problem, their differing perspectives will lead to the emergence of divergent motives. Each is under strains that as they interact provide the major dynamic leverage of the treatment (see Friedman, 1982).

The analysand will be under all the strains and tensions brought to the analysis as a consequence of the full accumulation of unresolved regulatory disturbances and conflicts from the past. In the analysis, the analysand will feel pulled toward an internally obligatory (and analytically necessary) full expression of his or her perceived needs and wishes—as an immediate "demand." At the same time the analysand will be drawn by the desire to comply with the goal shared with the analyst, to confine action and interaction to exploring meanings.

Similarly, the strains on the analyst have interactional and historical origins. In the interaction, the analyst must sense the analysand's wishes and needs as well as his or her own subjective inclinations in response to them; but the analyst must perforce restrain a direct reaction and instead organize the response to further the goal of exploring meanings. In trying to explore the meanings of the information the patient is communicating, the analyst is pulled toward an ideal of being free from preconceptions so as to be fully responsive to the individuality of the patient's experience. At the same time, as an analyst, he or she shares in a tradition based on the inspiration of Freud's case histories and clinical writings. To these, the analyst has added the explications of typical developmental crises formulated by one or more of the analytic schools. These known configurations serve as indispensable guides organizing the seemingly infinite variety of data. A tension is thus set up for the analyst in shifting between maximal immersion in the particular analysand's immediate state of mind and use of a more removed cognitive level to achieve matching of patterns.

The analytic relationship is therefore constituted by varying degrees of strain at the junction of the activities of two people, each of whom is simultaneously under varying degrees of internal tension. As a result of the shifting strain, the analysand produces associations that provide the basic information of the analysis. Through empathy and immersion into that information, and guided by an introspective understanding of his or her own tensions, the analyst learns about its meanings and conveys this to the patient through constructions and interpretations. However, achieving conscious awareness of unconscious configurations by means of pattern matching does not, in itself, constitute the most significant informational exchange. These patterns have meaning only as they apply to a context in a relationship. A unique feature of analysis is that the shifting strains at the junction of the analysand's and analyst's activities create a relational exchange, one that calls for definition and a comprehensible set of emotion-laden meanings. Thus, the relationship between analyst and analysand provides more than the working basis for the analysis; its shifting strains provide crucial data, from which the most significant aspects of understanding are derived.

An experiential vantage point is necessary to follow my reasoning. In the initial phase of analysis, a point of entry into the analysand's state of mind might be the success or failure of the analysand's effort to convey his or her experience of the ups and downs of the engagement itself. Another point of entry might be the analyst's empathic effort to sense the meaning of the analysand's eagerness or resistance to engage in the relationship, the calming or excitement that accompanies this, and so on. Throughout the analysis, all the experiences I have referred to as curative in one or another theory can be regarded as momentarily lessening the strain at the working junction. Because of the sense of benefit that results, they can provide a source for further understanding as the meaning of this effect itself is explored. A listing in summary fashion of analytic effects that have been regarded as curative includes: the experience of catharsis or abreaction, the sense of being empathically understood, a linking of a current unconscious wish to its source in childhood that leads to renunciation of the wish and a shift in goals, repair of a fragmented sense of the continuity of life experience, exposure of a vulnerability to idiosyncratic perceptual readings, the feeling of rich insight that replaces painful mystification, recognition of a disturbance in regulation of sleep or eating or excitement that allows for remedial action, and a successful confrontation that leads to a greater sense of autonomy and clears the air. Each of these beneficial effects, when it occurs during the analysis, can be understood in the context of the reduced strain in the analyst-analysand relationship. Yet these instances of beneficial experience do not provide the critical dynamic force leading to analytic cure. Rather, the *impetus* for change comes from the gross to partial failures that precede the successes. These failures force attention on understanding the nature of the problem areas.

Gross failures occur when analysands' messages are so unknown to themselves (dynamically unconscious) and they have so much to work against in their habitual self-obscuring (unconscious defense) that their communications are obscure, strained, and repetitious. The analyst's attempt at empathic perception meets this barrier. For a time the analyst's attention may focus on a sense of frustration based on mutual noncomprehension. Feeling frustrated and uncertain, the analyst may need to resist a possible inclination to rely on theory to effect a premature closure, before gaining access to the full inner experience of the patient. As in the case of the patient who, so to speak, had turned himself off and the TV on, neither making nor expecting meaningful communication, the analyst and analysand must constantly struggle to find each other in such situations. When analyst and analysand (largely through verbal exchanges, augmented at times by nonverbal signals) begin to bridge the gap, the recognition of the analysand's inner state by both partners is communicated in exchanges that are commonly partial failures. The back-and-forth activity by both partners to explore and negotiate these partial failures, occurring in the context of efforts to bridge, is, I believe, the most important analog between the process of analysis and the process of normal development.

In normal development, the child's growth, exemplified in shifting needs and increasing capacities, is facilitated by the caretakers' efforts to bridge gaps in their divergent motives. The divergent motives of child and parent produce strain. The effort to reduce this strain through empathic understanding and appropriate responses, first by the parent and later by both, brings the two together. The sharing that results is the context in which the growth process prospers. The value of this analogy for psychoanalysis is that we can identify what promotes a curative experience. Similarly, through the remarkable neonatal and infancy studies I have reviewed, we learn what potentiates and what interferes with normal development. But the essential process by which cure occurs is in continuity with growth and, like it, unknown—and experientially unknowable.

In summary, the analytic "cure" comes about as the result of an inherent process of growth, facilitated by a sequence of intrapsychic activities, communicated primarily through verbal exchanges (free association and interpretation). At one moment the analyst uses the empathic mode of perception and the patient uses introspection to place, in a meaningful relational context, some foreground information provided by the analysand's associations (such as a fight with a spouse). At another moment the analysand's subjective sense of reducing or intensifying of the strain at the working junction, brought about by success or partial failure in understanding, may become the focus for the further work. What happens in the relationship makes inquiry necessary, and success possible; the successful and unsuccessful search for meaning facilitates the study of the relationship in its conscious and unconscious, current and transferential forms. It is the combination of the unique interaction of a relationship with tension at its junction and the joint search for meaning that constitute the analysis, or rather, that constitute the curative experience that a successful analysis is.

References

Abelin, B. (1977), The role of the father in core gender identity and in psychosexual differentiation. Presented at meeting of American Psychoanalytic Association, Quebec, May.

Ablon, S., & Mack, J. (1980), Children's dreams reconsidered. *The Psychoanalytic Study of the Child,* 35:179-218. New Haven: Yale University Press.

Agosta, L. (1983), Empathy and intersubjectivity. In: *Empathy,* ed. J. Lichtenberg, M. Bornstein, & D. Silver. Hillsdale, N.J.: Analytic Press.

Ainsworth, M. D. (1979), Attachment as related to mother-infant interaction. In: *Advances in the Study of Behavior,* ed. J. B. Rosenblatt, R. A. Hinde, C. Beer, & M. Bushel. New York: Academic Press, pp. 1-51.

——— & Bell, (1969), Some contemporary patterns of mother-infant interaction in the feeding situation. In: *Stimulation in Early Infancy,* ed. A. Ambrose. London: Academic Press, pp. 133-170.

Aleksandrowicz, M., & Aleksandrowicz, D. (1976), Precursors of ego in neonates. *J. Amer. Acad. Child Psychiat.,* 15:257-268.

Amsterdam, B., & Levitt, M. (1980), Consciousness of self and painful self-consciousness. *The Psychoanalytic Study of the Child,* 35:67-84. New Haven: Yale University Press.

Arlow, J. (1963), Conflict, regression, and symptom formation. *Int. J. Psychoanal.,* 44:12-22.

Barnett, C., Leiderman, P., Grobstein, R., & Klaus, M. (1970), Neonatal separation: Maternal side of interactional deprivation. *Pediatrics,* 46:197-205.

Basch, M. F. (1975), Toward a theory that encompasses depression: A revision of existing causal hypotheses in psychoanalysis. In: *Depression and Human Existence,* ed. E. J. Anthony & T. Benedek. Boston: Little, Brown, pp. 485-534.

——— (1976), The concept of affect: A re-examination. *J. Amer. Psychoanal. Assn.,* 24:759-778.

——— (1977), Developmental psychology and explanatory theory in psychoanalysis. *The Annual of Psychoanalysis,* 5:229-266. New York: International Universities Press.

——— (1981), Psychoanalytic interpretation and cognitive transformation. *Int. J. Psychoanal.,* 62:151-176.

Beebe, B., & Sloate, P. (1982), Assessment and treatment in mother-infant attunement in the first three years of life: A case history. *Psychoanal. Inquiry,* 1:601-624.

_____ & Stern, D. (1977), Engagement-disengagement and early object experiences. In: *Communicative Structures and Psychic Structures,* ed. M. Freedman & S. Grand. New York: Plenum Press, pp. 35–55.

Bell, R. Q. (1975), A congenital contribution to emotional response in early infancy and the preschool period. In: *Parent-Infant Interaction* (CIBA Foundation Symposium 33). New York: Elsevier, pp. 201–212.

Bennett, S. (1976), Infant-caretaker interactions. In: *Infant Psychiatry,* ed. E. Rexford, L. Sander, & A. Shapiro. New Haven: Yale University Press, pp. 79–90.

Blum, H. P. (1978), Symbolic processes and symbol formation. *Int. J. Psychoanal.,* 59:455–471.

Bower, T. (1971), The object in the world of the infant. *Sci. Amer.,* 225:30–38.

_____ (1976), Receptive process in child development. *Sci. Amer.,* 235:38–47. 38–47.

Bowlby, J. (1969), *Attachment and Loss,* Vol. 1: *Attachment.* New York: Basic Books.

Brazelton, T. B. (1973), *Neonatal Behavioral Assessment Scale* (National Spastics Society Monograph). London: Heinemann.

_____ (1980a), Neonatal assessment. In: *The Course of Life: Psychoanalytic Contributions toward Understanding Personality Development,* Vol. 1: *Infancy and Early Childhood,* ed. S. I. Greenspan & G. H. Pollock. Rockville, Md.: NIMH, pp. 203–234.

_____ (1980b), New knowledge about the infant from current research: Implications for psychoanalysis. Presented at meeting of American Psychoanalytic Association, San Francisco, May 3.

_____ & Als, H. (1979), Four early stages in the development of mother-infant interaction. *The Psychoanalytic Study of the Child,* 34:349–371. New Haven: Yale University Press.

_____, Trolnick, E., Adamson, L., Als, H., & Wise, S. (1975), Early mother-infant reciprocity. In: *Parent-Infant Interaction* (Ciba Foundation Symposium). New York: Associated Scientific Publishers.

Brenner, C. (1974), On the nature and development of affects: A unified theory. *Psychoanal. Quart.,* 43:532–556.

Bridger, W. (1961), Sensory habituation and discrimination in the human infant. *J. Amer. Psychiat. Assn.,* 118:991–996.

Brody, S. (1982), Psychoanalytic theories of infant development and its disturbances: A critical evaluation. *Psychoanal. Quart.,* 51:526–597.

Brooks, J., & Lewis, M. (1976), Visual self recognition in infancy: Contingency and the self-other distinction. Presented at Southeastern Conference on Human Development, Nashville, April.

_____ _____ (1974), Infants' responses to pictures of self, mother and other. Princeton: Educational Testing Service, No. 100 (unpublished).

Brooks-Gunn, J., & Lewis, M. (1979), Infant social perception: Responses to pictures of parents and strangers. Princeton: Educational Testing Service, No. 215 (unpublished).

Broucek, F. (1979), Efficacy in infancy: A review of some experimental studies and their possible implications for clinical theory. *Int. J. Psycho-Anal.,* 60: 311-316.

———— (1982), Shame and its relationship to early narcissistic developments. *Int. J. Psychoanal.,* 65:369-378.

Bruner, J., & Sherwood, V. (1980), Thought, language, and interaction in infancy. Presented at First World Congress on Infant Psychiatry, Portugal, March 30-April 3.

Bühler, K. (1930), *Kindheit und Jugend.* Leipzig: Hirzel.

Call, J. (1980), Some prelinguistic aspects of language development. *J. Amer. Psychoanal. Assn.,* 28:259-290.

———— & Marschak, (1976), Styles and games in infancy. In: *Infant Psychiatry,* ed. E. Rexford, L. Sander, & A. Shapiro. New Haven: Yale University Press, pp. 104-112.

Carpenter, G. (1974), Mother's face and the newborn. *New Scientist,* 61:742.

————, Tecce, J., Stechler, G., & Friedman, S. (1970), Differential visual behavior to human and humanoid faces in early infancy. *Merrill-Palmer Quart.,* 16:91-108.

Cobliner, W. (1968), Appendix: The Geneva School of Genetic Psychology and psychoanalysis: Parallels and counterparts. In: *The First Year of Life,* by R. Spitz. New York: International Universities Press, pp. 301-356.

Condon, W. S. (1977), A primary phase in the organization of infant responding. In: *Studies in Mother-Infant Interaction,* ed. H. R. Schaffer. New York: Academic Press, pp. 153-176.

———— & Sander, L. (1974), Neonate movement is synchronized with adult speech. *Science,* 183:99-101.

Décarie, T. G. (1962), *Intelligence and Affectivity in Early Childhood.* New York: International Universities Press, 1965.

Demos, V. (1982), Affect in early infancy: Physiology or psychology. *Psychoanal. Inquiry,* 1:533-574.

Dowling, S. (1977), Seven infants with esophageal astresia: A developmental study. *Psychoanalytic Study of the Child,* 32:215-256. New Haven: Yale University Press.

———— (1982), Dreams and dreaming in relation to trauma in childhood. *Int. J. Psychoanal.,* 63:157-166.

Emde, R. N. (1980), Toward a psychoanalytic theory of affect. In: *The Course of Life: Psychoanalytic Contributions toward Understanding Personality Development,* Vol. 1: *Infancy and Early Childhood,* ed. S. I. Greenspan & G. H. Pollock. Rockville, Md.: NIMH, pp. 63-112.

———— (1981a), Changing models of infancy and the nature of early development: Remodeling the foundation. *J. Amer. Psychoanal. Assn.,* 29:179-219.

_____ (1981b), Presented to Interdisciplinary Colloquium on Infant Research, American Psychoanalytic Association, New York, December.

_____, Gaensbauer, T., & Harmon, R. (1976), *Emotional Expression in Infancy: A Biobehavioral Study (Psychol. Issues,* Monogr. 37). New York: International Universities Press.

_____, _____, Metcalf, D., Koenig, K., & Wagonfeld, S. (1971), Stress and neonatal sleep. *Psychosom. Med.,* 33:491–497.

_____ & Robinson, J. (1979), The first two months: Recent research in developmental psychobiology and the changing view of the newborn. In: *Basic Handbook of Child Psychiatry,* Vol. 1, ed. J. Noshpitz. New York: Basic Books, pp. 72–105.

Engel, G. (1962), Anxiety and depression-withdrawal: The primary affects of unpleasure. *Int. J. Psycho-Anal.,* 43:89–97.

_____ (1979), Monica: A 25-year longitudinal study of the consequences of trauma in infancy. Presented at meeting of the American Psychoanalytic Association,

Erikson, E. H. (1950), Growth and crises of the "healthy personality." In: *The Healthy Personality,* Suppl. 2. Caldwell, N.J.: Progress Associates.

_____ (1959), *Identity and the Life Cycle (Psychol. Issues,* Monogr. 1). New York: International Universities Press.

Fantz, R. (1961), The origin of form perception. *Sci. Amer.,* 204:66–84.

Fast, I. (1979), Developments in gender identity: Gender differentiation in girls. *Int. J. Psychoanal.,* 60:443–453.

Field, T., Woodson, R., Greenberg, R., & Cohen, D. (1982), Discrimination and imitation of facial expressions by neonates. *Science,* 218:179–181.

Flavell, J. (1963), *The Developmental Psychology of Jean Piaget.* Princeton, N.J.: Van Nostrand.

Fox, R., & McDaniel, C. (1982), The perception of biological motion by human infants. *Science,* 218:486–487.

Fraiberg, S. (1969), Libidinal object constancy and mental representation. *The Psychoanalytic Study of the Child,* 24:9–47. New York: International Universities Press.

_____ (1971), Smiling and stranger reaction in blind infants. In: *Exceptional Infant,* Vol. 2: *Studies in Abnormalities,* ed. J. Hellmuth. New York: Brunner/ Mazel, pp. 110–127.

_____ (1974), Blind infants and their mothers: An examination of the sign system. In: *The Effect of the Infant on Its Caregiver,* ed. M. Lewis & L. Rosenblum. New York: Wiley-Interscience.

_____ & Freedman, D. (1964), Studies in the ego development of the congenitally blind child. *The Psychoanalytic Study of the Child,* 19:113–169. New York: International Universities Press.

Frankel, S., & Sherick, I. (1977), Observations on the development of normal envy. *The Psychoanalytic Study of the Child,* 32:257–282. New Haven: Yale University Press.

Freud, A. (1936), *The Ego and the Mechanisms of Defense.* New York: International Universities Press, 1946.

———— (1965), *Normality and Pathology in Childhood.* New York: International Universities Press.

Freud, S. (1895), Project for a scientific psychology. *Standard Edition,* 1:295–387. London: Hogarth Press, 1966.

———— (1905), Three essays on the theory of sexuality. *Standard Edition,* 7:135–243. London: Hogarth Press, 1953.

———— (1909), Analysis of a phobia in a five-year-old boy. *Standard Edition,* 10:3–152. London: Hogarth Press, 1955.

———— (1912), Recommendations to physicians practicing psycho-analysis. *Standard Edition,* 12:109–120. London: Hogarth Press, 1958.

———— (1915), Repression. *Standard Edition,* 14:146–158. London: Hogarth Press, 1957.

———— (1926), Inhibitions, symptoms and anxiety. *Standard Edition,* 20:87–172. London: Hogarth Press, 1959.

Friedman, L. (1980), The barren prospect of a representational world. *Psychoanal. Quart.,* 49:215–233.

———— (1982), How does the analyst know what's what? Presented to Baltimore–D.C. Society for Psychoanalysis, April 17.

Galenson, E., & Roiphe, H. (1974), The emergence of genital awareness during the second year of life. In: *Sex Differences in Behavior,* ed. R. Friedman, R. Richart, & R. Van-de Wides. New York: Wiley, pp. 223–231.

Gay, E., & Hyson, M. (1976), Blankets, bears, and bunnies: Studies of children's contacts with treasured objects. In: *Psychoanalysis and Contemporary Science,* Vol. 5, ed. T. Shapiro. New York: International Universities Press, pp. 271–316.

Gedo, J. E. (1979), *Beyond Interpretation: Toward a Revised Theory for Psychoanalysis.* New York: International Universities Press.

Gill, M. M. (1963), *Topography and Systems in Psychoanalytic Theory (Psychol. Issues,* Monogr. 10). New York: International Universities Press.

Glauber, I. P. (1982), Dysautomatization: A disorder of preconscious ego functioning. In: *Stuttering—A Psychoanalytic Understanding,* ed. H. M. Glauber. New York: Human Sciences Press.

Goldberg, A. (1983), Self psychology and alternative perspectives on internalization. In: *Reflections on Self Psychology,* ed. J. Lichtenberg & S. Kaplan. Hillsdale, N.J.: Analytic Press.

Goldberg, S., & Lewis, M. (1969), Play behavior in the year-old infant: Early sex differences. *Child Devel.,* 40:21–31.

Graves, P. (1980), The functioning fetus. In: *The Course of Life: Psychoanaytic*

Contributions toward Understanding Personality Development, Vol. 1: *Infancy and Early Childhood,* ed. S. I. Greenspan & G. H. Pollock. Rockville, Md.: NIMH, pp. 235–256.

Greenacre, P. (1941), The predisposition to anxiety. In: *Trauma, Growth, and Personality.* New York: International Universities Press, 1952, pp. 27–52.

———— (1954), Problems of infantile neurosis: A discussion. *The Psychoanalytic Study of the Child,* 9:18–24. New York: International Universities Press.

Greenspan, S. I. (1979), *Intelligence and Adaptation (Psychol. Issues,* Monogr. 47/48). New York: International Universities Press.

———— (1981), *Psychopathology and Adaptation in Infancy and Early Childhood (Clinical Infant Reports,* No. 1). New York: International Universities Press.

———— (1982), Three levels of learning: A developmental approach to "awareness" and mind-body relations. *Psychoanal. Inquiry,* 1:659–694.

Hales, D., Losoff, B., Sosa, R., & Kennell, J. (1977), Defining the limits of the maternal sensitive period. *Devel. Med. Child Neurol.,* 19:454–461.

Hartmann, H. (1933), An experimental contribution to the psychology of obsessive-compulsive neurosis: On remembering completed and uncompleted tasks. In: *Essays on Ego Psychology.* New York: International Universities Press, 1964, pp. 404–418.

———— (1939), *Ego Psychology and the Problem of Adaptation.* New York: International Universities Press, 1958.

———— (1956), Notes on the reality principle. In: *Essays on Ego Psychology.* New York: International Universities Press, 1964, pp. 241–267.

———— (1964), *Essays on Ego Psychology.* New York: International Universities Press.

————, Kris, E., & Loewenstein, R. M. (1946), Comments on the formation of psychic structure. In: *Papers on Psychoanalytic Psychology (Psychol. Issues,* Monogr. 14). New York: International Universities Press, 1964, pp. 27–55.

———— ———— ———— (1964), *Papers on Psychoanalytic Psychology (Psychol. Issues,* Monogr. 14). New York: International Universities Press.

Hendrick, I. (1942), Instinct and the ego during infancy. *Psychoanal. Quart.,* 2.

Herzog, J. (1980), Sleep disturbance and father hunger in 18- to 20-month-old boys: The Erlkonig syndrome. *The Psychoanalytic Study of the Child,* 35:219–236. New Haven: Yale University Press.

Holt, R. R. (1967), The development of the primary process. In: *Motives and Thought (Psychol. Issues,* Monogr. 18/19), ed. R. R. Holt. New York: International Universities Press, pp. 344–383.

Inhelder, B., & Piaget, J. (1955), *The Growth of Logical Thinking from Childhood to Adolescence.* New York: Basic Books, 1958.

Izard, C. (1977), *Human Emotions.* New York: Plenum Press.

Jacobs, T. (1973), Posture, gesture and movement in the analyst: Cues to interpretation and countertransference. *J. Amer. Psychoanal. Assn.*, 21:77–92.

Jacobson, E. (1964), *The Self and the Object World*. New York: International Universities Press.

James, W. (1890), *Principles of Psychology*. New York: Dover, 1950.

Jones, J. (1981), Affects: A nonsymbolic information processing system. Unpublished manuscript.

Kagan, J., Kearsley, R., & Zelazo, P. (1978), *Infancy: Its Place In Human Development*. Cambridge, Mass.: Harvard University Press.

Kaufman, I. (1976), Developmental considerations of anxiety and depression: Psychobiological studies in monkeys. *Psychoanalysis and Contemporary Science*, Vol. 5, ed. T. Shapiro. New York: International Universities Press, pp. 317–366.

Keiser, S. (1977), Discussion group: Reconstruction and unconscious fantasy in psychoanalytic treatment.

Kennell, J., Gordon, D., & Klaus, M. (1970), The effect of early mother-infant separation on later maternal performance. *Pedia. Res.,* 4:473–474.

Kernberg, O. F. (1975), *Borderline Conditions and Pathological Narcissism*. New York: Aronson.

———— (1976), *Object Relations Theory and Clinical Psychoanalysis*. New York: Aronson.

Klaus, M. H. et al. (1972), Maternal attachment: The importance of the first postpartum days. *New Eng. J. Med.,* 286:460–463.

Kleeman, J. (1973), The peek-a-boo game: Its evolution and associated behavior, especially bye-bye and shame expression, during the second year. *J. Amer. Acad. Child Psychiat.,* 12:1–23.

———— (1975), Genital self-stimulation in infant and toddler girls. In: *Masturbation: From Infancy to Senescence,* ed. I. Marcus & J. Francis. New York: International Universities Press, pp. 77–106.

Klein, M. (1952), *Development in Psycho-Analysis,* ed. J. Riviere. London: Hogarth Press.

Kohut, H. (1971), *The Analysis of the Self*. New York: International Universities Press.

———— (1977), *The Restoration of the Self*. New York: International Universities Press.

———— (1980), Reflections. In: *Advances in Self Psychology,* ed. A. Goldberg. New York: International Universities Press, pp. 473–554.

———— (1983), Selected problems of self psychological theory. In: *Reflections on Self Psychology,* ed. J. Lichtenberg & S. Kaplan. Hillsdale, N.J.: Analytic Press.

Korner, A. (1973), Sex differences in newborns with special reference to differences in the organization of oral behavior. *J. Child Psychol. Psychiat.,* 14: 19–29.

_____ (1974), The effect of the infant's state, level of arousal, sex and onto-genetic stage on the caregiver. In: *The Effect of the Infant on Its Caregiver,* ed. M. Lewis & L. Rosenblum. New York: Wiley-Interscience, pp. 105–121.

_____, & Thoman, (1970), Visual alertness in neonates as evoked by maternal care. *J. Exp. Child. Psychol.,* 10:67–78.

Krystal, H. (1974), The genetic development of affects and affect regression. *The Annual of Psychoanalysis,* 2:98–126. New York: International Universities Press.

_____ (1979), Alexithymia and psychotherapy. *Amer. J. Psychother.,* 33:17–31.

La Barre, W. (1978), Freudian biology, magic, and religion. *J. Amer. Psychoanal. Assn.,* 26:813–830.

Langer, S. K. (1951), *Philosophy in a New Key,* 2nd Ed. Cambridge, Mass.: Harvard University Press.

Laplanche, J., & Pontalis, J.-B. (1967), *The Language of Psycho-Analysis.* New York: Norton, 1973.

Lester, E., Rep. (1982), Panel: New directions in affect theory. *J. Amer. Psychoanal. Assn.,* 30:197–212.

Lewin, B. (1950), *The Psychoanalysis of Elation.* New York: Norton.

Lewis, M., & Brooks-Gunn, J. (1979), *Social Cognition and the Acquisition of Self.* New York: Plenum Press.

Lichtenberg, J. (1975), The development of the sense of self. *J. Amer. Psychoanal. Assn.,* 23:413–484.

_____ (1978a), The testing of reality from the standpoint of the body self. *J. Amer. Psychoanal. Assn.,* 26:357–385.

_____ (1978b), Transmuting internalization and developmental change. Presented to Psychology of Self Conference, Chicago.

_____ (1979), Factors in the development of the sense of the object. *J. Amer. Psychoanal. Assn.,* 27:375–386.

_____ (1981a), The empathic mode of perception and alternative vantage points for psychoanalytic work. *Psychoanal. Inquiry,* 1:329–356.

_____ (1981b), Implications for psychoanalytic theory of research on the neonate. *Int. Rev. Psychoanal.,* 8:35–52.

_____ (1982a), Categories of aggression and frames of reference within which to view them. *Psychoanal. Inquiry,* 2:213–231.

_____ (1982b), Continuities and transformations between infancy and adolescence. In: *Adolescent Psychiatry,* Vol. 10, ed. Fernstein, Looney, Schwartzberg, & Sorosky, pp. 182–198.

_____ (1982c), Reflections on the first year of life. *Psychoanal. Inquiry,* 1:695–730.

_____ (1983), An application of the self-psychological viewpoint to psychoanalytic technique. In: *Reflections in Self Psychology,* ed. J. Lichtenberg & S. Kaplan. Hillsdale, N.J.: Analytic Press.

————, & Pao, P.-N. (1974), Delusion fantasy and desire. *Int. J. Psychoanal.*, 55:273–281.

————, & Slap, J. (1971), On the defensive organization. *Int. J. Psychoanal.*, 52:451–457.

———— ———— (1972), On the defense mechanism: A survey and synthesis. *J. Amer. Psychoanal. Assn.*, 20:776–792.

———— ———— (1973), Notes on the concept of splitting and the defense mechanism of splitting of representations. *J. Amer. Psychoanal. Assn.*, 21:772–787.

———— ———— (1977), Comments on the general functioning of the analyst in the psychoanalytic situation. *The Annual of Psychoanalysis*, 5:295–312. New York: International Universities Press.

Loewald, H. (1971), On motivation and instinct theory. *The Psychoanalytic Study of the Child*, 26:91–128. New York: Quadrangle.

———— (1978), Instinct theory, object relations and psychic-structure information. *J. Amer. Psychoanal. Assn.*, 26:493–506.

London, N. (1981), The play element of regression in the psychoanalytic process. *Psychoanalytic Inquiry*, 1:7–28.

Lustman, S. (1957), Psychic energy and the mechanism of defense. *The Psychoanalytic Study of the Child*, 12:157–165. New York: International Universities Press.

MacFarlane, J. (1975), In: *Parent-Infant Interaction* (Ciba Foundation Symposium 33). New York: Elsevier, pp. 103–118.

Mahler, M. S. (1967), On human symbiosis and vicissitudes of individuation. *J. Amer. Psychoanal. Assn.*, 15:740–763.

———— (1968), *On Human Symbiosis and the Vicissitudes of Individuation.* New York: International Universities Press.

————, Pine, F., & Bergman, A. (1975), *The Psychological Birth of the Human Infant.* New York: Basic Books.

Major, R., & Miller, P. (1981), Empathy, antipathy, and telepathy in the analytic process. *Psychoanal. Inquiry*, 1:449–470.

Malcolm, J. (1981), *The Impossible Profession.* New York: Knopf.

Massie, H. (1978), The early natural history of childhood psychosis. Ten cases studied by analysis of family home movies of the infancies of the children. *J. Amer. Acad. Child Psychiat.*, 17:29–45.

McKinnon, J. (1979), Two semantic forms: Neuropsychological and psychoanalytic descriptions. *Psychoanal. Contemp. Thought*, 2:25–76.

McLaughlin, J. (1982), Issues stimulated by the 32nd Congress. *Int. J. Psychoanal.*, 63:229–240.

Meltzoff, A., & Borton, R. (1979), Intermodal matching by human neonates. *Nature*, 282:403–404.

————, & Moore, M. (1977), Imitation of facial and manual gestures by human neonates. *Science*, 198:75–78.

Messer, S., & Lewis, M. (1970), Social class and sex differences in the attachment and play behavior of the year-old infant. In: *The Female Orgasm,* ed. S. Fisher. London: Lane, 1973, pp. 71–72.

Modarressi, T. (1980), An experimental study of "double" (amphiscious) imagery during infancy and childhood. Presented at meeting of American Psychoanalytic Association, New York, December.

———— (1981), An experimental study of mirror imagery during infancy and childhood: The evolution of the self and its developmental vicissitudes (unpublished).

————, & Kenny, T. (1977), Children's response to their true and distorted mirror images. *Child Psychiat. Human Develop.,* 8(2):94–101.

Moore, B., & Fine, B. (1967), *A Glossary of Psychoanalytic Terms and Concepts.* New York: American Psychoanalytic Association.

Moss, H., & Robson, K. (1968), The role of protest behavior in the development of mother-infant attachment. Presented at meeting of American Psychological Association, San Francisco.

Murphy, L. (1973), Some mutual contributions of psychoanalysis and child development. In: *Psychoanalysis and Contemporary Science,* Vol. 2, ed. New York: International Universities Press, pp. 99–123.

Nemiah, J. (1975), Denial revisited: Reflections on psychosomatic theory. *Psychother. Psychosom.,* 26:140–147.

Nicolich, L. (1977), Beyond sensorimotor intelligence: Assessment of symbolic maturity through analysis of pretend play. *Merrill-Palmer Quart.,* 28:89–99.

Noy, P. (1979), The psychoanalytic theory of cognitive development. *The Psychoanalytic Study of the Child,* 34:169–216. New Haven: Yale University Press.

Papousek, H., & Papousek, M. (1975), Cognitive aspects of preverbal social interaction between human infant and adults. In: *Parent-Infant Interaction* (Ciba Foundation Symposium). New York: Associated Scientific Publishers.

Parens, H. (1979a), *The Development of Aggression in Early Childhood.* New York: Aronson.

———— (1979b), Developmental considerations of ambivalence: An exploration of the relations of instinctual drives and the symbiosis–separation-individuation process. *The Psychoanalytic Study of the Child,* 34:385–420. New Haven: Yale University Press.

Peterfreund, E. (1978), Some critical comments on psychoanalytic conceptualizations of infancy. *Int. J. Psychoanal.,* 59:427–441.

Peterson, G., & Mehl, L. (1978), Some determinants of maternal attachment. *Amer. J. Psychiat.,* 135:1168–1173.

Piaget, J. (1936), *The Origins of Intelligence.* New York: International Universities Press, 1952.

———— (1937), *The Construction of Reality in the Child.* New York: Basic Books, 1954.

_____ (1945), *Play, Dreams and Imitation in Childhood.* New York: Norton, 1951.

_____, & Inhelder, B. (1966), *The Psychology of the Child.* New York: Basic Books, 1969.

Pine, F. (1981), In the beginning: Contributions to a psychoanalytic developmental psychology. *Int. Rev. Psychoanal.,* 8:15–34.

Prechtl, H. F. (1963), The mother-child interaction in babies with mimimal brain damage. In: *Determinants of Infant Behavior,* Vol. II, ed. B. M. Foss. New York: Wiley, pp. 53–66.

Rapaport, D. (1959), A historical survey of psychoanalytic ego psychology. In: *Identity and the Life Cycle (Psychol. Issues,* Monogr. 1), by E. H. Erikson. New York: International Universities Press, pp. 5–7.

_____ (1960), *The Structure of Psychoanalytic Theory (Psychol. Issues,* Monogr. 6). New York: International Universities Press.

Reinisch, J. (1981), Prenatal exposure to synthetic progestin increases potential for aggression in humans. *Science,* 211:1171–1173.

Renik, O., Spielman, P., & Afterman, J. (1978), Bamboo phobia in an eighteen-month-old boy. *J. Amer. Psychoanal. Assn.,* 26:255–282.

Roffwarg, H. P., Muzio, J. N., & Dement, W. C. (1966), Ontogenetic development of the human sleep-dream cycle. *Science,* 152:604–619.

Roiphe, H. (1968), On an early genital phase. *The Psychoanalytic Study of the Child,* 23:349–365. New York: International Universities Press.

Rovee-Collier, C., Sullivan, M., Enright, M., Lucas, D., & Fagen, J. (1980), Reactivation of infant memory. *Science,* 208:1159–1161.

Rubinfine, D. (1961), Perception, reality testing, and symbolism. *The Psychoanalytic Study of the Child,* 16:73–89. New York: International Universities Press.

Rubinstein, B. (1976), Hope, fear, wish, expectation and fantasy. In: *Psychoanalysis and Contemporary Science,* Vol. 5, ed. T. Shapiro. New York: International Universities Press, pp. 3–60.

Sander, L. (1975), Infant and caretaking environment: Investigation and conceptualization of adaptive behavior in a system of increasing complexity. In: *Explorations in Child Psychiatry,* ed. E. J. Anthony. New York: Plenum Press, pp. 129–166.

_____ (1980a), Investigation of the infant and its caregiving environment as a biological system. In: *The Course of Life: Psychoanalytic Contributions toward Understanding Personality Development,* Vol. 1: *Infancy and Early Childhood,* ed. S. I. Greenspan & G. H. Pollock. Rockville, Md.: NIMH, pp. 177–202.

_____, Rep. (1980b), Panel: New knowledge about the infant from current research: Implications for psychoanalysis. *J. Amer. Psychoanal. Assn.,* 28: 181–198.

_____ (1980c), Polarity, paradox, and the organizing process in development.

Presented at First World Congress of Infant Psychiatry, Portugal, March 30–April 3.

———— (1983), To begin with—reflections on ontogeny. In: *Reflections on Self Psychology,* ed. J. Lichtenberg & S. Kaplan. Hillsdale, N.J.: Analytic Press.

————, Stechler, G., Julia, H., & Burns, P. (1976), Primary prevention and some aspects of temporal organization in early infant-caretaker interaction. In: *Infant Psychiatry,* ed. E. Rexford, L. Sander, & T. Shapiro. New Haven: Yale University Press, pp. 187–204.

Sandler, J. (1960), The background of safety. *Int. J. Psychoanal.,* 41:352–356.

———— , & Joffe (1969), Towards a basic psychoanalytic model. *Int. J. Psychoanal.,* 50:79–90.

————, & Rosenblatt, B. (1962), The concept of the representational world. *The Psychoanalytic Study of the Child,* 17:128–145. New York: International Universities Press.

Schaffer, H. R., & Emerson, P. (1964), Patterns of responses to physical contact in early human development. *J. Child Psychol. Psychiat.,* 5:1–13.

Schur, M. (1966), *The Id and the Regulatory Principles of Mental Functioning.* New York: International Universities Press.

———— (1969), Affects and cognition. *Int. J. Psychoanal.,* 50:647–653.

Schwaber, E. (1981), Empathy: A mode of analytic listening. *Psychoanal. Inquiry,* 1:357–392.

Shapiro, T. (1979), *Clinical Psycholinguistics.* New York: Plenum Press.

Sharpe, E. (1940), Psycho-physical problems revealed in language: An examination of metaphor. In: *Collected Papers on Psychoanalysis.* London: Hogarth Press, 1950.

Shevrin, H., & Tousseing, P. (1965), Vicissitudes of the need for tactile stimulation in instinctual development. *The Psychoanalytic Study of the Child,* 20:310–339. New York: International Universities Press.

Shopper, M. (1978), The role of audition in early psychic development with special reference to the use of the pull-toy in the separation-individuation phase. *J. Amer. Psychoanal. Assn.,* 26:283–310.

Silver, D. (1981), Ed. Commentaries on John Gedo's *Beyond Interpretation. Psychoanal. Inquiry,* 1:163–319.

Siqueland, & de Lucia, C. (1969), Visual reinforcement of non-nutritive sucking in human infants. *Science,* 165:1144–1146.

Spiegel, L. (1959), The self, the sense of self, and perception. *The Psychoanalytic Study of the Child,* 14:81–109. New York: International Universities Press.

Spitz, R. A. (1957), *No and Yes: On the Genesis of Human Communication.* New York: International Universities Press.

———— (1959), *A Genetic Field Theory of Ego Formation.* New York: International Universities Press.

————— (1965), *The First Year of Life*. New York: International Universities Press.

Sroufe, L. A. (1979), The coherence of individual development: Early care, attachment, and subsequent developmental issues. *Amer. Psychol.,* 34: 834–841.

—————(1982), The organization of emotional development. *Psychoanal. Inquiry,* 1:575–600.

Stechler, G. (1982), The dawn of awareness. *Psychoanal. Inquiry,* 1:503–532.

—————, & Carpenter, G. (1967), A viewpoint on early affective development. In: *The Exceptional Infant,* Vol. 1, ed. J. Hellmuth. New York: Brunner/ Mazel, pp. 165–189.

—————, & Kaplan, S. (1980), The development of the self: A psychoanalytic perspective. *The Psychoanalytic Study of the Child,* 35:85–106. New Haven: Yale University Press.

Stern, D. (1977), *The First Relationship.* Cambridge, Mass.: Harvard University Press.

————— (1982), Implications of infancy research for clinical theory and practice. Presented to meeting of the American Psychoanalytic Association, November.

————— (1983), The early development of schemas of self, of other, and of various experiences of "self with other." In: *Reflections on Self Psychology,* ed. J. Lichtenberg & S. Kaplan. Hillsdale, N.J.: Analytic Press.

Stoller, R. (1968), *Sex and Gender: On the Development of Masculinity and Femininity.* New York: Science House.

Stone, L. (1961), *The Psychoanalytic Situation.* New York: International Universities Press.

Terhune, C. (1979), The role of hearing in early ego organization. *The Psychoanalytic Study of the Child,* 34:349–370. New Haven: Yale University Press.

Tolpin, M. (1971), On the beginnings of the cohesive self. *The Psychoanalytic Study of the Child,* 26:316–352. New York: Quadrangle.

————— (1980), Discussion of "Psychoanalytic Theories of the Self: An Integration," by Morton Shane and Estelle Shane, In: *Advances in Self Psychology,* ed. A. Goldberg. New York: International Universities Press, pp. 47–68.

Tomkins, S. (1962), *Affect, Imagery, Consciousness,* Vol. 1: *The Positive Affects.* New York: Springer.

————— (1963), *Affect, Imagery, Consciousness,* Vol. 2: *The Negative Affects.* New York: Springer.

————— (1981), The quest for primary motives: Biography and autobiography of an idea. *J. Pers. Soc. Psychol.,* 41:306–329.

Trevarthen, C. (1974), Converstations with a two-month-old. *New Scientist,* 62:230.

————— (1977), Descriptive analyses of infant communicative behavior. In: *Studies in Mother-Infant Interaction,* ed. H. Schaffer. London: Academic Press, pp. 227–270.

Tyson, P. (1982), A developmental line of gender identity, gender role, and choice of love object. *J. Amer. Psychoanal. Assn.,* 30:61–68.

Weil, A. P. (1970), The basic core. *The Psychoanalytic Study of the Child,* 25:442–460. New York: International Universities Press.

_____ (1976), The first year: Metapsychological inferences of infant observation. *The Process of Child Development.*

_____ (1977), Learning disturbances with special consideration of dyslexia. *Issues Child Ment. Health,* 5:52–66.

_____ (1978), Maturational variations and genetic-dynamic issues. *J. Amer. Psychoanal. Assn.,* 26:461–491.

Werner, H., & Kaplan, B. (1963), *Symbol Formation.* New York: Wiley.

Wilson, R. (1978), Synchronies in mental development: an epigenetic perspective. *Science,* 202:939–948.

Winnicott, D. (1953), Transitional objects and transitional phenomena. In: *Collected Papers.* London: Tavistock, 1958, pp. 229–242.

_____ (1963), Communicating and not communicating leading to a study of certain opposites. In: *The Maturational Processes and the Facilitating Environment.* New York: International Universities Press, 1965, pp. 179–192.

Wolff, P. H. (1966), *The Causes, Controls, and Organization of Behavior in the Neonate (Psychol. Issues,* Monogr. 17). New York: International Universities Press.

_____ (1969), What we must and must not teach our young children from what we know about early cognitive development. In: *Planning for Better Learning,* ed. P. Wolff, & M. MacKeith. London: Heinemann, pp. 7–19.

Woolf, V. (1927), *To the Lighthouse.* New York: Harcourt, Brace, 1955.

Wurmser, L. (1981), *The Mask of Shame.* Baltimore: Johns Hopkins University Press.

ATTRIBUTIONS FOR PSA AND INF. RES.

Chapters 1 and 2 are based on Implications for Psychoanalytic Theory of Research on the Neonate. *Int. Rev. Psychoanal,* 8:35–52.

Chapters 3, 4, 5 and 6 are based on Reflections on the First Year of Life. *Psychoanal. Inquiry,* 1:695–730.

Chapters 7, 8, 9 and 10 are based on Reflections on the Second Year of Life. Presented at the Amer. Psychoanal. Assn. Meeting, Boston: May 1982.

Chapter 12 is based on Infancy and the Psychoanalytic Situation. Presented at Fifty Years of Psychoanalysis in Chicago: Vital Issues, Nov. 1981. To be published in *The Vital Issues,* (ed.) J. Gedo and G. Pollack.

Chapter 13 is based on An Experiential Conception of What is Curative in Psychoanalysis. Presented at the Amer. Psychoanal. Assn. Meeting, New York, Dec. 1982.

Author Index

Subject Index

A

Adaptedness, 14, 28–29, 43–55, 157, 161–162
Affects
  as experience markers, 169–178
  in first year, 65–67, 73, 175–176
  imaging capacity and, 116 fn., 125
  in neonate, 21–27, 70, 72–78
  regulatory deficits in, 198
Aggression, 86, 122–123, 126, 189, 191–192, 221
Alexithymia, 198
Ambivalence, 122–123, 126, 144
Ambitendency, 64, 212
Analytic relationship, 235–238
Anger, 25, 73, 78, 81, 86, 93, 122, 123, 177, 190
Anticipation, 77–78, 98, 99
Arousal, internal, 91
Assertiveness, 122–127, 191, 199
Attachment, 18–19, 92, 157–158
  departure and, 82–83, 163, 164
  selective, 98–99, 103, 111
Automatisms, 52
Awareness, 31–32, 115, 120
  genital, 127–131, 199

B, C

Borderline personality disorders, 188
Cathartic method, 216
Circumcision, 5, 6
Cognition, 26, 37, 176; *see also* Imaging
  Capacity, Symbolic representation
Cognitive deficits, 203–205
"Colic," 22
  beginning, 50–51, 98–100
  foreground/background in, 207–209
  imaging capacity and, 100, 102
Communication

Competence pleasure, 89–90, 118, 162, 191, 192
Conflict, 16, 38–39, 43, 122–124, 147, 165, 178, 184, 199, 212
  resolution of, 216, 217, 222
Cooing, 23
Crawling, 52
Critical period, 15
Cruelty, 65, 67
Crying, 19, 21–22, 24–26, 53–54, 73, 78, 86, 176
Cure, psychoanalytic, 206–207, 214–239
  cathartic view of, 216
  experiential view of, 227–229
  self versus object relations in, 219–227
  structural view of, 217–219

D

Defense mechanisms, 80–83, 142, 186
Denial, 82
Departure-reunion studies, 82–83, 163, 164
Director, sense of self as, 117–123, 125
Discriminatory abilities, in neonate, 7, 10–12, 14, 49, 57–58, 105
Disengagement, 158
Dream interpretation, 151–154
Drive theory, 4–10, 91, 154–156; *see also* Id
Dystonic stimulation, regulation of, 6, 12–13, 53–55, 80–81

E

Efficacy pleasure; *see* Competence pleasure
Ego, 217
  in first year, 10–17, 84, 87–94
Ego psychology, 10–17, 161 fn., 183, 186
Emotion, 66, 73–77, 172; *see also* Affects
Empathy, 20, 173, 226
  psychoanalytic situation and, 209–211, 220, 222–227, 229, 231, 234